1992

GROUPS FOR GROWTH AND CHANGE

LEONARD N. BROWN
Rutgers University

Longman
New York & London

Groups for Growth and Change

Copyright © 1991 by Longman Publishing Group

Longman, 95 Church Street, White Plains, N.Y. 10601

Associated companies:
Longman Group Ltd., London
Longman Cheshire Pty., Melbourne
Longman Paul Pty., Auckland
Copp Clark Pitman, Toronto

Senior editor: David J. Estrin
Development editor: Virginia Blanford
Production editor: Janice Baillie
Cover design: Paul Agule Design
Text art: Burmar
Production supervisor: Kathleen M. Ryan

Library of Congress Cataloging in Publication Data

Brown, Leonard N.
    Groups for growth and change / Leonard N. Brown
        p.   cm.
    Includes index.
    ISBN 0-8013-0044-4
    1. Social group work.   I. Title.
    HV45.B745   1990
    361.4—dc20   90-37631
                                                                              CIP

ABCDEFGHIJ–MA–99 98 97 96 95 94 93 92 91 90

To my wife, Marilyn,
a woman of valor, who lived life to the fullest
and inspired others along the way.

Contents

Preface   **ix**

PART I: BACKGROUND

Chapter 1: Social Work with Groups as Integrative Practice   **3**
Definitions   **3**
Essential Elements of Social Work with Groups   **5**
Practice with Groups as Integrative and Health-Oriented   **21**
Where to Find the Ten Dimensions of Social Work with Groups   **22**
Summary   **24**
References   **25**
Teaching and Learning Ideas   **26**

Chapter 2: Historical Influences   **28**
The Roots of Group Work   **28**
Branches of Group Work   **31**
Models of Social Group Work   **38**
Practice Developments and Refinements   **39**
Groups in Direct Practice   **40**
Groups for Health, Prevention, and Productivity   **41**
Returning to Our Roots   **42**
Summary   **42**
References   **43**
Teaching and Learning Ideas   **46**

Chapter 3: Types of Groups   **47**
Treatment Group   **47**
Socioeducation Group   **50**

Social Action Group   **52**
Administrative Group   **55**
Similarities and Differences in Worker Role   **58**
Summary   **61**
References   **61**
Teaching and Learning Ideas   **62**

PART II: FRAMEWORKS FOR UNDERSTANDING

Chapter 4: Knowledge and Values   **65**
Relevant Knowledge   **65**
Values   **83**
Summary   **86**
References   **87**
Teaching and Learning Ideas   **88**

Chapter 5: Practice Principles with Oppressed and Vulnerable Populations   **91**
Definitions   **91**
Continuum of Behavior   **92**
Practice Principles   **94**
Summary   **108**
References   **110**
Teaching and Learning Ideas   **111**

Chapter 6: Use of Techniques   **112**
Techniques   **113**
Techniques Applied to a Group   **117**
Analysis of Group and Worker Activity   **135**
Summary   **138**
References   **138**
Teaching and Learning Ideas   **139**

PART III: PHASES OF WORK

Chapter 7: Pregroup Planning   **143**
Reasons to Form Groups   **144**
Who Should Be in Groups   **145**
Group Composition   **147**

Dealing with Resistances **148**
Referrals and Recruitment **149**
Conditions for the Group Meetings **150**
Preparing Group Members **152**
Leadership Preparation **154**
Pregroup Planning Illustration **155**
Summary **158**
References **158**
Teaching and Learning Ideas **159**

Chapter 8: The Beginning   **161**
Emergence of Group Structure **161**
Interrelationship of the Person, Group, and Environment **163**
Tasks of the Group Worker **164**
Summary **186**
References **186**
Teaching and Learning Ideas **187**

Chapter 9: The Middle   **189**
Tasks of the Group Worker **190**
Summary **216**
References **216**
Teaching and Learning Ideas **217**

Chapter 10: The Ending   **218**
Ending the Group Session **219**
Planned Ending with the Group **220**
Tasks of the Group Worker **221**
Unplanned Endings **229**
Transformation **231**
Summary **232**
References **232**
Teaching and Learning Ideas **233**

Chapter 11: Social Action and System Development   **234**
A Social Action and Systems Development Model **236**
Techniques of Intervention **240**
Group as Part of the Environment **241**
Groups Organized in Relation to Environmental Need or Problem **244**
Summary **247**

References   **247**
Teaching and Learning Ideas   **249**

Index   **251**

Preface

Working with groups, whether they comprise family, client, community, or administrative groups, is basic and essential to social work practice. The small group forms the link between individual and environment; it is the medium of socialization, nurturance, and problem solving. Every social worker will fulfill the roles, frequently or infrequently, of facilitator, participant, or organizer, and must therefore understand the knowledge and techniques that make group work effective. The purpose of this book is twofold: to provide an overview of social work with groups—its history, underlying theory, and purposes; and to demonstrate step by step the process that constitutes working with groups.

One may wonder how social work with groups differs from social work in general or, alternatively, how social work with groups differs from other kinds of group work, such as group therapy. In fact, social work with groups is similar to many forms of group work practiced by nonsocial workers, where the focus is on helping the individual within the group. Many of the therapeutic techniques are the same and, in some cases, the knowledge base is similar as well. The difference is that social work with groups encompasses a broad range of groups, including those for psychological healing, social skill development, environmental change, and task accomplishment. The values of social work place a high priority on working with persons who face oppression because of race, ethnicity, or economic or social disadvantage. Such persons often will not seek out agency help, therefore appropriate outreach structures must be developed to meet their needs. Agencies must also develop preventive activities to reduce the incidence of psychological and social trauma, as well as the costly drain of economic and human resources in rehabilitation centers or institutionalization. It is the particular constellation of all these characteristics—the breadth of group types with both personal and social goals, the use of the group process to foster mutual aid, the focus on serving vulnerable populations and the concomitant need for outreach and preventive services—that defines social work with groups.

In writing this book, I have drawn on my work experiences in both clinical and community social work, as well as in administration and social work education. I have taken special care to make the book clear and accessible to students; ample illustrations, chapter overviews, chapter summaries, and teaching and learning ideas are included. The tasks and techniques of the group worker are defined on the basis of a clear conceptual model. Although the book is written primarily for social work students, it is also applicable for all those in the helping professions who work with groups. The essential elements of this text are the following:

- A health orientation, or wellness perspective, emphasizing the challenge and creative tension inherent in personal and group growth
- An integrative approach that relates individual, group, and environmental issues
- An emphasis on a problem-solving methodology, applicable to all kinds of groups, from those that focus on personal change to those that focus on social change
- A conceptual model that describes tasks and techniques for the group worker in relation to the stages of group development and the various needs of person, group, and environment
- An emphasis on work with disadvantaged populations
- Sensitivity to the psychological, social, and cultural factors that often prevent minority or disadvantaged populations from seeking help, and an emphasis on the need for appropriate outreach
- Attention to prevention
- An emphasis on the professional's own need for self-awareness as an essential dimension of practice.

I would like to thank my wife, Marilyn, for her patience, understanding, and love. The students in my group work classes were extremely helpful in making the book more useful to students. Paula Friedman and Ann Nelke assisted me during the original organization of the manuscript. Kathleen Fahmie, as a student and now a colleague, was invaluable for her research assistance, critical review, and friendship. The faculty at the Rutgers School of Social Work were supportive throughout the writing, especially David Antebi, Martin Bloom, Eleanor Brilliant, Paul Glasser, Daniel Katz, Elfriede Schlesinger, and Marcos Leiderman for their practical comments. My friend and colleague, Martin Birnbaum, provided insights for changes and was a willing listener. Florence Schwartz and George Getzel, from the Hunter School of Social Work, were encouraging. To my international friends, Florence Mittwock of Israel and Carol Irzarry of Australia, I offer thanks for their review of the manuscript. Much appreciation to the social workers who provided practice illustrations—Nancy Brail, Brinda Breese-Wederich, Russell Filsinger, Kathleen Gebhardt, Patricia Morris, Linda Meisel, Marianne Polinski, Barbara Rabinowitz, Louise Rodgers, Rose D. Selzer, Melissa Starr, Florence Weisfeld. Beatrice Saunders was a wonderful teacher in the onging writing and organization of the book. Hally Abbott was the able word processor who contributed expertise and good humor during the many changes. My son Samuel Brown contributed his expertise in developing the index. And finally, I would like to thank David Estrin, senior editor at Longman, for his patience and encouragement, as well as Virginia Blanford, for her constructive suggestions.

PART I
Background

CHAPTER 1

Social Work with Groups as Integrative Practice

Social work with groups addresses the interdependent relationship of person, group, and social environment. It is holistic in the sense of working with the whole person, including involvement of significant other persons in the lives of the group members. A particular emphasis in this text will be on how to work with disadvantaged populations, including those facing poverty or discrimination because of race, ethnicity, gender, sexual preference, or a particular mental or physical handicap. This health-oriented approach helps the person and group to bring out and work with personal strengths and to create sources of support in the group and the community.

Four basic types of groups will be examined: the *treatment group* for behavioral and social change; the *socioeducation group* for support, socialization, and education; the *social action group* for community change; and the *administrative group* for accomplishing tasks within organizations. These will be explained in Chapter 3.

DEFINITIONS

A *group* is considered a small, face-to-face collection of persons who interact to accomplish some purpose. The group will meet for one or more sessions, have open-ended (persons coming and going all the time) or closed membership (persons not added after the initial session) and time limited (a fixed number of meetings) or ongoing (without a definite ending date). Groups will usually be formed by an agency staff person to fulfill a purpose that is within the guidelines of the agency's mission. There are also natural or informal groups, self-selected on the basis of friendship, similar interests, or problems.

Group work is the generic term for all kinds of professional work with groups. It is used to describe an array of approaches from education, recreation, social work, psychology, and related helping professions. The basic ingredient in group work is that the worker (group worker) enables group members to engage in collaborative problem solving. The literature also refers to the worker as the leader, meaning the person designated by the agency to implement the group's purpose. This is sometimes confusing, since actual leadership may also come from the group members. In this case, it means indigenous leadership. "Group facilitator" is often used synonymously with "group leader" and connotes a less directive role, although in actual practice there may not be much difference.

Group work has traditionally been referred to as *social group work*—a method of using the group process to enhance the social functioning of group members and the group itself. Chapter 2 describes the strong influence of education, recreation, and social action for community change in the evolution of social group work. More recently, a distinction has been made between social group work and social work with groups (Middleman and Goldberg, 1987, 714–729).

Social work with groups includes most aspects of social group work but also brings in more of the personal change or treatment dimension. It is broadly conceived for the fuller range of social work functions when the small group is used along the continuum from treatment to community change. Perhaps it amounts to semantic hairsplitting, but for social workers not trained in "social group work" and thinking of themselves as direct practitioners or community planners, "social work with groups" seems more acceptable and compatible to their thinking.

Integrative practice, as used in this text, views the group as the link between the individual and social environment. The group has the function of increasing the coping capacities of the individual and influencing the environment to be more receptive and nurturing. The group itself becomes an environment for constructive growth and problem solving, including characteristics of trust, acceptance, challenge, and mutual aid. The group may also be a source of changing the larger environment—families, organizations, and segments of the community—where persons or procedures in these other systems interfere with the potential for personal or group enhancement. While the target of change may be these other systems, such as the group's social action to change a policy that is discriminatory, it is more likely that the change will occur in the reciprocal interaction between group members and their environments. This notion implies a different and—one hopes—a healthier way that persons relate to one another. In integrative practice the worker needs to conceptualize five areas, separately and together:

1. Self-awareness as a professional, whereby the worker attempts to recognize and understand how his or her ideas and feelings may influence the manner of relating to others
2. The assessment and interventions with group members
3. The assessment and interventions with the small group
4. The assessment and interventions with the social environment
5. The purpose and meaning of interaction with two or more of the above

ESSENTIAL ELEMENTS OF SOCIAL WORK WITH GROUPS

Ten dimensions of social work with groups will be described in this chapter. This material provides a general overview of social work practice, but the particular emphasis here is on group work. These ten areas are the organizing framework for this integrative approach:

1. Contacting prospective group members
2. Understanding presenting needs or problems
3. Locating resources to benefit group members
4. Preparing for the group
5. Planning with group members
6. Using professional self-awareness in a helpful way
7. Knowing how active or directive to be
8. Acting in a variety of social work roles
9. Making use of group process and problem solving
10. Encouraging psychological and social health

As these dimensions are explained, the reader will be referred to sections of this book where each will be discussed more thoroughly.

Contacting Prospective Group Members

There are various ways that social workers meet prospective group members. The social agency, as an organization providing a type of community service, will attract persons who have needs, interests, or problems that are consistent with the agency's mission. Persons may come voluntarily or be mandated by legal authorities, or the agency may reach out to resistant clients. Some agencies develop activities that help prevent problems from occurring. In the area of prevention, social workers may consult with neighborhood leaders and staff of community organizations in order to mobilize resources for additional services. For persons who are unwilling or unable to come to the agency, staff may go into the local neighborhood to make services more accessible. Each of these forms of engagement (see Figure 1.1) is discussed in the following sections.

Voluntarily Seek Services. Some persons, families, and groups voluntarily seek professional services in social agencies. They may simply come on their own or be referred by a friend, relative, or professional in the community. The needs and problems will vary—some being specific needs such as recreation, education, medical attention, housing, or child care, and others being more general, such as marital discord, emotional distress, or fulfillment in social relationships.

Mandated to Seek Services. Others seek social services under duress, such as by court mandate because of substance abuse. More subtle coercion to seek help may come from family members or the school environment. There is usually an overt or veiled threat in these requests by someone with power or authority over the client. Needless to say, it is difficult to help someone who is only there because he or she has to be.

Outreach. Many people who have needs for services will not come to the agency on their own. This is especially true for those who live in poverty or have ethnic or racial differences, conditions that can be perceived by the client as a barrier to receiving help. Other people may feel that they will not be accepted because of a social, physical, or emotional problem and will stay away from

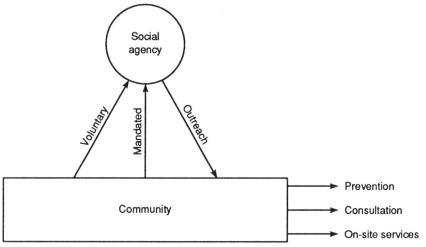

Figure 1.1

agencies. Still others, at risk and in need of professional intervention, may not recognize that they have a problem at all.

Consultation and Prevention. The agency may find that the best way to deal with a social problem, such as drug abuse or homelessness, is to provide consultation to professional or lay persons in the community. If another organization is already offering such services to the target population, the agency may join forces with them, thus helping professionals deal more ably with the problem being considered.

On-site Services. Some clients will avoid visiting the agency but may indicate during initial contacts that they will avail themselves of services if some of the barriers are removed: financial restrictions, transportation, time, fear of the formal structure of an agency, or ethnic constraints. In this case, it could be desirable to develop on-site activities close to the area of the target population. This may mean setting up services in a school, a church or synagogue, or a local community building.

Some agency on-site services may be of long-term duration, but they may also be brief—if, for example, a specific problem needs immediate attention. The outreach worker must be well informed of community resources, since it is often necessary to refer persons to other agencies in the community for help with particular problems.

In the end, a person who inquires may not be interested in any formal offer of services. However, if this initial contact demonstrates caring and concern, the inquirer may return at a later point to use the agency. The worker's attitude should encourage prospective clients to feel secure about making a return visit.

Understanding Presenting Needs or Problems

This particular phase, during which the worker attempts to understand the meaning of a presenting need or problem, is usually termed "assessment." It may involve an intake or psychosocial evaluation to help the client define the problem and its possible causes, and to plan further if the person is eligible for services. However, I've labeled this section "understanding" because this term implies a more mutual engagement between worker and client.

The term "assessment," by itself, may suggest that the worker is gathering information and making judgments about the client. In this book, "assessment" is meant to include both people in the process. Recipients of helping services can understand their situations more fully when they participate jointly in the assessment of needs, problems, and the environment.

During this process, the worker must always remember that, although the biological, psychological, social, and cultural aspects of behavior are being considered distinctly, in practice these influences are all interrelated. It is helpful to separate causes periodically, but the worker must always have a holistic view of the problem.

During this phase of assessment and understanding, the social worker will find out the client's reasons for coming to the agency, the background of the problem, and what the prospective client would like to do about it, and will explain what the agency is prepared to offer. The client's degree of commitment is assessed by his or her willingness to take responsibility for resolving the problem and by his or her particular strengths and limitations. It is also useful at this time to work with the person in identifying other people who are perceived as being important and related to the problem in some way. They are considered "significant others" who will be meaningful in understanding the problem, and may eventually be involved in its solution.

As shown in Figure 1.2, the biological, psychological, social, and cultural components are all interrelated and part of how people function and cope with their environment. The person, family, and group also influence one another. In seeking understanding about presenting needs or problems, the worker must take into consideration the totality of the experiences. Clausen (1986, 9) distinguishes four types of influences on a person's development which support this type of thinking:

1. The person's own attributes, constitutionally given or developed—intelligence, appearance, strength, health, temperament.
2. The sources of socialization, support, and guidance that initially orient persons to the work in which they will function and subsequently assist them to cope with problems or offer emotional support when effective solutions are limited.
3. The opportunities available to the person or the obstacles that are encountered in the environment, as influenced by social class, ethnic group, age, sex, and social network; as well as the effects of war, depression, and other

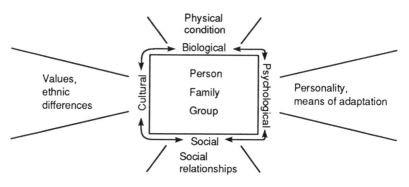

Figure 1.2

major social changes that affect particular birth cohorts differently; and, not least, the vagaries of chance.

4. Investments of effort that persons make in their own behalf (commitments) and the mobilization of resources to attain desired goals.

Locating Resources to Benefit Group Members

Friends, family members, and group and community resources can be potentially helpful to clients (see Figure 1.3), acting as a buffer against distress or aiding in problem solving. People who have the capacity to lend their support are part of a natural helping network (Collins, 1976). Maguire (1980) describes personal networks as support systems that counteract the stress of emotional upheavals in a person's life.

Different helping networks may be available, depending on the situation. The social worker may be able to identify potential sources of help which clients have not recognized. For instance, the clients may be unaware that self-help groups have been formed in their neighborhoods, designed for the very problems they presented.

The identification of resources is done jointly by the worker and group member(s), which gives more responsibility for problem solving to the group. As the network of potential help is expanded—including family, friends, or work associates—resources become more available if and when they are needed. The

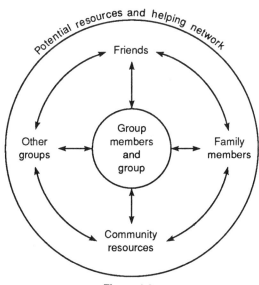

Figure 1.3

aim of this cooperative planning is to begin building a supportive environment for solving problems. Knowing what resources persons have used or would like to use also helps the worker assess the prospective client's capacity for exercising initiative on his or her own behalf.

When persons from outside the group are involved in helping solve problems, the number of potential helpers expand. This is consistent with an integrative approach, since it reinforces the concept of interdependence and interrelationship of person, group, and environment. The location and use of resources is especially beneficial when the group is part of an institution, hospital, residence, school, or work place. The worker may engage staff as part of a team effort on behalf of the client, and thus the environment becomes a therapeutic milieu—a place where there are consistent policies and practices to support healthy growth and development.

Preparing for the Group

The preparation involved in getting a group started seems undervalued in group work. Considerable effort may be necessary to arrange for people to be in the group. Figure 1.4 shows five basic aspects of good group preparation, the completion of which will increase the possibility of success.

Clarity of Purpose. The worker should be clear about the purpose of the group. The purpose should be consistent with the function of the agency and within its context for social services. If the reasons for participation are clear, it is more likely that the persons selected will be appropriate for the group.

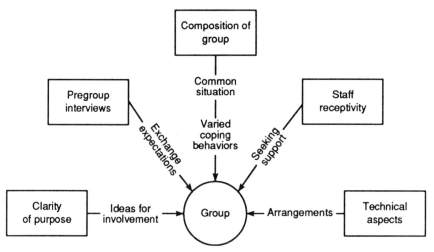

Figure 1.4

The worker should think about appropriate ways to involve group members, in order to foster interaction, inclusion, and relationship building. For certain groups, especially children, the use of an activity helps to encourage participation—in, of course, a structured, safe place.

Pregroup Interviews. It is not always possible to see prospective group members beforehand, but when it can occur, people should be prepared for what to expect in the group. This allays anxieties and can enhance the development of a working relationship, bringing up additional material for assessment and further understanding of the client's needs and problems. Persons about to participate in a group may resist involving themselves or they may be willing. The pregroup interview can be used to explore and begin to resolve any ambivalent feelings about being in the group.

Composition of the Group. In composing the group, depending on its purposes the workers should include people with something in common and with some differences. Usually, they should have shared needs or problems, such as persons facing loss or a housing problem, or persons with a similar social and educational background. Their common life experiences draw them together and provide a basis for solving problems.

The need for differences should call for people with varied abilities and coping behaviors, to enrich a problem-solving process. If the purpose of the group is to improve relationships between whites and minorities, the composition should include a racial or ethnic mix. Often a shared like experience—a serious illness in the family, a problem with drugs—is powerful enough to keep such a group together. Their differences will enable them to exchange ideas on how to use personal resources to cope with the problem.

Building Staff Receptivity. If the agency has approved the organizing of the group, presumably support and encouragement will exist. But there may also be resistance from some staff. In an agency where the predominant mode of helping is a one-to-one relationship, some may see groups as unnecessary or even damaging. Some people believe that group life is superficial, or that persons who have their own problems will not be able to help someone else. Staff who are seeing clients individually may also develop a possessiveness about "their" clients and may resist sharing them with another staff person. Childrens' groups tend to be noisy and may be perceived by professional and clerical staff as troublesome. Groups require a lot more administrative time in keeping track of people and making the physical arrangements necessary for meetings. All these factors may cause staff to resist referring a client to a group or starting one at the agency.

The worker who is planning a group should discuss these plans with the staff, including clerical personnel, so they understand the reasons for the group and can express their reservations early. In this way the worker will be better prepared to answer their questions and even enlist their ideas in the planning.

Technical Aspects. Technical aspects involve all the arrangements for the group. The place where they are to meet should have a comfortable atmosphere conducive to the sharing of ideas and feelings that are expected. If the group will be using activities, there should be space and freedom for unrestricted movement. The time to meet should be convenient so that it will not be a hardship for group members to attend. If equipment is to be used, such as a movie projector or video tape deck, it should be tested beforehand.

Adequate preparation requires that all obstructions to a group be cleared beforehand—everything from a clear proposal to an adequate number of chairs. Otherwise, valuable group time will be wasted on avoidable administrative problems.

Planning with Group Members

Everything we have discussed thus far has involved preparing for the creation of the group. In order to begin the work that brought social worker and group together, all the participants should develop a working agreement—their reasons for being in the group. Each person has some piece to contribute to the whole, but the group purpose is more than a collection of individual interests. By sharing ideas and feelings, examining different values, beliefs, and ranges of purpose, group members can understand how their expectations fit within the boundary of what the agency is prepared to offer.

Expectations are also shared about the roles of group members and social worker. The worker talks about what he or she is doing—explaining why she is required to do this or that. The client should also be encouraged to discuss the expectations of his or her role. Unless there is clarity about the "contract" between social worker and group members, a mutual agreement about purposes and roles, it is likely that there will be dissatisfaction in the group (Maluccio and Marlow, 1974, 28).

The negotiation that takes place in clarifying these multiple purposes and roles is the group's first task. It sets the tone for future communication and establishes a social climate in which indigenous leadership can exert its strength. It is the beginning of a collaborative relationship. The structure that is introduced at this time—smoking or not, confidentiality, how people can participate, responsibilities—provides security to group members in knowing what they can expect.

While the group's common needs and interests are their basis for working together, their differences should not be seen as an impediment. The varying expressions of values, ideas, and feelings by members are important to the group and should be appreciated as a measure of individuality and a reflection of everyone's self-image.

Figure 1.5 shows how the expectations and purposes of the group consider worker, members, and agency. The ideas and feelings of these participants attempt to mesh into a clear direction and focus for the group. The group member is recognized as an individual, a member of a group, and a participant in the larger context of the agency. Despite an initial understanding of the reasons for the group being together, the contract is dynamic and changing, depending on the changes that take place in the group members and in the group itself. Within the larger context of the prevailing contract, there will be minicontracts—agreements for each session that establish the agenda or plan for that particular meeting.

Using Professional Self-Awareness in a Helpful Way

During the evolution of the client/worker relationship, workers must be constantly self-aware. In working with groups, social workers learn to develop a four part focus: on each group member individually; on the group as a whole; on themselves as helping people; and on the agency as a context for service delivery (see Figure 1.6). Not only must workers be aware of each of these dimensions, but they must decide how their use of self will best benefit the group. A worker's reaction may be different from what others in the group are experiencing, or

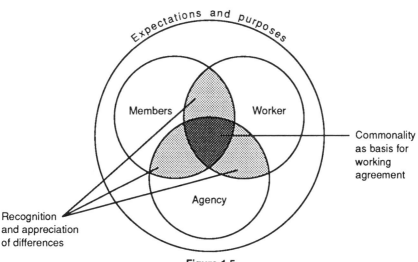

Figure 1.5

Figure 1.6

similar to it, and in order to deal accurately and sensitively with the group interaction, the worker must be aware of this distinction.

Group workers can use their own self-awareness positively in several ways. They can invite group members who seem to be having similar reactions to share their thoughts or feelings, and in that way bring certain perceptions into the life of the group. Or workers may offer direct feedback or provide empathy to one or more group members, reinforcing an important realization. A third possibility is for workers to share their own perceptions in order to present themselves as genuine and caring. However, self-disclosure must be presented in an appropriate way, which means that workers must use personal sharing to assist the group, and not for their own release of tension or in a play for sympathy.

Finally, the worker should create an atmosphere that allows for mutual feedback. In this way the worker and group are placing a value on self-understanding for all those in the group. The worker should be open to what the group members are saying, which will increase professional self-awareness and present the social worker as a role model willing to listen and learn from others.

Knowing How Active or Directive to Be

The social worker's ability to lead the group is crucial to all phases and types of groups. However, the worker must be sensitive to the needs of the group and adjust himself or herself accordingly. The group worker's leadership will be more or less active, depending on a number of factors. The ability of the worker to change his or her behavior is a measure of professional skill.

The worker must always listen actively and be responsive to leadership overtures from the group. Depending on the level of this indigenous leadership, workers will vary how much they initiate ideas or structures, set boundaries of permissible behaviors, lead a discussion or activity, and communicate in the group (see Figure 1.7). A worker will take a more active role if the group is in an early stage of development, if the group has low coping and less mature members, if little indigenous leadership exists, or if the group's purpose is more task-oriented. A worker should try to become less active if the group is in a later stage of development, if there are high coping and more mature members, if indigenous leadership is strong, or if the group's purpose is oriented to personal growth or change.

Flexible leadership is important to all kinds of social work. For work with groups, it is vital to allow for the growth of group members. Some persons may not have had much opportunity to assume leadership roles. By allowing them to take on responsibilities as they grow more comfortable, the worker helps increase confidence that they will be able to assume leadership outside the group.

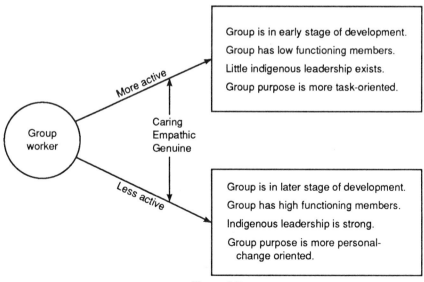

Figure 1.7

Acting in a Variety of Social Work Roles

There are many roles for the social worker with groups, as is shown in Figure 1.8.

Within Group: In the *therapist* role, the social worker focuses on helping group members achieve personal change through self-understanding and ability to solve problems. As an *educator,* the worker may impart knowledge, teach social skills, and support appropriate behavior. The *mediator* role enhances communication between group members or subgroups in resolving problems or making constructive use of conflict. In the role of *discussion leader,* the worker may direct, focus, or summarize content and use techniques to involve group members toward maximum participation and decision making.

Usually the worker will perform *all* of these roles, sometimes in the same group. The emphasis on which roles are used will depend on the type and purpose of the group, as well as the phase of group development.

Within Agency: As a staff member, team member, and supervisor/administrator, the group worker often has a responsibility to the agency. Committees and staff meetings require knowledge and skills of how groups accomplish tasks. The role of *team member* or *leader* necessitates collaborative activity, usually pooling the resources of other team members to benefit the client. The *supervisor/*

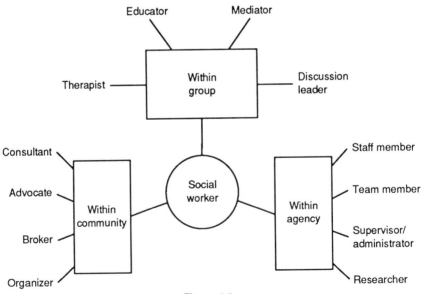

Figure 1.8

administrator may work alone, but more likely he or she meets in groups to achieve the goals of the organization. The *researcher* role may not require group participation but it is becoming more and more necessary to study group effectiveness, develop theory, and refine skills in group work.

Within Community: The *consultant* role may involve training staff in methods of working with groups, particularly in specialized forms of group work such as that dealing with children. Consultants in group work are also called upon to train peer leaders for self-help groups and to be available as a resource for these groups.

As an *advocate,* the worker will attempt to use his or her influence or expertise in behalf of group members or the group as a whole. The *broker* role involves making arrangements with group members for the use of other services; the broker function requires that the worker have broad knowledge of community resources. The role of *organizer* is necessary to carry out social action activities, whereby people with similar interests are brought together to achieve organizational or community change.

These various roles are a reflection of the many facets of integrative practice, whereby the worker assumes different responsibilities at different times, according to the needs and interests of group members, the group as a whole, the agency, and the community. When any one system is strengthened, that is presumed to have a positive effect on the others.

Making Use of Group Process and Problem Solving

Tension often builds up within groups when the interests and needs of a group member conflict with those of the group. The process of individuation, whereby persons differentiate themselves from others, is an attempt to define self-identity in relation to significant other persons. In groups, this kind of socialization goes on constantly. If the tension is resolved completely in favor of either personal or group needs, the result is either anarchy or "groupthink." Janis (1982) describes groupthink as excessive group conformity—an unwillingness to exercise critical, independent judgment to examine or challenge decision making in the group.

The tension that results from this duality can be a source of creative growth, as shown in Figure 1.9. For a successful resolution, the group must establish a norm for the acceptable expression of differences. Each individual's contribution will be seen as benefiting both the individual and the group, and a balance is achieved between individual and group needs. Resolving conflict can lead to an increased intimacy and respect for differences, a characteristic of a more advanced stage—see Chapter 4. For group development to advance to its most productive level, the values of self-determination and collaboration must pervade the functioning of the group, a climate fostered by the worker.

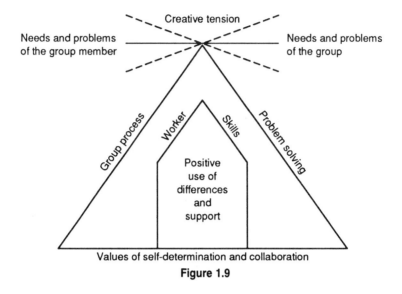

Figure 1.9

The value of mutual aid should be made clear early in the group. The worker's helping tasks and techniques will come to be shared by all group members, once they feel more comfortable and learn how to solve problems collaboratively. Development of these skills is essential for the success of the integrative approach, especially as the diverse needs and concerns of the group come into conflict.

Encouraging Psychological and Social Health

People have the capacity to grow and develop to their fullest potential only when the conditions are favorable (see Figure 1.10). Physical well-being, emotional stability, spiritual sustenance, and cognitive understanding are all interrelated. Six elements contribute to personal, group, and environmental change—outlined in Figure 1.10—and all seem necessary for growth to occur. The worker and group are both responsible for implementing this growth.

Clear Purpose. The first step in resolving problems is becoming clear about the nature of a need. When individuals are focused on the changes they want to make, they begin to take control of their personal situations. Such focusing may become even more complicated when a group is involved. Although they may have joined a group in order to accomplish a specific task or to solve a problem, the array of personal interpretations and perceptions they encounter from other group members may clash with their own. Unless the initial meetings are spent in

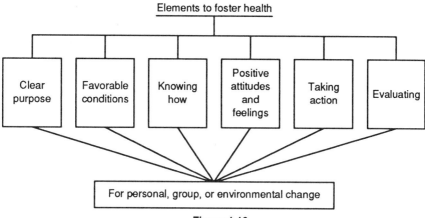

Figure 1.10

clarifying these individual perceptions and identifying common needs or problems, participants may become discouraged, fearing that their personal expectations will not be met.

At first, needs or problems can seem large and overwhelming, so it is useful to separate out parts of them (partializing) in order to set priorities. Which areas seem most accessible, manageable, or immediate? Identify them, and zero in on the most pressing. In this way the energies within the group can be more focused. Once even a small part of a problem is solved, this successful step can be stimulus for further work.

Favorable Conditions. The group worker must create a relationship with group members on the basis of genuine caring, empathic listening, and respect, in order to foster growth within the group. Both the group and the worker need to appreciate the ability of the group members to work together in ways that will produce desirable outcomes. Faith in the group process will help to release the latent strengths of group members.

The influence of persons in the family, organization, or community make an impact on the functioning of the group members. The group uses its problem-solving abilities to improve relations with persons outside the group and to change organization and community policies when these procedures place negative constraints upon group members.

Knowing How. The problem-solving process includes the gathering of appropriate information before making relevant decisions. In group work the members and the worker share their personal resources—knowledge, values, and skills— as they are needed to fulfill the purposes of the group. The extent to which knowledge is imparted will depend on the type of group: Socioeducation groups will gather more particular information than treatment groups will. Knowledge needs to be related to what is necessary to solve a problem or to deal with a specific task, such as a job or a social encounter. It should also belong within a generally accepted value system. Delinquents may have a great deal of "street savvy," but their use of this knowledge could be destructive to themselves and others.

Besides knowledge and values, the third dimension is skills. However knowledgeable and honorable people are, they may be at a disadvantage if they have not learned sufficient skills to behave acceptably. Lack of effective role behavior prevents the individual from using himself or herself constructively when confrontations arise. Moreover, the successful person is skilled at adapting his role behavior to new and constantly changing circumstances. Adopting a role entails a synthesis of knowledge, values, and skills to meet an interpersonal encounter. Knowing-how is a powerful mechanism for growth and change.

Positive Attitudes and Feelings. The relationship between the mind and the body is nothing new; this interdependence keeps getting rediscovered as new research highlights the powerful effects of the mind. Imagery, in which persons imagine their bodies fighting cancer cells, has been used to bolster the immune system of cancer patients (Justice, 1987, 319–321). Imagery has also been used to induce relaxation or to recall earlier memories that may help with problems, such as feelings of separation.

We also know that the way people feel about learning affects their ability to grasp new information or gain new skills. Similarly, in a therapeutic encounter, a client or patient will only be able to change behavior if he or she wants to change. If a client resists modifying negative behavior, the professional helper will assist him or her in overcoming this block.

A great deal of personal energy goes into denying certain attitudes and feelings. The need to cover up or explain away real feelings limits people in using their resources for personal enrichment. In group work there are many techniques to help members of a group explore their feelings and become more aware of them. When these feelings are released, it can seem like a tremendous weight has been lifted from the person.

Taking Action. Growth and change will not occur unless there is action in the direction of change. Change is usually regarded as taking place in an orderly process of problem solving. Although this is true generally, sometimes change can be stimulated by an experience—an unexpected encounter will elicit a certain feeling, demonstrate caring, provide linkage with others, or bring out a dimension of a problem that had been unrecognized. The use of experience or activity is especially desirable when persons have little or underdeveloped conceptual ability, as in childhood. The experience provides a frame of reference in which to locate feelings and ideas. John Dewey recognized experience and thinking as a basic part of education (Dewey, 1916, 139). For instance, in training group leaders, the trainer might do a role play of a situation in which persons (potential group leaders) come together to form a group and bring out feelings of anxiety, caution, anticipation, joy, and rejection. In the role play, the trainer can discuss with the trainees how their feelings about group formation are related to what is known in the literature about initiating the formation of a group. After the participants experience being a new member of a group, they should be better able to understand the relationship of knowledge and feelings. The role play activity provides a means of integrating theory and practice.

Action also means a commitment. It says that there is motivation to change and willingness to risk the possibility of not succeeding in what one is attempting to do. Group members are usually more willing to initiate action if there is a supportive environment for change, a positive outlook, and knowledge and skills to lower the possibility of failure. When the action is manageable and contains low risk, it is likely that these experiences, if successful, will provide positive reinforcement for additional advances. The group can offer a safe environment in which to gain confidence in their abilities.

Evaluating. Evaluating the process of growth and change enhances self-awareness and increases the possibility that the individual will continue to function at a high level and even improve. One aspect of evaluation is reflection, thinking over an encounter, in order to discover what went well and what might have been done differently. Perhaps it will help the group discover new ways of learning. It also enables the worker and group members to recognize feelings that accompany episodes, and this in turn opens them up to feedback about patterns of behavior.

Self-examination—and in the case of a group, reflection on the group interaction—clarifies thoughts, feelings, and the meaning of change. Either from personal introspection or the reaction of others, people can consciously weigh the benefits or costs of certain ways of behaving or thinking. Without these periods of reflection, it is likely that group members will continue doing the same self-defeating things, even though there were negative consequences to such past actions. The use of self-study provides a corrective mechanism to human behavior, and evaluation allows the group to refine its attitudes and change its reactions.

Periodic review makes it possible to redefine problems. After an evaluation process, people may perceive their original need or problem in a new light and adjust their priorities accordingly.

PRACTICE WITH GROUPS AS INTEGRATIVE AND HEALTH-ORIENTED

Integrative practice encompasses the aforementioned elements of social work with groups. The worker must maintain a flexible stance that responds to the needs and problems of a situation, whether he or she is intervening with a group member, the group, the social environment, or some combination. The integration interrelates these systems so that the group member is viewed as a unique person, a functioning member of a group, and part of a larger social environ-ment. The worker demonstrates self-awareness and conscious use of this understanding to engage group members, the group, and significant other persons in the lives of the group members. The holistic nature of social work views people in their multiple roles. It is also health-oriented since the values of self-determination and collaboration assume a partnership with societal resources to build on the strengths of the individual and the group as a whole. The use of differences and conflict is seen as an opportunity for growth, while the combination of challenge and support provide the balance necessary for resolving problems and enabling the group members to learn coping behaviors.

WHERE TO FIND THE TEN DIMENSIONS
OF SOCIAL WORK WITH GROUPS

This first chapter is meant to be an outline of essential elements in social work with groups as well as a guide to where the material will be found throughout the book. In this next section each of the ten dimensions will be identified with the appropriate chapter.

1. *Contacting prospective group members.* An understanding of types of groups in social work will prepare the reader for possible choices when they first encounter prospective group members. Chapter 3, "Types of Groups," describes four different kinds of groups that could be adapted to the particular needs of individuals. Chapter 5, "Practice Principles with Oppressed and Vulnerable Populations," notes guidelines for reaching the more resistant clients and describes the worker self-awareness necessary during initial contacts. Chapter 7, "Pregroup Planning," outlines the necessary steps in forming a group, so that the worker can prepare the agency as well as the prospective group members, and thus lessen resistance and increase the possibilities of success.

2. *Understanding presenting needs or problems.* The holistic nature of social work, and group work in particular, is brought out in the history of social work with groups (Chapter 2). The tradition here has always stressed a social-change purpose as well as individual and group growth. Chapter 4, "Knowledge and Values," and 5, "Practice Principles with Oppressed and Vulnerable Populations," assesses the relationship of individual, group, family, and community needs. Theories about social systems, small groups, roles, learning, and ego psychology are explained to assist the reader in comprehending human behavior in a broad perspective. Chapter 5 offers considerable informa-tion about the application of practice principles to various ethnic groups. Since assessment is an ongoing process that includes group members in joint problem solving, "Phases of Work" (Part III) is all relevant. In Chapter 7, for instance, the needs of the agency and staff are seen as having a bearing on how services are planned and implemented.

3. *Locating resources to benefit group members.* Part II, "Frameworks for Understanding," shows how to use resources to support, reinforce, and possibly affect changes in behavior. In Chapters 8, "The Beginning," 9, "The Middle," and 10, "The Ending," an environmental focus is shown helping group members become engaged with significant others or community resources as a dimension of helping. Chapter 11, "Social Action and System Development," demonstrates the location of resources as a vital step in achieving community or organizational development. In this formulation the expansion of helping efforts through people who are caring and accessible, and can offer a particular kind of knowledge or skill, increases the possibilities of growth and change for members of the group.

4. *Preparing for the group.* The practice principles in Chapter 5 offer specific guidelines for what to do with vulnerable groups. Being clear about expectations and group purpose is an essential part of being prepared. In Chapter 7, various aspects of the preparation phase are identified in some detail. These include approaches to work with the agency staff and potential group members in order to increase possibilities for success. A pregroup planning illustration reveals how the elements of planning are implemented with a specific group.

5. *Planning with group members.* The nature of group work requires that decision making become a joint process of working. Part II, "Frameworks for Understanding," highlights the values of this collaborative approach. The specific ways of accomplishing group involvement and problem solving are outlined in Chapter 6, "Use of Techniques," with examples of how this is done. The chapters in Part III, "Phases of Work" emphasize the importance of planning in discussing the goals of building self-esteem and empowerment. Chapter 8, in particular, which deals with the Beginning Phase, identifies tasks of the worker that involve group members in defining their purposes for being in the group and how they will work together. In Chapter 11, "Social Action and System Change," the planning process is shown as an essential element of initiating social action.

6. *Using professional self-awareness in a helpful way.* In Chapter 3, "Types of Groups," the worker becomes more understanding of appropriate role behavior, according to the type of group. Some of the principles in Chapter 5, "Practice Principles with Oppressed and Vulnerable Populations," refer directly to worker preparation, including self-awareness and realistic expectations. In Chapter 6, "Use of Techniques," self-disclosure is shown to be a helpful technique in building relationships with group members, especially those who may initially be more resistant to the formal role of social worker. In using the technique of reflection, the worker will often rely on his or her judgment or feelings to engage the group in a discussion of the meaning of events the group has taken part in. In Chapters 8–10, the self-awareness factor is used in the performance of worker tasks and techniques.

7. *Knowing how active or directive to be.* The discussion of small group theory in Chapter 4 describes stages of group development. The level of

worker/group member activity will vary according to the phase of the group. For instance, the worker is usually more active at the beginning and end of the group.

In Chapter 5, "Practice Principles," determining the nature of intervention will depend on a number of variables. If group members are particularly vulnerable because of a traumatic recent event or have low coping ability, the worker will initiate activity. But for groups with an abundance of indigenous leaders (leaders from within), the worker will encourage the balance of active leadership to shift toward them. This is discussed further in Chapter 8.

8. *Acting in a variety of social work roles.* Some of the similarities and differences of worker role are described in Chapter 3, "Types of Groups." The roles of staff member, team member, and supervisor/administrator are mentioned, but the researcher role, while important, was not discussed in the book because of space limitations. The roles within the group or community are discussed in Part III, "Phases of Work." Each worker task includes an environmental aspect, such as broker (Chapter 8), mediator, advocate, and collaborator or team member (Chapter 9), and referral agent (Chapter 10). The organizer role is amply demonstrated in Chapter 11, "Social Action and System Development." The roles within the group, such as therapist, educator, mediator, and discussion leader, are all described in Chapters 8–10 and in "Use of Techniques" (Chapter 6).

9. *Making use of group process and problem solving.* Group process as it unfolds through stages of group development is described in Chapter 4, "Knowledge and Values." The specific applications of group process and problem solving are brought out in Chapter 5, "Practice Principles." In Chapter 6, "Use of Techniques," relevant techniques engage the group in problem solving, especially the ones on Self-Awareness and Task Accomplishment. The twenty-seven tasks of work phases are elaborated upon in Chapters 8–10. Each of these chapters focuses on the aspects of individual and group functioning, as well as the environment surrounding the group. The dimension of the group is relevant to problem solving, especially in recognizing where conflict can become a source of creative tension. Chapter 8 outlines the task of planning with the group to accomplish its purposes.

10. *Encouraging psychological and social health.* This dimension permeates much of Parts II and III of the text. Part II, "Frameworks for Understanding," provides the conceptual rationale for what the worker and group members do. Part III, "Phases of Work," deals more with the specifics of what is done, primarily by the worker, in terms of actually helping group members achieve higher levels of coping behavior.

SUMMARY

The group worker is faced with a variety of persons and systems and works with them in response to their needs and problems. The model includes outreach and prevention, and applies particularly to those experiencing hardship because of social and economic disadvantage. In this holistic form of social work, attention is paid to system change as well as to change in personal attitudes and behavior. The group is the medium that enables members and significant others (family, friends, persons in communities) to develop helping relationships with one another.

The bio-psycho-social-cultural assessment offers a broad framework for understanding behavior in the social environment. In view of the many factors shaping the way people think, feel, and act, it is essential to partialize problems in order to set priorities.

Adequate time must be spent in preparing group members and the agency staff for the group, to lessen resistance and improve receptivity. A balance of homogeneity and heterogeneity in group composition will help to create the optimum conditions for growth and change in the group. With self-determination and collaborative problem solving as underlying values, the first task of the group is to clarify its reasons for meeting—establishing the working agreement. Throughout the process of working with the group, the practitioner must be self-aware and flexible, adjusting activity in accordance with the stage of group development, the functioning of members, the extent of indigenous leadership, and the basic reason for forming the group. The group worker should portray caring, empathy, and genuineness.

The social worker has many professional roles within the group, agency, and community. Often these roles are related such as practitioner/researcher, where the problem-solving framework is the common core for thinking and actions. In the practitioner roles within the group, as it evolves through various stages, the worker must maintain as goals the enhancement of mutual aid and task accomplishment. As the issues of personal versus group need are resolved, challenges abound, so that creative growth is possible for both the individual and the group. This can only take place if the group is a place where members feel safe and self-confident.

A goal of social work with groups is to foster psychological and social health through personal, group, and environmental change. Various techniques of the worker, often shared by group members, contribute to this health perspective: (1) clarifying the nature of the need or problem; (2) providing favorable conditions; (3) contributing the necessary knowledge, values, and skills; (4) emphasizing positive awareness of attitudes, behavior, and feelings; (5) taking action; and (6) evaluating the process and outcome.

REFERENCES

Clausen, J. A. (1986). *The life course: A sociological perspective*. Englewood Cliffs, NJ: Prentice Hall.

Collins, A. H. (1976). *Natural helping networks*. Washington, D.C.: National Association of Social Workers.

Dewey, J. (1916). *Democracy and education*. New York: Free Press.

Janis, I. L. (1982). *Groupthink*. Boston: Houghton Mifflin.

Justice, B. (1987). *Who gets sick: Thinking and health*. Houston: Peak Press.

Maguire, L. (1980). The interface of social workers with personal networks. *Social Work with Groups, 3*(3), 39–49.

Maluccio, A. N., & Marlow, W. D. (1974). The case for the contract. *Social Work, 19*(1), 28–36.

Middleman, R. R., & Goldberg, G. (1987). Social work practice with groups. In A. Minahan et al. (Eds.), *Encyclopedia of social work* (18th ed.) (pp. 714–729). New York: National Association of Social Workers.

TEACHING AND LEARNING IDEAS

Using the questions that follow, write an analysis of a group based upon the ten dimensions discussed in the chapter. The questions can also be used for discussion by student groups who are observing a group in action. An understanding of the knowledge, skills, and values from the remaining chapters will be necessary to fulfill this assignment in its entirety. However, parts of it could be used, after this chapter is read, as a means of examining the issues from the different sections.

Analysis of a Group

1. Describe the means of engaging people in the group. What is their motivation for coming to the group and how does their relative interest or accessibility affect participation and involvement?

2. What is the range of environmental resources and support available to the group member? How can an enlarged and effective helping network be encouraged, either by the group member taking more responsibility for increasing contacts or by the worker initiating further involvement by the significant other persons?

3. What are the essential elements of assessing individual and group behavior? Consider the physical condition, personality factors, social relationships, and cultural aspects of the individuals. What is the stage of group development, pattern of communication, norms, and values, structure of indigenous leadership, and interpersonal relationships in the group?

4. How did you prepare for the group? Consider this in terms of (a) defining the purpose; (b) arranging for pregroup interviews (if possible); (c) composing the group in regard to a common need, problem, or interest and varied coping patterns and abilities among group members; (d) preparing agency staff, if necessary; (e) arranging for the facilities of the agency to be available to group members.

5. How did you develop a contract or working agreement with the group so that they had an opportunity to exchange expectations with you and work toward a mutual understanding of group purpose and roles of group members and worker?

6. To what extent are you aware of how your own needs and biases might interfere with your judgment in making decisions or relating to group members? Are you discussing personal feelings or experiences appropriately?

7. Are you using yourself flexibly so that you may be more active or less active, depending on the needs of group members and stage of group development? To what extent are you able to demonstrate caring, offer empathic responses, and act out of genuine concern?

8. What are the various professional roles that are useful in the group or in the community or agency in behalf of the group? Are you experiencing any role conflict, and if so, what can you do about it?

9. How do you foster mutual aid and collaborative problem solving in the group? How do you help the group deal with the tension that may result from group members wanting to satisfy personal needs and yet accommodate themselves to the needs of the group? What are the techniques that are most useful and appropriate for this particular group? What are the tasks to help the group during its stage of group development?

10. Discuss how you have created favorable conditions for growth in the group. What does it mean for you to share power and control for the group with its members? How is activity used as a vehicle for interaction and building cohesion? What is the relative importance of imparting knowledge, skill development, release of feelings, and self-awareness for group members? How are you able to evaluate process and progress with the group?

CHAPTER 2

Historical Influences

This chapter traces the evolution of social group work from its earliest beginnings to the present day. This history provides a background for understanding group work as a problem-solving process, which treats psychological and social problems, enhances learning and socialization, and achieves system or social change. This kind of group work has become the property of many helping professions. Social workers may think of group work and social work as synonymous, but, in a bibliography of group work in the helping professions (Zimpfer, 1984), the author cites references in ninety journals of which only five concern social work.

There are many common elements in all forms of group work, but workers will shape practice with groups to fit their own particular values and purposes. In social group work these purposes are usually defined as corrective purposes, preventive purposes, normal social growth, personal enhancement, and citizen responsibility and participation (Hartford, 1964, 5–6). The emphasis has shifted recently toward the therapeutic use of groups, more in line with current clinical practice. However, the social-change direction for group work is enjoying a renewal of interest, especially in empowering oppressed and vulnerable populations to seek changes in their environment.

THE ROOTS OF GROUP WORK

Groups as social services were first developed in response to the social upheaval caused by the Industrial Revolution in England. Workers who came to the cities from rural areas found inadequate housing. Crime and delinquency were rampant. In the last half of the nineteenth century, a number of organizations were set up, primarily under religious auspices, to fulfill the spiritual and recreational needs of this vast new urban population.

Similarly, group service organizations were formed in the United States in response to the Industrial Revolution of the 1850s. Poverty, social isolation, long working hours, and little recreation created unstable social conditions. As in England, the agencies were rooted in the Judaic-Christian tradition that highlighted the dignity of people. Religious zeal activated the reformers for improving the living conditions of the poor and humanistic values underlying their belief that each person had the right to achieve maximum fulfillment.

Nevertheless, the prevailing view was that people were afflicted with poverty because of some personal shortcoming—a character defect or moral deficiency. Then in the late 1800s, a challenge to this view arose. Edward T. Devine (1867–1948), an economist and general secretary of the New York Charity Organization Society (Quaim, 1987, 920), pointed out that unhealthy social conditions contribute to the problems of individuals. He called for social action to improve the environment, and others who were attempting to help the poor also began to report the damaging effects of deteriorating neighborhoods (Reid, 1981, 51). A number of organizations, like Devine's New York Society, started to form private coordinating agencies to dispense relief funds; the first of these was established in Buffalo, New York, in 1877. They were instrumental in calling for the improvement of urban decay and supported legislation for better housing in the slums, improved penal institutions, and more desirable health care for poor families (Reid, 1981, 52).

Well-meaning volunteers, at first college students in England, went to live in poor neighborhoods, their mission to offer help to those less fortunate than themselves. The idea spread to the United States, primarily through the efforts of Stanton Coit (1857–1944), who had visited Toynbee Hall, a settlement house in England, and wanted to duplicate such efforts in this country. College-educated women lived in these early settlement houses, the first of which was the Neighborhood Guild (later University Settlement) in New York City (1886). These women wanted the trust of the neighborhood people and felt that the only way to gain their respect and acceptance would be to live among them. They were friendly neighbors, who responded to local needs. Being so close to the problems of the neighborhood, these volunteers often emphasized social reform above individual improvement. They were willing to be avant-garde in introducing new services, such as kindergartens, day nurseries, baths, art classes, baby clinics, workrooms for the unemployed, and many more (Bremner, 1956, 64–65).

Other group service agencies were formed to strengthen the character of young boys and girls: the Young Men's (and Young Women's) Christian Association, Boy Scouts and Girl Scouts, Catholic Boy's Brigade, Young Men's (and Young Women's) Hebrew Association, Boys Clubs and Girls Clubs. The programs in these agencies offered all forms of sports, crafts, singing, recreation, skill training, nature and camping, community service projects and vocational help (Reid, 1981, 63). They emphasized group activities to support normal growth and development of young people.

During the first years of the twentieth century, the sociologist Charles Horton Cooley (1864–1929) was responsible for developing the concept of the *primary group* (Cooley, 1909), such as a family or friendship group, which he envisioned as strongly influencing morality and socialization. Cooley's work, along with that of other sociologists of his day, paved the way for studying the small group as a transmitter of norms and social behavior.

Group services continued to be found mainly in leisure-time agencies and agencies for youths, each with a strong emphasis on religious values, moral development, and character building (Wilson, 1976, 6). Their closest professional tie was to progressive education and adult education. John Dewey, an educator at the University of Chicago (later Columbia), saw in this form of voluntary group association the potential for a creative form of learning. Through his close relationship with Jane Addams, who in 1889 had founded the famous Chicago settlement house, Hull House, Dewey was instrumental in moving group work toward a more scientific method. He believed there was a natural tendency for people to act impulsively in relation to a need, and that a more intelligent approach would be to direct action "into channels of examination of conditions, and doings that are tentative and preparatory" (Dewey, 1929, 223).

Dewey recognized that the small group contributed to the vitalization of local community life, so that democracy could be active and alive. He believed that continuous inquiry into all conditions of the community was essential, and that the actual means of accomplishing this kind of public awareness was through "face-to-face relationships by means of direct give and take" (Ratner, 1928, 484).

Mary P. Follett (1868–1933) was another pioneer in the use of group process and problem solving. She was active in industrial relations and as a vocational counselor with poor working families in Boston. According to Follett, the richness of groups lies in the contribution and unification of different ideas and values, and the creation of something new in the group process. Follett stated that "The complex reciprocal action, the intricate interweaving of the members of the group, is the social process" (Follett, 1918, 33).

In the 1920s, through the efforts of Wilbur Newstetter, Clara Kaiser, and the staff of the University Settlement in Cleveland, studies were organized to document leadership and group interaction. Newstetter used a sociometric analysis of groups at a summer camp to study group life, which was a way of looking at patterns of how group members related to one another. Grace Coyle, educated as a sociologist and social worker, published *Social Process in Organized Groups* (1930), and in 1929 Margaretta Williamson, in *The Social Worker in Group Work,* found that there were increasing commonalities of beliefs and techniques relating to work with people in groups (Williamson,

1929). Most practitioners believed that group work was an educational process, which, usually by means of activity or program, built character and fulfilled the growth and socialization needs of a normal population. However, practitioners also believed in participating in social action when it was necessary to strengthen community life and prevent social disorganization.

In the early 1900s group work was often referred to as club work. Young people would meet in leisure time settings such as Ys, community centers, and settlements, and take part in recreation-oriented groups. Neva Boyd (1876–1963) is particularly well-recognized for writing about recreation as an active means of personal fulfillment. She believed that activity could be used creatively in accordance with the needs of the group, and later wrote about the therapeutic effects of play for patients in a mental hospital (Boyd, 1936, 339–52).

Adult education was another important ingredient of group work during the formative years. Eduard Lindeman (1885–1953) was a pioneer in writing about group methods in adult education, describing education as the active participation of the learner in the social discovery process (Lindeman, 1926). Lindeman was an advocate, along with Dewey, of strong citizen participation in the affairs of the community. Many scholars and practitioners saw the small group as a means of educating people in democratic decision making that would prepare citizens for more active participation and responsibility in social change efforts within their neighborhoods.

BRANCHES OF GROUP WORK

Until the 1930s, group work had been a mixture of progressive and adult education, recreation, social action, and the research interest of social psychologists. Strong religious underpinnings remained from the earlier settlement-house days and from the sectarian agencies that emphasized moral development and cultural enrichment. With such a diversity of interests and beliefs about the use and value of groups, it is not surprising that we find group work growing into four separate and relatively distinct branches: social group work, group therapy, group relations, and research. Figure 2.1 outlines this in detail, and can be referred to during the discussion of these branches that follows.

Social Group Work

During the early 1900s, group workers and caseworkers shared common interests, especially in wanting to remedy poor social conditions. Mary Richmond, a casework pioneer, mentions group work as one of the forms of social work (Richmond, 1930). However, the eventual joining of group work into the social work family did not flow smoothly. Caseworkers were concerned that group work lacked professionalism, and they identified themselves with the growing popularity and status of psychiatry. In the 1920s, casework focused on

Historical events: The evolution of groups

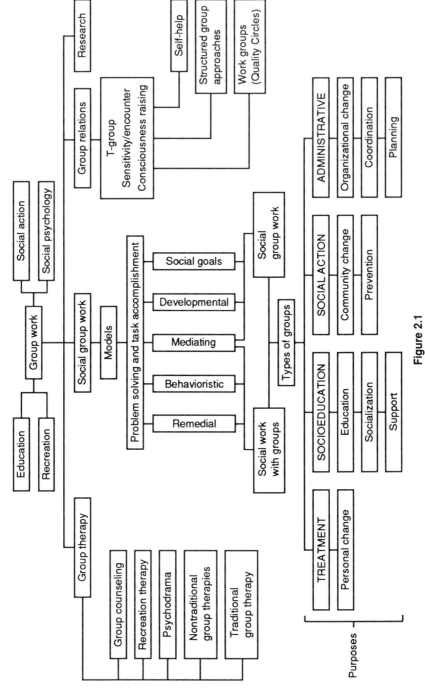

Figure 2.1

32

Freudian theory, emphasizing work with individuals and paying less attention to the impact of social conditions on human behavior. With its tradition of relying on education and recreation to provide healthy growth experiences for individuals and groups, group work did not find a receptive climate from the psychoanalytically oriented casework faculties at schools of social work. Somewhat earlier, in 1915, a report on social work education questioned whether group work had sufficient depth to be taught in a university setting (*Education for social work* 1915, 345–48).

The leaders in group work recognized the need for more research on the group method and wanted to develop educational materials with which to teach about professional practice. In 1930, faculty members at Western Reserve University in Cleveland and students from its School of Applied Social Sciences developed group records for teaching and a form on which to record and identify relevant aspects of group functioning (Reid, 1981, 120). Starting in 1929, Wilbur Newstetter's research with boys' groups at Camp Wawokiye provided further documentation about the properties of groups, how the needs of individuals are met through small groups, and the role of the group leader (Newstetter et al. 1938).

At the 1935 National Conference of Social Work, papers on group work were presented for the first time. These papers covered a wide range of subjects, including "Group Work and Social Change," by Grace Coyle, "The Integration of Group Work and Case Work," by Claudia Wanamaker, "Group Work Experiments in State Institutions in Illinois," by Neva Boyd and "What Is Social Group Work?" by Wilbur Newstetter. Newstetter's paper emphasized group work as a process, as a field, and as a range of techniques. He emphasized the group work process needs to include "both individual growth and social results" (Newstetter, 1938, 291), and went on to say that "the acceptance of group workers into the fraternity of social workers bears testimony to the broadening base of social work and an emphasis on generic concepts" (Newstetter, 1935, 299).

The establishment of the National Association for the Study of Group Work in 1936 helped to deepen the understanding of group work and move it toward professionalism. This group of professionals represented a wide range of interests in group work, reflecting the earlier historic ties to education, recreation, and social work. Some of these varied interests were also represented in a publication of the National Association of Social Workers, *New Trends in Group Work*, edited by Joshua Lieberman in 1938. Lieberman's first sentence of the preface indicates his orientation: "Group Work's outstanding contribution to the field of education is the experience it provides in social living" (Lieberman, 1938, v). In a 1939 publication, Samuel Slavson, an influential and active member of the association, writes:

> Until comparatively recently group or club work was a leisure-time occupation, with no educational or any other far reaching implication. Within the last

few years group work has come to be considered as a major educational influence. As a result, it is now referred to as *group education*. (Slavson, 1939, 126)

This was a time of ferment. People in group work began to move in different directions—toward social work, education, recreation, therapy, or research. The American Association for the Study of Group Work (changed from National to American Association in respect for Canadian colleagues) became the American Association of Group Workers (AAGW) in 1946—another big step toward social work for a large segment of practitioners. When AAGW joined the group work section of the National Conference of Social Work, the marriage with social work was becoming real.

In addition, two major books on social group work were published in the forties: *Group Work with American Youth* by Grace Longwell Coyle (1948) and the classic *Social Group Work Practice* by Gertrude Wilson and Gladys Ryland (1949). Both books added greatly to the quality of practice and education in social group work. The Wilson and Ryland text, in particular, had a broad focus on social group work for all ages and an in-depth analysis of program media.

But also within social work, various specializations and interest groups were developing, such as medical and psychiatric social work. In order to create a unified professional social work organization, the Temporary Inter-Association Council of Social Work (TIAC) was formed. In 1952 the AAGW voted to participate in TIAC, but there were some who dissented, because they did not want group work to lose its commitment toward fulfilling normal growth needs and social action in communities. Nevertheless, when the National Association of Social Workers was formed in 1955, group work was one of the major partners of the new alliance, solidifying its relationship with social work.

Group Therapy

During this time others explored the uses of small groups in psychiatric treatment. Samuel Slavson was a strong advocate of group work as an educational process. He was also the primary leader in the development of group therapy, which viewed the group as part of treatment in a program of psychotherapy. Slavson's early experiences were with children in what he called activity group therapy, in which the group leader creates a permissive climate for the children to express their feelings through craft activities and in discussion (Slavson, 1939, 132–133). Slavson continued his interest in group therapy with children and adults, using a psychoanalytic framework as a basis for his writings and practice.

Other developments in therapeutic group work preceded Slavson's. Neva Boyd's paper at the 1935 National Conference of Social Work discussed work at a state mental hospital begun in 1918. The recreational activities developed by the group leaders were geared to the needs of the patients. Boyd also described group activities at a training school for girls and a school for "mental defectives," which were used as vehicles for modifying behavior. She described the work as recreational group therapy (Boyd, 1935, 339–345).

Albert Alissi discusses the variety of group therapies, including those used in medical practice and other clinical group approaches, such as Freudian and neo-Freudian, adaptive approaches, psychodrama, reality therapy, transactional analysis, behavior therapy, existential group psychotherapy, bioenergetic therapy, primal scream, therapeutic social clubs and communities, repressive-inspirational groups, and the curative factors in group psychotherapy that were identified by the research and experiences of Irvin Yalom (Alissi, 1980, 341–353).

Although J. L. Moreno was a psychiatrist and is associated with group psychotherapy, his major contribution was in developing sociometric studies and psychodrama. By using a sociogram, which is a diagram of relationships in a group created from member choices, Moreno was able to identify patterns of group structure. The psychodrama is an experiential method in which participants enact life situations, those in the group playing significant roles associated with the dramatic episode (Moreno, 1985).

Of all the types of group psychotherapy, Yalom's approach is probably the most widespread today. He relied to a large extent on dealing with what was happening in the here and now of the group to the patient's environment outside the group. These models of group psychotherapy might be practiced by professionals from a variety of disciplines, including psychiatry, psychology, education, nursing or social work. Persons usually have an advanced degree in one of these fields and sometimes additional specialized training in the specific modality.

A range of group methods is also available, referred to as group counseling and guidance. While there may be a fine line between group counseling and group therapy, counseling is described in terms of developmental approaches (social experiences related to developmental problems), goal-directed methods, problem solving, Adlerian counseling, functional approach (principles of learning), group-centered counseling (Rogerian), and family group counseling. Usually these approaches are practiced in educational settings (Alissi, 1980, 353–357). The professional background of the group leader in these kinds of groups will likely be in educational psychology, guidance, or counseling, as well as in social work.

Group therapy is distinct from social group work, but many of the techniques and philosophies are shared. Just as social work incorporated into its repertoire Freudian theory and work with small groups, so psychotherapy developed a use for small groups.

Group Relations

The group-relations branch of group work focuses on increasing social and psychological awareness, rather than on individual treatment or social action. One of the most important group relations developments was the T (Training)

Group, a forerunner of the sensitivity and encounter group developed in 1946 by social psychologists, including Kenneth Benne, Leland Bradford, Ronald Lippitt, and Kurt Lewin. It started as a workshop in New Britain, Connecticut, to train leaders to be more effective in facilitating compliance with the Fair Employment Practices Act. The sponsor of the program, the Research Center for Group Dynamics located at the Massachusetts Institute of Technology, was interested in how the trainees would be able to apply leadership techniques to real-life situations. After the success of the initial workshop, the trainers continued the following year (1947) in Bethel, Maine, with what is now known as the T-Group. Persons participate in these groups to learn more about being an effective group leader or member rather than to solve a particular social or emotional problem. Members generally attempt to discover more about their behavior in an unstructured situation from the feedback of others on how they assume roles and react to members in creating a group (Benne, 1964, 80–83).

Other types of groups in this category include the following: the Group Relations Conference and S (Study) Groups, originated by A. K. Rice of the Tavistock Institute in London, which emphasized the examination of group processes and especially authority issues; the encounter group, an offshoot of the T-Group and sensitivity group, which relies on confrontation of group members to elicit self-awareness; the marathon group, which is like the encounter group but meets for one long session, supposedly wearing down defenses so that group members are more willing to risk the sharing of real feelings; Gestalt Therapy, influenced by Fritz Perls, which helps people become more aware of their total selves (physical, emotional, and cognitive) in the reality of the present moment; sensory awareness groups, created primarily by Bernard Gunther at Esalen, California, which seek to help people rediscover the joy of experiencing the senses and appreciating one's body and mind; and, finally, est groups, originated by Werner Erhard, which attempt to change people's thinking toward more positive belief systems (Alissi, 1980, 357–364).

Self-help groups, such as Alcoholics Anonymous, have proliferated in the last two decades. Although professionals do not lead these kinds of groups, they are a great source of support and resources for persons who are sharing similar problems or life experiences. The "support group," once associated with the consciousness raising of the women's movement, is a generally accepted type of growth group in our society, suitable for anybody, with no stigma attached. The role of the professional may be as a resource, helping the group get started or offering consultation to the facilitators once they are in progress.

Another major development in the use of small groups has been the Quality Circle, used mostly in business and industry as a means of involving employees in problem solving to insure better work. These are task-oriented groups, where the workers are not expected to bring in personal problems. However, workers often feel involved and appreciated for what they can contribute to better service or manufacture of goods.

The use of socioeducation groups in social work has drawn from the experience of people in the group-relations field. Actually, the educational component in these groups is nothing new, since this dimension was part of the historical development of social group work mentioned earlier. However, the combination of education and support make this type of group a powerful force for nurturance and personal growth that continues to the present day.

Research

Kurt Lewin (1890–1947) had a major impact on social group work through his research on small groups and the development of field theory—a way of explaining behavior as a response to interactive forces within the environment of the individual. When group work was struggling to find its identity in the 1920s and 1930s, social psychologists also made contributions while studying the properties of small groups. Ronald Lippitt, who collaborated with Lewin in the study of democratic, autocratic, and laissez-faire leadership (Lewin, Lippitt, and White, 1939, 271–299) was part of this research team.

However, there were some in group work who did not approve of research because they thought that people were being manipulated. They were not accustomed to group members being treated as subjects in an experiment, and for this reason there was a split between those who favored research and those who rejected it. This is one of the reasons why research in social group work was slow in coming.

But eventually, as social work with groups became more professionalized, use of research has increased in group work theory and practice. Garvin, writing in the *Encyclopedia of Social Work* (1987, 689), discusses several research papers that were published in the 1950s and 1960s, including Vinter's "Small Group Theory and Research: Implications for Group Work Practice Theory and Research" (1960) and Schwartz's "Small Group Science and Group Work Practice" (1963). Marvin Silverman (1966) reviewed social-group-work articles during an eight-year period (1956–1964) and found little research carried out during that time. Feldman (1986) did a follow-up study almost twenty years later (1975–1983) and concluded that actual research in social group work had enjoyed a modest increase, but the quantity and quality were still below what seemed desirable for a profession that wanted to be scientifically based. In 1985, the Symposium on Empirical Foundations of Group Work was formed to bolster research and has continued each year.

Anderson, writing in a special issue of *Social Work with Groups* (1986), discusses the need to integrate research and practice—a development that holds promise for building knowledge about group work and refining practice skills. In the next decade, demands for accountability of what social workers do will increase, along with more careful measuring of their effectiveness in work with groups.

MODELS OF SOCIAL GROUP WORK

Therapeutic group work increased substantially after World War II. During the war years, social workers worked closely with psychologists and psychiatrists in treating the emotional disorders of military personnel, and they were impressed by the therapeutic results of small group work in treating service-related problems. Fritz Redl, Gisela Konopka, and others who were to make substantial contributions in group work came from central Europe during the war and brought with them their backgrounds in psychoanalytic techniques.

As therapeutic group work became more and more common and workers took jobs in these specialized settings, new strains developed in the professional ranks. Those who were strongly committed to groups as a means to social action and to meeting leisure time needs saw the shift to psychosocial treatment as a threat. They felt that social group work was slipping away from the values of socialization, normal development, education, use of activity, and community involvement that had all been so much part of its tradition (Konopka, 1983, 8–9).

From 1959 to 1963, a committee of the Group Work Section of the National Association of Social Workers, chaired by Bernard Shiffman, met to clarify the definition of social group work. In a publication edited by Margaret Hartford, the committee reaffirmed that the focus of the social group worker is to address simultaneously the needs of the individual and the needs of the group:

> The social group work method is used to maintain or improve the personal and social functioning of group members within a range of purposes. Groups may be served for corrective purposes when the problem is in the person of group members or in the social situation or both, for prevention where group members are in danger of dysfunction, for normal growth purposes particularly at critical growth periods, for enhancement of the person and for the purpose of education and citizen participation. Any group may be served for any one or all of these purposes simultaneously, and the purposes of the service may change through time, but are related to the social functoning needs of the particular group members within their social context and within agency focus and goal. (Hartford, 1964, 5)

Ten working papers were included in this volume, along with an analysis of the contents. The committee's definition was an attempt to integrate the early group work tradition of normal social growth and social responsibility with the newer demands for clinical practice.

In the 1960s, when federal funds became available through the War on Poverty, group workers renewed their commitment to community work. Lines sometimes blurred between group work and community organization, as programs were developed to provide direct services and initiate social change. Traditionally, group workers had focused on self-determination and democratic decision making within the group, since the process of involvement and individual fulfillment was considered as important as the outcome of the completion of a task. Many community organizers were more task-oriented. Just as strains had developed between group workers with individual therapeutic aims and those who felt groups should emphasize social growth, now new strains developed between those who wanted to emphasize the group model and those who wanted to work for community change.

During the 1960s, workers with community organization backgrounds were often hired in settlement houses, since group workers often emphasized clinical goals, whereas settlements saw their functions as initiating social change. On the other hand, some institutions—YMCAs, YWCAs, and Jewish Community Centers, for example—continued to fulfill their traditional functions in providing education, recreation, and cultural awareness. Thus group work continued to shift in many directions.

PRACTICE DEVELOPMENTS AND REFINEMENTS

In the 1960s and 1970s there was an attempt to clarify models of practice. In 1966, Papell and Rothman wrote their classic article outlining three models of group work—the social goals, the remedial, and the reciprocal models—which still organize current thinking about practice with groups (Papell and Rothman, 1966, 66–77).

The *social goals model* reflected the writings of traditionalists who wanted to preserve the social action dimension of social group work. The *remedial model*, developed by Robert Vinter and colleagues at the University of Michigan, defined the use of groups for therapeutic purposes, to serve individuals who were most in need of services. In defining the remedial mode, the Michigan faculty made an important contribution in clarifying what they considered to be a "problem-oriented approach to practice" (Vinter, 1967, 1). William Schwartz was the leading exponent of the *reciprocal model*, in which the social worker mediates the differences between the individual and his or her social environment. This was done in the context of the group as a mutual aid system. The writings of Schwartz, using a social systems approach (see Chapter 4), provided a way of conceptualizing integrative practice with the person, group, and environment (Schwartz, 1961).

As a further development toward integrative practice, Roberts and Northen published their anthology, *Theories of Social Work with Groups* (1976), which included several theorists (Hartford, Northen, Schwartz, Parad et al., and Somers) who attempted to link group work with generic social work practice. The other significant development of the 1970s was the use of behavior-modification in group treatment (Rose, 1977). Since it was clear, specific, and easily researchable, behavior modification quickly became popular.

There was an attempt to clarify different group models not only within social work but also between social work and other human service professions. Lang, comparing therapeutic uses, found there were important differences between social work with groups and other group therapies. Other professions had "only partial correspondence to the core group concepts utilized by the social worker in the group" (Lang, 1979a, 107). For the most part, these other group therapies used psychological rather than sociological terms. Lang urged social workers to make use of the rich heritage and creative potential of social group work rather than consider themselves therapists doing group therapy (Lang, 1979b, 216). Papell and Rothman (1980, 7) define a mainstream group in social work as "characterized by common goals, mutual aid, and non-synthetic experiences," compared to group psychotherapy and a structured-group approach.

While many of the helping professions were discovering groups as a valuable addition to their treatment repertoire, the social work profession began to develop toward generic practice. Hearn used general systems theory as a way to formulate a unified conception of social work. He was hopeful for the prospects of a generic theory of practice (Hearn, 1958). Pincus and Minahan proposed a model based on systems thinking that addressed itself to working with target systems and action systems as well as the traditional client system. The social worker was identified as a change-agent system (Pincus and Minahan, 1973). There were changes in schools of social work to design more generic and integrated curricula.

As schools of social work have attempted to integrate work with individuals and small groups in a direct practice course, work with groups has taken on secondary importance and in some cases the group has not been used at all (Goldberg and Lamont, 1986). Part of the reason for this development is that few persons teaching this kind of course have formal education and practice experience with social work groups. If the group dimension is covered, it is more likely that it is group treatment, possibly fashioned after group therapy with psychiatrists or psychologists as the role models.

GROUPS IN DIRECT PRACTICE

There has been a resurgence of interest in group work, as evidenced by the formation of the Committee for the Advancement of Social Work with Groups in 1978, now called the Association for the Advancement of Social Work with Groups. The use of the group is now an integral part of all aspects of social work. The task group in social policy, planning, or administration has also taken on renewed significance as the importance of groups in the decision-making process gains increased recognition. Zimpfer found that in comparing his first edition (1976) on *Group Work in the Helping Professions* to the second edition (1984), there was "creativity, vitality, and explosive increase in the use of the group in delivering helping service" (Zimpfer, 1984, 5).

The challenge within the profession of social work is to continue the tradition of using groups for environmental change and personal development, along with treatment of psychosocial dysfunction. The humanistic framework of Tropp, which focuses on "group-oriented efforts that revolve around common concerns or common life situations" (Tropp, 1969, 1), is part of this tradition, and is described as a developmental model (Tropp, 1976, 198–237). Gitterman and Shulman (1985/1986) have continued writing in the tradition of Schwartz. They have also deepened the integration of mutual aid groups in relation to stages of the life cycle (1986).

The creative use of activity is another aspect of social group work that should not be lost in the trend toward direct practice. For certain kinds of group members, especially children, the planning of activities or program is the most effective way to fulfill the purpose of the group. Activities can also be used spontaneously according to individual and group needs in the here-and-now of the group experience (Middleman, 1983). It is viewed as a means to individual or group change rather than as an end in itself.

GROUPS FOR HEALTH, PREVENTION AND PRODUCTIVITY

One of the most significant developments in health care in the United States in the last twenty years has been the widespread use of support groups, sometimes called self-help groups. Meyer reports that there are over 6 million such groups, and sufficient research evidence has surfaced to demonstrate the link between social supports and health (Meyer, 1985, 291). It has been found that people can actually bolster their immune systems to prevent illness when there are strong social supports available to them (Justice, 1987, 127–140). Not all social supports are in the form of small groups. The formal and informal relationships in the family, work, or neighborhood environment can also contribute significantly to self-esteem and a positive outlook. However, for those persons who are socially isolated or need someone to share a common problem or situation, the small group can have tremendous preventive/supportive importance. It is reported that participation in such groups can reduce the need to seek professional help (Gottlieb, 1985, 293–300).

With reduced funding for social programs and greatly increased spending for health care, there is less time and fewer staff resources to provide direct services. It is likely that we will need to redefine the role of the professional helper to include training of indigenous and peer leaders so that support networks can be expanded in lieu of longer-term professional care. As we look ahead into the next decade, the small group should take on even more importance because of its potential for strengthening individuals and preventing problems.

Another place where small groups have made an impact is in business and industry. The Quality Circle, where employees meet in small groups to share ideas and information about how to produce a better product, has saved a great deal of money for companies. It is simply good business to involve workers in some forms of participation and decision making. For this reason perhaps as many as 90 percent of the Fortune 500 companies are now using Quality Circles as a means of employee involvement and idea sharing (Lawler and Mohrman, 1985).

Human service organizations have made less use of the Quality Circles than industry, perhaps because they are set up to be task-oriented and do not deal with the socioemotional aspects of behavior. Nevertheless, such organizations often find it helpful for staff to engage in stress management groups to reduce or prevent the powerful effects of burnout (Brown, 1984, 55–66).

Social workers with an expertise in work with groups can offer help within organizations and communities as resource persons, trainers, and consultants. If group work increases substantially in the health care system, there will be a need for more staff and peer leaders of self-help groups in the future, to understand group dynamics and offer leadership in helping groups to function successfully.

RETURNING TO OUR ROOTS

In examining the history of group work, with its long traditions, it becomes clear that old values are still with us: helping people to reach their fullest potential; increasing mutual aid through social relationships; improving social conditions. Today groups emhasize short-term problem solving rather than longer intrapsychic treatment. We still use activity—mainly in children's groups—but it more often takes the form of structured exercises than that of involving the group members in decision making or the creative use of communication and interaction to meet their needs. Groups providing services to high risk or disadvantaged populations are on the rise. The cry for prevention will be a major priority. With resources scarce and shrinking and staff size decreasing, agencies will turn more to groups as a way of serving a greater number of people. Meanwhile, the crisis of training for work with groups continues, just as the curricula of schools of social work are lessening their emphasis on group work.

Other professional disciplines are filling in the void created by social work. Perhaps the lesson that we have learned throughout all these years is that group work does not belong solely to one profession. The use of the group is valuable enough to be shared by those professionals who wish to help people become empowered and active in their own behalf and to benefit others.

SUMMARY

There has been a progression in the development of groups in social work—from group work as essentially an educational process to a social-treatment orientation. In this shift, schools of social work pay less attention to teaching group work as a separate helping method. The current direction is toward the inclusion of social work with groups within a direct practice curriculum. The traditional values and strengths of social group work—such as attention to prevention, socialization, education, and social action—are receiving less of a priority than the treatment approach.

Today, demand is increasing for expertise in specialist areas, such as intervention with families. How then can social work educators help students gain proficiency in work with groups? On the one hand, a generalist must understand unified ways of dealing with social problems. On the other, the specialist needs skills in working with specific persons or groups. The challenge for the educator is to locate skills available among individuals, families, and small groups, and show how these skills can be applied in accordance with the needs and problems of the population being served.

The history of social work with groups reveals that integrated practice has been with us since the settlement houses first attempted to meet the needs of slum residents and to help them improve their living conditions. The attention was on the social problems in the community, and work with individuals, families, and groups was directed toward solving those problems.

In the next chapter on types of groups, the commonalities and differences in the role of the social worker with four types of groups will be explained: the treatment group; the socioeducation group; the social action group; and the administrative group.

REFERENCES

Alissi, A. S. (1980). Comparative group methods. In A. S. Alissi (Ed.), *Perspectives on social group work practice* (pp. 341–377). New York: The Free Press.

Anderson, J. D. (1986). Integrating research and practice in social work with groups. *Social Work with Groups, 9*(3), 11–124.

Benne, K. D. (1964). History of the T group in the laboratory setting. In L. P. Bradford, J. R. Gibb & K. D. Benne (Eds.), *T-group theory and laboratory method*. New York: John Wiley and Sons.

Boyd, N. (1935). Group work experiments in state institutions in Illinois. *Proceedings of the National Conference of Social Work, 1935*. Chicago: University of Chicago Press.

Bremner, R. H. (1956). *From the depths*. New York: New York University Press.

Brown, L. N. (1984). Mutual help staff groups to manage work stress. *Social Work with Groups, 7*(2), 55–66.

Cooley, C. H. (1909). *Social organization*. New York: Charles Scribner's & Sons.

Coyle, G. L. (1930). Social process in organized groups. New York: Richard R. Smith.

———(1948). *Group work with American youth*. New York: Harper and Brothers.

Dewey, J. (1929). *The quest for certainty: A study of the relation of knowledge and action*. New York: Mentor, Balch and Company.

Education for social work (1915). Reprinted from the Report of the Commissioner of Education for the Year ended June 30, 1985. Washington, DC: U.S. Government Printing Office.

Feldman, R. (1986). Group work knowledge and research: A two decade comparison. *Social Work with Groups, 9*(3), 7–14.

Follett, M. P. (1918). *The new state.* New York: Longmans, Green and Co.

Garvin, C. (1987). Group theory and research. In A. Minahan et al. (Eds.), *Encyclopedia of social work.* New York: National Association of Social Workers.

Gitterman, A., & Shulman, L. (Eds). (1985/1986). The legacy of William Schwartz: Group practice as shared interaction. *Social Work with Groups, 8*(4). New York: Haworth.

———(1986). *Mutual aid groups and the life cycle.* Itasca, IL: F. E. Peacock.

Goldberg, T., & Lamont, A. (1986). Do group work standards work? Results from an empirical exploration. *Social Work with Groups, 9*(3), 89–109.

Gottlieb, B. H. (1985). Assessing and strengthening the impact of social support on mental health. *Social Work 30*(4), 293–300.

Hartford, M. E. (1964). Frame of reference for social group work. In M. E. Hartford (Ed.), *Working papers toward a frame of reference for social group work* (pp.4–10). New York: National Association of Social Workers.

———(1976). Group methods and generic practice. In R. W. Roberts and H. Northen (Eds.), *Theories of social work with groups* (pp. 45–74). New York: Columbia University Press.

Hearn, G. (1958). *Theory building in social work.* Toronto: University of Toronto Press.

Justice, B. (1987). *Who gets sick: Thinking and health.* Houston: Peak Press.

Konopka, G. (1983). *Social group work: A helping process* (3rd ed.). New York: Prentice Hall.

Lang, N. (1979a). A comparative examination of therapeutic uses of groups in social work and in adjacent human service professions: Part I—The literature from 1955–1968. *Social Work with Groups, 2*(2), 101–115.

———(1979b). A comparative examination of therapeutic uses of groups in social work and in adjacent human service professions: Part II—The literature from 1969–1978, *Social Work with Groups, 2* (3), 197–220.

Lawler III, E. E., & Mohrman, S. A. (1985). Quality Circles after the fad. *Harvard Business Review, 63*(1), 65–71.

Lewin, K., Lippitt, R., & White, R. (1939). Patterns of aggressive behavior in experimentally created "social climates." *Journal of Social Psychology 10,* 271–299.

Lieberman, J. (1938). *New trends in group work.* New York: Association Press.

Lindeman, E. (1926). *The meaning of adult education.* New York: New Republic.

Meyer, C. (1985). Social supports and social workers: Collaboration or conflict? *Social Work 30*(4), 291.

Middleman, R. R., & Goldberg, G. (1987). Social work practice with groups. In A. Minahan et al. (Eds.) *Encyclopedia of social work* (18th ed.) (pp. 714–729). New York: National Association of Social Workers.

Middleman, R. R. (Ed.). (1983). Activities and action in groupwork. *Social Work with Groups, 6*(1). New York: Haworth.

Moreno, J. L. (1985). *Psychodrama,* vol. I (4th ed.). Ambler, PA: Beacon House.

Newstetter, W. I. (1935). What is social group work? *Proceedings of the National Conference of Social Work.* Chicago: The University of Chicago Press.

———,W. I., Feldstein, M. J., & Newcomb, T. M. (1938). *Group adjustment: A study of experimental sociology.* Cleveland: School of Applied Social Sciences, Western Reserve University Press.

Northen, H. (1976). Psychosocial practice in small groups. In R. W. Roberts and H. Northen (Eds.), *Theories of social work with groups* (pp. 116–152). New York: Columbia University Press.

Papell, C. P., & Rothman, B. (1966). Social group work: Possession and heritage. *Journal of Education for Social Work, 2* (2), 66–77.

———(1980). Relating the mainstream model of social work with groups to group psychotherapy and the structured group approach. *Social Work with Groups, 3*(2), 5–23.

Parad, H. J., Selby, L., & Quinlan, J. (1976). Crisis intervention with families and groups. In R. W. Roberts and H. Northen (Eds.), *Theories of social work with groups* (pp. 304–330). New York: Columbia University Press.

Pincus, A., and Minahan, A. (1973). *Social work practice: Model and method*. Itasca, IL: F. E. Peacock.

Quaim, J. K. (1987). Edward Thomas Devine. In A. Minahan et al. (Eds.), *Encyclopedia of social work*. New York: National Association of Social Workers.

Ratner, J. (1928). *The philosophy of John Dewey*. New York: Henry Holt.

Reid, K. E. (1981). *From character building to social treatment*. Westport, CT: Greenwood Press.

Richmond, M. E. (1930). Some next steps in social treatment. *The long view: Papers and addresses by Mary E. Richmond* (pp. 484–491). New York: Russell Sage Foundation.

Roberts, R. W., & Northen, H. (Eds.) (1976). *Theories of social work with groups*. New York: Columbia University Press.

Rose, S. D. (1977). *Group therapy: A behavioral approach*. Englewood Cliffs, NJ: Prentice Hall.

Schwartz, W. (1961). The social worker in the group. *New perspectives on services to groups: Theory, organization, practice: Social work with groups, 1961*. New York: National Association of Social Workers.

——— (1963). Small group science and group work practice. *Social Work, 8*(4), 39–46.

——— (1976) Between client and system: The mediating function. In R. W. Roberts and H. Northen (Eds.), *Theories of social work with groups* (pp. 171–197). New York: Columbia University Press.

Silverman, M. (1966). Knowledge in social group work: A review of the literature. *Social Work, 11*(3), 56–62.

Slavson, S. R. (1939). *Character education in a democracy*. New York: Association Press.

Somers, M. L. (1976). Problem solving in small groups. In R. W. Roberts and H. Northen (Eds.), *Theories of social work with groups* (pp. 331–367). New York: Columbia University Press.

Tropp, E. (1969). *A humanistic foundation for group work practice*. New York: Selected Academic Readings.

———(1976). A developmental theory. In R. W. Roberts and H. Northen (Eds.), *Theories of social work with groups*. New York: Columbia University Press.

Vinter, R. D. (Ed.). (1967). *Readings in group work practice*. Ann Arbor, MI: Campus Publishers.

Vinter, R. (1960). Small group theory and research: Implications for group work practice theory and research. In L. Kogan (Ed.), *Social science theory and social work research*. New York: National Association of Social Workers.

Williamson, M. (1929). *The social worker in group work*. New York: Harper.

Wilson, G. (1976). From practice to theory: A personalized history. In R. W. Roberts and H. Northen (Eds.), *Theories of social work with groups*. New York: Columbia University Press.

Wilson, G., & Ryland, G. (1949). *Social group work practice*. Boston: Houghton Mifflin.

Zimpfer, D. G. (1976). *Group work in the helping professions*. Muncie, IN: Accelerated Development.

———(1984). *Group work in the helping professions* (2nd ed.). Muncie, IN: Accelerated Development.

TEACHING AND LEARNING IDEAS

1. Divide the class into small discussion groups, each group taking one of the following topics:

    (a) How do the origins and developments in group work help us to understand current issues and problems in social work, such as the increase in treatment groups compared to prevention and social action groups or how group work can be used in problems of homelessness.

    (b) What is the relationship of social work with groups compared to the use of groups in other helping professions?

    (c) Has social work with groups evolved toward more integrative practice? If so, in what way?

After the groups have met for a period of time, have a person from each group give a report on a panel, followed by a discussion.

2. Visit a settlement house, if one is located in your community, and look for group work's historical influences in what is happening in the agency.

3. Interview a social worker who was educated as a social-group-work major over twenty-five years ago. Find out from him or her what the differences are in group work now compared to an earlier time.

CHAPTER 3
Types of Groups

The groups which social workers lead or with which they interact form a continuum, from those that focus on personal change through those that focus on enrichment or socialization to those that focus on task accomplishment. Even at the far ends of the continuum, some elements of other emphases remain: Personal growth groups almost always need to accomplish certain tasks, and social action groups almost always require some self-awareness. Groups can be considered the link between micro and macro practice, since all groups deal to some extent with both the socioemotional and the task dimensions.

In the first chapter, four types of group were identified: the treatment group, socioeducation group, social action group, and administrative group. These four types will be examined more closely, to highlight their similarities and differences and show how the role of the worker may vary with each group.

TREATMENT GROUP

Where personal change or therapy is the main purpose of a group, attention focuses on the presenting problems of group members. Group therapy is defined as "A systematic process and activity designed to remedy, cure, or abate some disease, disability, or problem" (Barker, 1987, 164). Treatment groups represent the continuing evolution of the group therapy movement, which emerged during and after World War II. Such groups engage in resolving emotional or social issues, and the emphasis is on sharing information and feelings, both for greater understanding of the problem and to implement change.

Treatment groups are most effective when group members are able to share leadership, either by offering support to others, by providing information, or by offering feedback to those in the group about the meaning and effects of their behavior. A therapeutic relationship based on caring, respect, and empathic listening should be fostered, although group workers may become more directive if members with many deficits cannot assume indigenous leadership. The worker initiates action to help treatment group members recognize and evaluate their strengths and limitations, so that members will be able to use themselves constructively in making choices about alternative ways of resolving problems. Workers should be focused on assisting in the modification of individual behavior, but they should also attempt to strengthen group bonds, so that the group itself can develop more fully and become a healthier place for change to occur.

Members of treatment groups may be more inclined than members of other groups to use defense mechanisms to protect themselves from the pain of intrapsychic conflict, the experience of loss, or the awareness of physical or mental deterioration. These defenses need to be respected, since they may represent the only way that individuals can respond to the pain of the conflict. However, as one of the goals of the treatment group is to help participants use constructive methods of solving problems or dealing with life issues, group members should be encouraged to seek alternative behaviors or roles that will, in the long run, offer them more satisfaction. In order for people to be willing to change, they must activate latent strengths and receive support and affection from the worker and group members. The extent to which the group can be mobilized to offer mutual aid will often be the determining factor in motivating group members to give up unhealthy or unproductive behavior. Once that happens, they will be open to new approaches to solving problems.

If the environmental conditions of group members are favorable, they are more likely to be supported in their efforts to make changes in their lives. Members should be encouraged to strengthen relationships with persons outside the group or modify living arrangements that may adversely affect the problem. In most cases this will be done solely by the individuals. However, there may be times when the worker will act as a mediator, advocate, or broker and work with persons in the family or community to strengthen the therapeutic potential of the member's environment. This will be done with the group member, or when the worker acts alone, the group member will be involved in joint planning of the activity.

Example of a Treatment Group

A women's group meets weekly at a community mental health center. All the women have symptoms of anxiety or depression, and several have been hospitalized for emotional problems. While in the group, members are encouraged to bring out personal issues and use the group for problem-solving.

> Betty presented a problem to the group. She was having overwhelming feelings of fear, sadness, and anger toward her family and especially her husband. He had been gravely ill with a massive heart attack. Betty felt guilty for these feelings and thought she should be "strong and control herself and her feelings." Betty had a history of recurring major depressive episodes and had been in psychiatric hospitals many times. Group sessions had discussed how Betty tended to use depression as a means of avoiding her anger. In response to what Betty said about needing to control her anger, the worker asked Betty if she could see her behavior now as a pattern of previous behavior. The worker also asked the group if they could recognize the pattern. Other group members could understand Betty's feelings.
>
> Rose started talking about her own separate issue. The worker suggested they stay on Betty's topic before moving on and then asked Rose if she could identify with Betty's issue herself. After some further discussion by the group members about illness, the worker suggested that the group members explore their feelings about illness. At that point Betty started to talk about the possibility of her husband dying. It was obvious that she was fighting back the tears.
>
> Shirley jumped in and minimized the situation. The worker interpreted her action as an avoidance of sadness. Shirley agreed and related that the issue brought back memories of when her own husband died two years earlier.
>
> The worker asked the group how they were feeling. Several group members talked about the difficulty of seeing someone sad and their need to change that feeling of sadness. The worker talked about the need to express sad feelings when they occur and tried to normalize these feelings with the group. This led to further group interaction, which in turn led to crying by the members. They were comforting one another during this expression of emotion. In the last ten minutes, the worker asked the group to discuss what they thought had taken place during the group session and encouraged them to express any leftover concerns.

During this group session the worker is particularly aware of the possible relationship between withholding anger and symptoms of depression. She encourages group members to express their anger in the accepting climate of the group. It is also necessary for the worker to recognize the meaning of the avoidance and how important this defense may be for them. A skill of the worker is to understand when it is appropriate to challenge their avoidance and encourage them to express feelings and when to face them only minimally with this resistance. This will depend on the strengths of group members, the stage of group development, how able they are to support one another, and the nature of the issue being addressed. Some problems are too sensitive to be confronted unless the worker is assured that there is sufficient acceptance within the group and inner resources among group members to risk personal disclosure.

Even though the treatment group is especially responsive to individual change, attention must also be paid to group cohesiveness, in order to strengthen mutual aid and interaction among the members. The worker will probe gently to encourage the expression of feelings and always support strengths.

SOCIOEDUCATION GROUP

Socioeducation groups are formed for purposes of education, socialization, and support, and are the natural outgrowth of the earliest group work efforts. Some groups focus on educating group members in regard to a particular interest or problem—members, for instance, who are mandated to participate in an alcoholism program because of drunken driving, or who have joined a parent-education program to bolster their parenting skills. Other socioeducation groups range from preadolescents who participate in after-school clubs to former mental patients who meet on a regular basis at a community mental health center for social activities; from women-in-transition groups for women facing similar life events to staff stress-management groups at human service agencies. In each case, members are learning behaviors appropriate to social interaction. Few groups in this category are purely education, purely socialization, or purely support-oriented. Instead, these ingredients are usually blended.

Workers facilitating socioeducation groups need to provide reinforcement of positive behavior and to encourage individuals to recognize their strengths and expand upon them. Supporting negative behavior is not desirable, since such behavior, if met with approval, will probably continue. Workers must differentiate between positive and negative behavior—not always an easy task.

There is a significant difference between acknowledging feelings, ideas, or behaviors and supporting them. With acknowledgement, individuals are recognized and accepted as having certain feelings or ideas, even if these feelings or ideas should not be encouraged, since they could prove dysfunctional. Among boys on probation for delinquency, for example, a favorite pastime might well be the sharing of "war stories"—experiences associated with delinquent acts. When this happens, the worker might use these stories as a way of encouraging the boys to acknowledge the feelings of hostility or disempowerment that led to their antisocial actions. The hostility or disempowerment might well be validated by the worker—but the next step would be to help the boys discover other ways of expressing these hostile feelings, which would bring attention but not trouble.

Workers should also assist group members in identifying the *roles* in their lives. Roles are socially determined behaviors, and members can often be encouraged to pursue these behaviors in ways that are more appropriate or more socially acceptable than what they have been doing up to that point. In other words, members can be encouraged to behave according to what society expects of people in those roles (Anderson and Carter, 1984, 232–233).

Some role behavior can be learned, and socioeducation groups can provide the context for learning. Garvin refers to these groups as role-attainment groups and discusses strategies of "social skills training, task-centered group work, and behavior modification in groups" in helping persons learn roles that they are already in or aspire to fulfill (Garvin, 1987, 240–253).

Socioeducation groups can also be used to train lay care givers in human services or to serve as a means of ongoing consultation. Agencies are sometimes unable to reach certain resistant populations, and in these cases, it may be feasible to work through those persons who do have access to them: teachers, parents, clergy, recreation staff, or their peers. Such groups, properly trained, could have great prevention value (Radin, 1985).

Example of a Socioeducation Group

A public welfare department offered a six-session group for people who were homeless. It took place at the county's shelter for homeless families. The purposes were to provide information and encouragement while persons were looking for housing. This was the fifth session.

> The group was asked to update the others about their housing search activity for the week. Since no one volunteered to begin the discussion, the worker asked Gloria to tell the group about the apartment she was close to getting last week. Gloria said that she did not get the apartment, and it became apparent that her race was the issue. The worker offered to look into having a Legal Services attorney attend a group session to discuss what could be done about housing discrimination. This seemed to interest the group members. All agreed that racism was a significant obstacle to black families.
>
> Wilma was also denied an apartment because of her race. The landlord was interested when she called, but when she went to meet him face to face, he changed his mind. Wilma expressed her anger about these experiences. It was significant that Wilma both offered to speak in the group and that she did so at length. Up till then, she had been silent, answered in monosyllables, or when pressed, literally shook with anxiety while speaking. During this session she appeared comfortable talking to the group.
>
> The other group members summarized their activities during the week. Bill reviewed a multitude of problems he had with his prior landlord, Mr. Davis. Bill was confronted by the worker for blaming the landlord for all his tenancy problems. The worker pointed out that last week Bill had revealed that he put his rent money "up his nose." Then Susan added that she and Bill had an argument during the week about his smoking pot. A long discussion followed regarding drug and alcohol dependence. Gloria brought up problems created by her former boyfriend's addiction. Bill appeared emotionally affected by the group.
>
> This was the first meeting where sensitive personal issues had been brought up and addressed. Enough trust between the members had developed to allow this to occur in five sessions, especially since there was a different collection of group members each week.

This kind of group offers all the dimensions of a socioeducation group: education (information about looking for housing, identifying obstacles, home-share arrangements, approaching a landlord, filling out applications), socialization (participating as a member and leader, social skills), and support (gaining approval, recognition, feelings of competency). The problems of racism were discussed from the experiences of the group members. Being able to bring out a personal encounter with landlord discrimination in the accepting environment of the group enabled Wilma to speak with more assurance. Members were learning to be more assertive in their role behavior.

It is significant that Bill was confronted with his drug problem even though this was not meant to be a treatment group. Was it appropriate for the worker to confront a member about a personal problem in this kind of group? Since Bill's use of drugs may have been one reason for his housing difficulties, it is acceptable practice for this issue to be raised. The next step would be to refer Bill to an agency where he could get help with this problem. The most that could be hoped for in the six sessions is that Bill has gained sufficient trust in the worker to follow through on the referral.

The socioeducation group blends education, socialization, and support with increased self-awareness. The severity of a problem does not determine whether the person should be in a treatment or socioeducation group. As a matter of fact, persons who are fragile as a result of emotional problems often do better, at least initially, in a socioeducation group, where there will be less challenge to their defenses. If sufficient ego strength has been developed, a member may go on to a treatment group.

SOCIAL ACTION GROUP

The social action group has strong roots in the profession of social work. The early reformers addressed issues such as poor housing, unsanitary conditions, and lack of recreation and adequate health facilities. More recently, social action groups have attempted to change policies, practices, and attitudes that are discriminatory or inhibit personal development of community residents. For instance, parents may organize to improve schools; the homeless may participate in a march to publicize their plight; or professionals in a community may join with neighborhood people for a conference on prevention of teen suicide. In the formation of such groups, group members are usually clear about what they want to accomplish, although some persons may have specific personal needs that will influence the direction of the group.

Although the group is task-focused, interpersonal issues sometimes interfere with the accomplishment of the task. The worker deals with these as the group-maintenance part of his or her role.

Since the primary purpose of the group is community development and change, the group is action-oriented and will spend its time planning strategy and initiating action. Presumably, persons in this type of group have strengths and the inner resources that will be needed to deal with the complexities that crop up when change is planned. The worker will do as much as necessary to mobilize the group to use its abilities in the problem-solving process. He or she will also share information about helpful resources.

Groups of this nature often seek larger changes than are feasible or manageable in a limited period of time. The worker must help them locate more realistic goals, even though these are smaller than members initially desired. Small accomplishments may lead to larger ones at a later time. In these smaller and more manageable tasks, the group can more readily exercise control of the decision making, or they can enlist the help of persons outside the group, who are more able to influence a process of change.

Even with a feasible plan for social change, persons affected by such change may resist. The worker, during these times, will need to offer support, recognize members' feelings of discouragement, and help them appreciate their successes, however small they may be. It may be possible to join forces with other groups who share common interests. Forming a larger group of this kind may create some instability in the original group at first. However, the gain in strength from such a union of forces could bring the combined group much closer to accomplishing its goals.

Example of a Social Action Group

The Inter-Agency Youth Council is an organization of agency staff persons, who meet on a monthly basis to discuss the needs and problems of adolescents in an interracial urban community. They have been together for several years, sharing agency practices in relation to young people, identifying specific areas of concern, and coordinating their efforts to deal with the problems. They have also attempted to plan ways to prevent problems. The worker for this group is a staff person from a family counseling agency, who initiated the idea of coordinating services for youths and their families.

It was suggested at one of the meetings that the group find out the extent to which youth problems exist in the community so they would be able to set priorities for action. They decided to do a survey of what certain population groups thought about the severity of a listing of problems. First, the Council identified areas to study: family stress, alcohol and drugs, pregnancy and venereal disease, recreation and socialization, employment opportunities, racial tension, school, and antisocial behavior. A twenty-four-item questionnaire was drawn up about these areas and distributed to high school students, parents, teachers, school administrators, and community agency staff. They were asked to indicate the degree to which the listed problems affected them personally or whether they know that the problem affects adolescents. The results of the questionnaire were compared. Responses from students and adults were remarkably similar. Use of drugs was identified as the most important problem, followed by not enough jobs, drinking alcohol, and being bored at school. Another part of the questionnaire asked the respondents to suggest ways of dealing with any of the problems. There were many useful suggestions.

With this information, the Council was able to focus their energies according to selected priorities. Since so many persons had been involved in the survey and in a discussion of its results, there was more awareness and readiness of people in the community to become engaged in the implementation stage. Committees were formed, representing students, parents, school, and agency personnel to evaluate the suggestions and propose action alternatives for the Council to consider.

This is just one type of social action group that involves coordination by agencies serving the same population. It seems logical to assume that, since resources in communities are scarce, there would be a pooling of expertise and collaboration in dealing with complex social problems. This does not always happen. Interagency communication is often lacking. Professionals claim that there isn't enough time to get together. Time is one factor, of course; however, agencies also perceive that the delivery of social services becomes more complicated when there is joint planning with other professionals. Conflict over responsibility, professional philosophy, the structure of services, and the policies of agencies may be raised when there is a collaborative effort. Often, it just seems easier to go it alone. Yet, agencies may be duplicating services, or for clients using several different agencies, expectations of one agency may be inconsistent with those of another, causing confusion. Agencies need to work together in the planning and delivery of services, and in preventing social problems. Moreover, social change often requires mass action by interested persons and groups. In the example of the Inter-Agency Youth Council, a staff person from one agency agreed to provide the leadership for bringing other professionals together. Such a joint planning effort might also be helpful for a United Fund organization or council of community agencies, agencies already part of the existing community structure.

A key to social action is the gathering of data to determine need and clarify the nature of the problem. The Inter-Agency Council also used the survey to involve members of the community in the problem-solving effort. In any implementation plan, people are more apt to cooperate in working toward the goals if they feel part of the undertaking. The survey also allowed the council to set priorities in regard to the many problems of adolescents. Recognizing their limited time, it was necessary to focus their attention on areas where people felt the most need and were most willing to invest their energy in finding solutions.

Social action could also be attempted within the agency, where staff might work by itself, or with community persons, to plan a community-change project. It could start simply as a way of determining the need for services with certain population groups in the community. Depending on the interest that is generated, this type of involvement could then lead to the emergence of community leaders willing to assume responsibility for further activity. Agencies that envision their mission as serving persons facing discrimination because of race, ethnicity, gender, or sexual preference should make special efforts to involve such persons in social action projects, encouraging them to act in their own behalf.

The social action group will attempt to mobilize resources within a community to improve social conditions. It is an example of democracy in action and was seen by the early reformers as a way to strengthen citizen participation and achieve social change. The empowerment that comes from taking more control of one's environment can also enhance feelings of personal competence.

ADMINISTRATIVE GROUP

The administrative group is formed within an organization to complete a task. Persons exercising the worker role are usually part of the organization and have a designated position as chairperson or team coordinator. The group may be either ongoing or time-limited. Group members may volunteer or be chosen by an administrator for a specific purpose. Because of the nature of the group composition, which includes persons with varying degrees of commitment and enthusiasm for the assigned task, there will often be mixed responses and an uneven willingness to focus on the purpose of the meeting. Since persons may represent different constituency groups within the organization, there could be vested interests in seeking opposing solutions. Personal agendas and the need to ventilate feelings may also interfere with the functioning of such a group.

The worker will need to balance the interpersonal aspects of group functioning with getting the job done. The task focus should be considered central, and yet persons should be allowed to share feelings and perceptions of how they are being affected by the group. Group members clarify the problem, share in providing relevant information, seek alternative solutions, and make decisions about a course of action. There are also structured ways for generating ideas and making decisions that facilitate problem solving. One such approach is brainstorming, where group members are encouraged to generate as many ideas as possible without criticism (Toseland and Rivas, 1984, 280–285). This technique is a data-gathering step that requires the selection of the most feasible ideas for solving problems. In all cases the worker encourages a desirable climate for shared participation and outcome.

The administrative group is influenced by the larger system of the agency, needing to adhere to its policies and procedures. This kind of work group may influence a change in agency policy, but it is most often used to solve problems of implementing policy or to facilitate staff working relationships. Employee involvement and participatory management is increasingly recognized as producing high staff morale and more constructive decision making for the organization (Katz and Kahn, 1978; Simmons and Mares, 1985; Tjosvold, 1986).

The team is another type of administrative group. Its purpose is to work together in behalf of clients. Usually persons on the team represent different specialties, each contributing to the overall goal. There may be a coordinator who maintains responsibility for the functioning of the team, but the leadership is usually shared. In some cases, interpersonal issues will disrupt team functioning. Unless the team is willing and able to confront these differences when they occur, such intragroup problems may interfere with client services. On the smallest possible level, there is the co-worker team of two persons. If co-workers cannot work together in a harmonious relationship, the group members will detect it and this lack of team unity can impede the progress of the group as a whole. It is suggested that teams, including co-workers, talk to one another about their process of working together. The communication needs to be open and constructive (Galinsky and Schopler, 1980, 57).

There are times when a consultant is called to an agency to help the staff deal with a particular kind of problem. The consultant may work with staff to involve them in clarifying their objectives and developing plans to implement them. He or she might also be called upon to assist staff with their working relationships, sometimes called team building.

In the example that follows the consultant is expected to help the staff in regard to both their objectives and the interpersonal area.

Example of an Administrative Group

A family-practice residency faculty, including physicians, behavioral science staff, and nurses, had formed the Family Practice Group but were having difficulty in working together as a team of eleven professionals. Besides the director of the program, who was a physician located at the hospital, the rest of the staff were about equally divided at two different regional family health centers. They came together at monthly meetings. A consultant was called in to help them with their problems as a total group. The consultant, recognizing that he was an outsider, needed first to establish a relationship with the staff members and to help them develop more trust in one another. This was done in an informal way by sharing information about themselves and with the consultant.

The next step was to clarify the purpose of their meeting together, the roles of the consultant and the participants, and how they might work together as a group. The staff groups from each of the family practice centers were asked to meet separately to identify their issues and concerns. In coming together they looked at their separate lists and identified commonalities and differences among them. Issues that were common from both lists included being competitive versus being cooperative, how much teaching versus service they should do, how decisions are made at the various levels, how much support they could expect from the hospital, and their desire to solve problems as a group.

Once these issues were presented it became necessary to set priorities from among them in order to develop work tasks. The staff group was involved in making the decisions about these priorities. They decided that the most basic issue and the primary reason for calling in the consultant was their interest in working more effectively as a problem-solving group. In regard to this concern, the consultant asked them to share their perceptions of the barriers that were interfering with being able to function well as a group. Issues were presented as impediments to their relating as a group: how decisions were made that affected them; divided loyalties between their staff at the branch and the total staff; unwillingness to express how they really felt about their work situation; and lack of trust.

The mediating role of the consultant was to help the staff members share information and feelings about the issues, such as how decisions were being made by the overall director, the branch director, and the participants as a group. The essential skill was to increase the communication flow among the participants regarding their differences and areas of agreement. As persons with varying perceptions of the problem heard from one another, it became more possible for them to understand another position or point of view.

Their first task was to develop a consensus about the issues and what they wanted to do together. This is similar to what any group needs to do in getting started. Their agreement defines the conditions under which they can work together harmoniously. Once the consultant was able to help them communicate with one another, on both a feeling and content level, they were more willing and able to accomplish the tasks that they had decided upon. When they had difficulty in facing the obstacles to their growth as a group, the consultant would ask them to examine how their process worked, so they could continually recognize some of their difficulties and consider alternatives ways to overcome them.

In administrative groups, there may be hidden agendas that interfere with the functioning of the group. In the Family Practice Group, there were tensions about status and role differences among the physicians, psychologists, social workers, and nurses. The nurses, for instance, felt that their input was minimized in the collective decision making of the group. Sometimes nonverbal communication, such as eye contact, will convey the message that certain members of the group can be overlooked or their contributions disregarded. After the consultant had met with the group a number of times and trust had increased, the members were able to risk discussion of their personal concerns. The consultant, as an outside person, provided a measure of safety, because he was free from the internal entanglements of their staff relationships.

As in the other types of groups, there is wide variation in the range and purpose of administrative groups. There are teams, committees, task forces, and problem-solving groups similar to the Family Practice Group. Groups that meet for training or supervisory purposes are a blending of the socioeducation and administrative group. A key to making a distinction among the types is to examine the purpose of the group, whether personal, community, or organizational change.

SIMILARITIES AND DIFFERENCES
IN WORKER ROLE

In each of these types of groups there are some worker behaviors that are basically the same. There are also differences. Even with different groups of the same type, the worker will use selective tasks and techniques, depending on what the group needs. For groups that have a different purpose, as in the types mentioned, there could be even more variation.

Similarities in Leadership

Group workers will often find themselves as facilitators or members of more than one of these groups. The types of groups have many overlapping features, or the group may change its focus, as when a group that starts out as a socioeducation group later contracts for more of a treatment emphasis. The educational, socialization, or support focus may have been what they needed initially. It enabled the group members to build the trust and low risk environment that was necessary for the self-disclosure of the treatment group. In other cases, groups that begin as a socioeducation or treatment group will recognize that some of the sources of problems are in the environment and will agree to add system change to their original agenda of personal growth. The accomplishments of being able to affect modifications in the environment can build self-esteem, expand the repertoires of role behavior, and increase cohesiveness in the group. In all cases there are many similarities in the worker role.

They fall into six basic categories:

1. Clarifying Group Purposes. In each type of situation, the purpose of the group needs to be clear for all parties concerned. Considering that group members may have varying perceptions or different personal agendas and needs, the first task of any group is to clarify its purpose, so that members' energies are aimed in the same direction.

2. Balancing Task and Maintenance Functions. The worker may emphasize either a task role or a maintenance role. Both are important, and the use of the one or the other will depend on the needs of group members and group purposes. There will be times when a task group (administrative, team, social action, or change) will get bogged down because of personal issues or legitimate differences that need to be reconciled. Conflict can be a part of any group, and if it is handled well, the group will profit from a rich diversity of views. During these times the worker will help persons bring out differences, share feelings, offer support, and raise group issues for further discussion and resolution (maintenance dimension). In a therapeutic or socialization group, the emphasis is on the socioemotional development of the group. However, these groups will want to move toward accomplishing goals that they set for themselves (the task dimension), and the worker attempts to help them take action in the direction of the changes that they envision.

3. Using a Problem-Solving Process. Within the boundary of each group's purpose, the worker will help the group to focus on an issue, problem, need, or interest. Usually he or she will facilitate sharing of information and collection of data to make the topic more understandable. Feelings as well as knowledge may be exchanged. The worker will elicit variations in how persons perceive the subject under discussion. Actions that might be taken are evaluated by the group members so that thoughtful, reasonable, and manageable solutions are sought. Once an activity is attempted, it is usually followed by an evaluation of the success or failure of the approach.

4. Developing a More Favorable Environment. At times the work or play of the group involves persons outside the group. These people might include a relative of a member in a therapeutic group, an agency director or staff person in a socioeducation group, a community person in a social action group, or a supervisor in an administrative group. These encounters with persons in the surrounding environment could be made by the worker and/or the group members. It would help create a more favorable overall climate for group members, either within the group or with persons associated with the members.

5. Using a Relationship. To a great extent, people are able to find personal fulfillment and accomplish goals with the help of others. This help should increase our own autonomy and ability to make responsible choices. A group worker needs to be this kind of individual, increasing the possibilities for group members to take on more constructive leadership, both in the group and in the larger environment. This relationship should emphasize caring, trust, empathy, respect, genuine sharing of oneself, an ability to really listen, and setting limits when necessary. If the worker achieves such a rapport with the group, the individual will feel that he or she is valued and can make use of existing strengths to develop a more positive self-image. Through honesty and trust, people can become aware of the less productive aspects of their behavior. They are encouraged to view their behavior as it affects others as well as themselves. The relationship encourages self-evaluation so that the person is in a better position to make changes.

6. Individualizing. Persons come to groups from different intellectual, physical, and emotional places. Their values may also be varied. The worker assesses where people are and starts to work with them in the framework of their readiness and willingness to participate in the group. When there is resistance to the task, the discussion of the group will center on being in the group or working on the task. The agenda is a joint one, not just something the worker or a single group member wants. Besides responding to group members on the basis of their personal characteristics and conditions, the worker must also consider the stage of group development and the physical setting as factors influencing behavior.

Differences in Leadership

Although there are more similarities than differences in worker roles vis-à-vis the various types of group, some differences are evident. In some cases, it may be only a matter of emphasis, or there may be substantial changes. However, the activity of the worker may also change within the same group, depending upon the stage of group development or the ability of group members to assume responsibilities. Hartford refers to the changing role of the group worker as the flexible stance (1971, 64–65) and Hersey and Blanchard (1977) describe situational leadership, where the leader will be more or less active according to the maturity level of the participants in the group. In the initial contracting with the group, roles of worker and members should be clarified. The type of group will often determine what the worker will and will not do. If and when this range of worker behavior changes, it should be discussed with the group.

1. Taking Responsibility. It is generally believed that workers in task-oriented groups will take more initial responsibility than those in other types of groups and will exercise authority. However, worker behavior should be less determined by type of group than by group composition. If group members are competent in demonstrating leadership to move the group forward, the worker should encourage this kind of development. In this case, leadership is defined as the ability to present ideas and feelings that will help group members accomplish their task(s) and pay attention to the socioemotional component of group life. When group members are passive, uninterested, destructive, or completely self-centered, the worker will want to be in control and demonstrate "healthy" behavior to encourage constructive leadership. The worker will continue this kind of activity until the group members are able to assume greater responsibility themselves for what happens in the group.

2. Emphasizing Exploration of Meaning of Behavior. This is a real difference. In a task-centered group, the worker will be aware of certain types of behavior, encourage expression of feelings, or deal with resistance in the group, but not explore the meaning of behavior—unless there was agreement during an initial group session that exploration of behavior would be an accepted practice. Above all else, it would violate confidentiality and respect for the person's right of privacy. It would also not be necessary in completing the task.

3. Determining extent of contact with persons in environment. This area is also a matter of emphasis rather than a question of whether or not this worker activity should be used. In groups for social action and change, this kind of intervention will obviously be very much a part of the work. For groups with a therapeutic purpose, the work will be focused more on individual and group behavior. To the extent that the small group is seen as a system in interaction with other systems, there may be involvement with persons in the environment, in relation to behavior and goals of group members.

4. Preplanning from One Meeting to the Next. For some of the task groups and socioeducation groups, there may be planning before the meeting about the nature of the agenda. Sometimes the chairperson or worker will arrange for what needs to be covered, and at other times the agenda will be decided upon jointly. This is often necessary so that participants will be able to read certain materials ahead of time, to be prepared with information necessary for the discussion or to make more astute decisions. Even in these more formal meetings, there should be room for immediate issues that have taken some priority of importance since the previous session. In therapeutic groups the agenda usually is an informal one that emerges from the pressing problems of individuals or from the interaction among members or with the worker.

SUMMARY

It may seem overwhelming for the beginning practitioner to be confronted by the many types and purposes of groups. There is some solace in knowing that a basic core of knowledge, values, and techniques underlies all groups. The many variables necessary to determine the specific application of knowledge and techniques includes agency context, purpose of group, personal characteristics of worker and group members, particular issue or problem, and phase of the group.

In the next chapter, knowledge and values are discussed as the conceptual background for practice with groups. The worker is constantly making choices about the most appropriate intervention. Theory from the social and behavioral sciences can provide some of the rationale for these decisions.

REFERENCES

Anderson, R. E., & Carter, I. (1984). *Human behavior in the social environment* (3rd ed.). New York: Aldine.

Barker, R. L. (1987). *The social work dictionary*. Silver Spring, MD: National Association of Social Workers.

Galinsky, M. J., & Schopler, J. H. (1980). Structuring co-leadership in social work training. *Social Work with Groups, 3* (4), 55–64.

Garvin, C. (1987). *Contemporary group work* (2nd ed.). Englewood Cliffs, NJ: Prentice-Hall.

Hartford, M. (1971). *Groups in social work*. New York: Columbia University Press.

Hersey, P., & Blanchard, K. H. (1977). *Management of organizational behavior: Utilizing human resources* (3rd ed.). Englewood Cliffs, NJ: Prentice-Hall.

Katz, D., & Kahn, R. L. (1978). *The social psychology of organizations* (2d ed.). New York: John Wiley.

Radin, N. (1985). Socioeducation groups. In M. Sundel, P. Glasser, R. Sarri, & R. Vinter (Eds.), *Individual change through small groups* (2nd ed.). New York: Free Press.

Simmons, J., & Mares, W. (1985). *Working together: Employee participation in action.* New York: New York University Press.

Tjosvold, D. (1986). *Working together to get things done.* Lexington, MA: D. C. Heath.

Toseland, R. W., & Rivas, R. F. (1984). *An introduction to group work practice.* New York: MacMillan.

TEACHING AND LEARNING IDEAS

1. Think of three different groups that you have participated in as a worker or member and identify its type. Meet with two or three other students and briefly describe the group. Also ask the others in this threesome or foursome to identify the type from your description. Compare the answers. If there were discrepancies, what would account for the differences?

2. Ask a supervisor or staff person at a social agency to identify three types of groups. See if this person would agree or disagree with the listing of similarities and differences in worker role in these groups.

3. Observe a role play or see a video tape/film of a group and discuss the type of group it is with others who have seen it. What are the reasons for your selection? Refer to the chapter.

PART II

Frameworks
for Understanding

CHAPTER 4

Knowledge and Values

The decisions about interventions are based upon an assessment of a situation: What is happening at a particular time that requires the use of specific actions? Knowledge, whether it is based upon research evidence or practice wisdom, allows the practitioner to make intervention choices that have the best chance of succeeding. Presumably, the knowledge areas become incorporated into the thinking of the practitioner. What may seem like a spontaneous reaction to group interaction is actually based upon a gradual building of the integration of theory and experience. For the student, it must seem like an overwhelming task to be "spontaneously integrative." To add another degree of complexity to the practice equation, the worker is expected to act on the basis of professional values. These are the ethical principles and judgments that are at the foundation of the professional's thinking. The worker needs to be clear about his or her own values as well as the values that may influence group member behavior.

Group workers must also be self-aware in order to recognize the impact of personal feelings and attitudes and to use this understanding constructively in a professional role. Professional knowledge and values, together with the worker's own knowledge and values, suggest a range of choices that require constant decision making. These choices should point to an array of techniques that can then be used to fit the needs of a particular situation.

RELEVANT KNOWLEDGE

In this chapter, we will focus on certain knowledge areas that have particular applicability to social work with groups. This discussion will prepare you to recognize the importance of using theoretical frameworks as a foundation for performing skills. In the practice examples that follow throughout the book, the knowledge base will be identified in the analysis of interpersonal situations.

Several perspectives are basic to our discussion here: a social systems approach, small group theory, role theory, learning theories, and ego psychology.

Social Systems

In groups, individuals interact within defined boundaries of purpose and expectation. A *social system* is the pattern of these reciprocal role relationships, or a "bounded set of interrelated activities that together constitute a single social entity" (Olsen, 1968, 228–229). Systems may be open or closed. We will use the concept of *open systems,* which are free to exchange energy and matter with their environment, in the model of social work practice discussed in this book.

Systems need to be conceptualized at different levels. For instance, although are speak about *a* system, this system may actually include many smaller systems, or subsystems, and the larger system may be a subsystem of a still larger system. We need to begin our discussion by defining our terms.

Boundary. Interaction with the environment occurs within a specified *boundary,* which is defined as the border or limited region within which more energy interchange takes place than outside it (Anderson and Carter, 1984, 24). A boundary, for instance, would define a family or small group. However, as we mentioned above, systems have subsystems, and therefore boundaries can be described according to how a problem is defined.

Polsky (1962) discusses children from a residential treatment center, who are seen for individual treatment by the clinical staff. The initial boundary, in this situation, is the social worker and child in relation to the child's problem. Progress seems to occur in the counseling sessions, but these boys then return to their living quarters, and any gains are overshadowed by the peer group structure; the boys are pressured to conform to the values within the cottage (Polsky, 1962, 160–161). In order to encourage behavioral change among the residents, we would need to redefine the boundary as the cottage itself, including the cottage house parent who wields great influence with the boys. To take it a step further, let us say that the policies and procedures of the institution's administration are creating tensions among the staff and residents so that therapeutic gains are minimized. Then the boundary would best be defined as the institution itself, so that the development of a therapeutic milieu becomes more possible.

When the system of administration joins in its efforts with staff and residents of the cottage, the process of *systemic linkage* has occurred. On these occasions two or more systems act as one. The boundary that was envisioned may actually become a reality—a more total and consistent approach to helping within the institution.

Energy. In any system there is an exchange of energy from inside and outside the boundary, and this energy can affect information, resources, or communication. Anderson and Carter define *energy* as the "capacity for action," "action," or "power to effect change" (1984, 10). If social systems become closed, with little energy flow from the outside to stimulate new thinking, they are in danger of limiting their growth, since they have little opportunity for creative problem solving. The very essence of finding new solutions to problems is to have varied sources of information as alternatives for action. Openness to ideas and feelings, from within and without the group, becomes a value for the group so that this energy flow can take place.

Leverage and Linkage. A goal of the worker is to increase mutual aid possibilities within the group and work toward the release of more positive energy, perhaps in terms of resources from the environment. The concept of leverage becomes important in this regard. Group members who are the natural or informal leaders (also known as indigenous leaders) have high status and can sway the group, usually because of the qualities or resources they possess. These indigenous leaders exercise leverage by influencing the group. Where it is desirable to enlarge the boundary, persons who demonstrate leverage from a larger system are enlisted for support. They may act as leverage points, because of their natural leadership or through the dominance of their position, such as a key supervisor or administrator who has access to resources or controls the flow of communication (Lippitt, Watson, Westley, 1958, 100–101). Linkage means that there are connections among people in regard to the common pursuit. Linkage is also defined as "the function of bringing together the resources of different agencies, personnel, voluntary groups, and relevant individuals and brokering or coordinating their efforts on behalf of a client or social objective" (Barker, 1988, 90). For people to assist in the process of systemic linkage, they must also be accessible and willing to participate. For instance, staff on a ward of a psychiatric hospital wanted to involve more of the withdrawn patients in activities. The social worker recognized that there were a few patients who did seem somewhat responsive. These patients met as a planning group with the worker to enlist their ideas about how to reach the less active patients. In this case they acted as a means of leverage to stimulate the interest of the patients on the ward. Patients who have more abilities to function and perhaps exercise indigenous leadership may be able to influence these more withdrawn patients to become more active.

Tension. Since the characteristics of people within systems are sometimes different, such as roles, ages, gender, ethnic background, race, or religion, tension may be caused by failure to understand these differences. Tension may also be caused by policies and practice within organizations and communities that are not understood or are injurious to people who belong to these systems. The tension is sometimes referred to as stress, which is considered energy and a normal part of living (Zerin and Zerin, 1986, 5). Strain or distress is the result of the inappropriate use of stress, which can lead to harm to oneself or others. It is damaging stress. For instance, social work students often experience stress because of the excessive demands on their time, considering the pressures of class *and* field work. This is a normal stress. If students believe that something is wrong with them because of not being able to keep up with all the work, lose sleep over it, and become depressed, they are in a state of distress. However, if they learn to set priorities, become assertive in discussing the management of their load with school or field faculty, or find techniques to do their work more efficiently, the stress does not necessarily become distress. When this happens, the student experiences what Zerin calls eustress, which is the constructive use of stress. The difference is that in eustress the person takes control of the situation and *chooses* to take action or to allow something to happen (Zerin and Zerin, 1986, 6).

There is also conflict, which is usually associated with differences between people. According to Chin, "When tensions gang up and become more or less sharply opposed along the lines of two or more components, we have *conflict*" (1961, 204). Northen (1988) proposes a social psychological way of viewing conflict, which is consistent with a holistic approach to practice. "It recognizes the need to understand the persons involved, the nature of the issues, the responses of others to the conflict, the social environment in which the conflict occurs, and the consequences of the conflict for all who are affected by it" (Northen, 1988, 38). Some of the techniques for resolving conflict will be discussed in Chapter 6 and in Part III, "Phases of Work."

It is helpful to separate out the meaning of these various concepts, since lumping them all together doesn't permit us to differentiate between the positives and negatives of a conflictual situation. If we recognize that tension within the person or between systems is a natural source of growth, then the differences that may create the tension are to be valued. However, if the situations are so overwhelming and powerful, it may be too much to handle. There can be excessive tension at one particular time: the effects of war, several losses at once, an economic disaster, or a severe illness. When such a crisis occurs, the person may need to protect himself or herself with emotional defenses.

During these times, the worker will need to respect the group member's distancing, but at the same time, help the person drawn upon personal or organizational resources to cope with the crisis. The worker emphasizes what the group member can do—what choices are available for action. Another approach is to help the group member view the situation in a more constructive way. This is called *reframing* and is discussed further in Chapter 6.

If members of the group have positive balancing factors to extreme tension—such as good friends, health, economic security, recognition at work, and enjoyable experiences—it is more likely that the tension will be used in a productive way. Any change creates ambivalence; we are delighted to anticipate improvement, but can we manage a new situation, a new type of behavior? The safety, security, and nurturing of these positive experiences will counteract the threatening aspects of change.

In a group, the degree of tension that is allowed or encouraged will depend on the level of competence, maturity, and coping capacities of the group members. If the level is low, the emphasis will be on increasing the positive influences, building self-esteem and support, helping group members to deal effectively with the tension in the group and in their lives outside the group. A guideline for the worker is to balance challenge with support.

Another important means of helping group members deal with distress and conflict is to focus on attitudinal change. If the causes of the distress are belief systems that create conflict, it will be necessary to consider alternative ways of thinking. For instance, if parents make a child think that he or she has to be perfect, anything less than perfection will be a source of distress. The worker can enable group members to explore their attitudes and possibly work toward a redirection in ways of thinking. The problem-solving process, including the use of specific techniques, will be discussed further in Chapter 6.

The concepts of boundary, energy, linkage and leverage, and tension have broad applicability to individuals, groups, and larger systems. We will now consider more specifically the nature of small groups and what happens in the life of a group.

Small Group Theory

Knowledge about small groups is organized here within a framework of stages of group development, drawing on the work of Garland, Jones, and Kolodny (1973), Hartford (1971), Sarri and Galinsky (1985), and Tuckman (1965). The stages that will be explained include origin, formation, power and control, intimacy, maturation, and separation. Various group processes occur during all of these stages, and these will be discussed as well. For instance, group structure evolves from a collection of individuals to patterned relationships with indigenous leadership assuming task and socioemotional roles; communication may take many forms, often depending on the purpose of the group, but usually shifting from communication with the designated leader (worker) to group members as mutual aid develops; goals will be determined early in the life of the group but may change as group members' needs shift in focus; the experiencing and resolution of conflict is a necessary part of moving the group to an advanced phase; norms are the way the group develops expectations and stability in the performance of its functions; cohesion increases as the group members form attachments with one another through collaborative problem-solving activity; and a group culture takes shape as rituals, symbols, and values add meaning and purpose to the group.

Origin Stage. Group organization begins with a private phase, when someone has the idea to form a group, usually in relation to a specific need. In the public phase, the idea is shared with others, and the decision to act on it is made. During this time, workers think about the purpose, size, time, frequency, location, and membership of the group. Hartford (1971, 67–77) refers to this stage as the *pregroup phase,* including convening of the group, and Sarri and Galinsky (1985, 73) mention it as the *origin phase* (see Chapter 7, "Pregroup Planning"). The group purpose should be understood by the social worker and agency at this time, so that group composition can be arranged in relation to it.

Formation. Schutz (1961) discusses the basic needs of inclusion, control, and affection. Since individuals are not assured that these needs will be met when they first enter a group, most have some ambivalence about becoming members during this initial period. People enter the group with varying degrees of acceptance or rejection from their experiences in living. Their abilities from previous positions outside the group may or may not contribute to leadership in the group.

During this beginning period, group members look to others who have similar characteristics and might be more willing to accept them, thus seeking to satisfy their need for *inclusion.* But unresolved issues and associated emotional pain from former experiences may make some members distance themselves from others to maintain safety. The worker will orient the group in accordance with the agency's purposes, plans, and procedures and set up the conditions for a mutual exchange and clarification of everyone's expectations. Group purposes emerge from the sharing and negotiation of the separate purposes of agency, worker, and group member. Group members may have questions about whether they will be able to maintain their individuality or become engulfed in the conformity of group standards.

At this time, group members depend heavily on the group worker, looking to persons in authority to set guidelines, since they don't know how they are expected to behave. Group members can feel vulnerable in turning over control to the formal leader, not yet knowing how to use their strengths and defenses in the most constructive way. Group members may test out group policies, procedures, or worker actions to determine their reality and efficacy. This testing activity may take the form of challenging worker and/or member behavior or the guidelines that were proposed for the group's continuance. The testing will be more pronounced if there is freedom in the group to engage in real contract negotiation and if there continues to be lack of clarity about group purposes and worker/member roles.

This stage is similar to Hartford's group formation (1971, 77–84), Sarri and Galinsky's formative stage (1985, 73–74), Garland, Jones, and Kolodny's preaffiliation (1973, 29–42) and Tuckman's forming stage (1965, 396), and we discuss it further in Chapter 8.

Power and Control. The desire to maintain personal values and behaviors poses a dilemma for group members, who may feel a simultaneous need to adapt to the diversity of views and actions of other group members. The group worker's authority may stir up latent feelings of being controlled by parental figures, thus causing resistance, and the emergence of indigenous leadership may also threaten some members for the same reasons. Uncertainty about what kind of responses will be rewarded is also cause for concern and may add to dependency feelings.

Differences become more apparent as the group develops an informal structure, with members assuming roles to accomplish task and socioemotional aspects of group life. Indigenous leadership becomes more evident, and subgroups form around common interests and needs. As communication fosters sharing of beliefs and positive regard for one another, members will begin to feel personally accepted and willing to withstand the strain of negotiating their differences. If acceptance is not forthcoming or members feel that their particular needs and goals will not be met, they are likely to drop out of the group, withdraw from participation, or become deviants in the group.

Conflict resolution begins to occur as members perceive a need for one another and reach toward common aspirations, referred to as *superordinate goals.* The sharing of similar experiences, perhaps through prearranged activity, can create joint problem solving and the commonality of reactions that will lead to greater respect, caring, and understanding of one another. This validation of different values and personal styles will add to the comfort of knowing that members can retain their individuality.

Hartford identifies this period as integration, disintegration, or reintegration (1971, 80–84). Often, just as the group appears stabilized, there is a turnaround. Perhaps the group established a premature agreement about issues when they began to meet. Since the need for inclusion and acceptance is great, group members will want to do what is expected of them. Once they perceive trust and safety, however, they may be willing to risk voicing less popular views or questioning persons in leadership positions, in order to assert a degree of power and control in the group. This can lead to a temporary destabilization, similar to what Sarri and Galinsky refer to as the *intermediate and revision phase* (1985, 74–75). Garland, Jones, and Kolodny describe this stage as power and control, where "problems of status, ranking, communication, choice making and 'influence' come to the fore" (1973, 42–43). Tuckman refers to this stage as *group structure: intragroup conflict*—a period of tension as group members attempt to express and resolve their differences, also characterized as storming (1965, 396).

Intimacy. When the socioemotional climate of the group is supportive of the varying personality characteristics of the group members, they will like one another more. If the worker is empathetic, members are often more willing to risk the expression of feelings and ideas. The group members' commonalities become more apparent as differences are resolved through increased communication and joint problem solving. Norms, or accepted patterns of behavior that grow out of mutual sharing of experiences, begin to take shape. An informal ranking along a status hierarchy may occur as members demonstrate leadership behavior to help the group accomplish its purposes. Increased affection for one another and greater ability to solve problems will lead to cohesiveness or a group bonding. This stage of intimacy is characterized by the development of norms, expressions of empathy in the sharing of personal experiences, and more clearly identified roles, which permit the group to satisfy personal and group goals.

In this stage, resistance is overcome, according to Tuckman, and an in-group feeling develops (1965, 396.) Standards of behavior that represent the values of the group become more apparent. Hartford's *group functioning and maintenance phase* is similar to the *norming* that Tuckman describes (1965, 84–87). The new standards of acceptable behavior and procedures are part of a developing group culture, where the members begin to feel its uniqueness as a group. The structure is more established, so that subgroups, leadership, and isolates or deviants are more noticeable. Sarri and Galinsky see this phase as approaching stability, an equilibrium following the earlier revision stage. The group becomes able to redirect its energies from clarification of interpersonal differences to activity that will satisfy its purposes for coming together (1985, 75–76). Garland, Jones, and Kolodny also discuss this stage as intimacy and identify an "intensification of personal involvement" (1973, 47). Although vestiges of interpersonal conflict remain, there is an increased ability to plan and carry out group projects. Members are more aware of their own abilities to meet their needs for growth and development within the group.

Maturation. With continuing leadership in the form of support and with goal-directed activity, the group is able to become mature. Not all groups progress to this stage, either because their time together is too limited or because the group composition does not have the necessary strength to negotiate the differences that arise in problem solving. During this period the group structure is fully developed, with an established pattern of indigenous leadership. Socioemotional and task activities are balanced, and participation by group members is shared. Members are comfortable about expressing their feelings, secure in the knowledge that they will be supported as individuals even though their behavior may be questioned at times. The most distinguishing feature of this stage is that group members can be themselves, without needing to impress others or only assume roles that will gain them more acceptance.

Conflict may continue, but it is qualitatively different from disagreements at an earlier stage. During the conflict stage, group members attempted to use controversy to establish power and control. In maturation, conflict is used to enhance the goals of the group. In fact, the differences that group members bring to the group can contribute to their problem-solving efforts; individuality is valued because the alternatives that are presented through individual contributions can add to the strength of the group.

Mature groups are strongly cohesive. An identifiable culture typifies the group through certain symbols and rituals, such as greeting one another with a hug, serving refreshments at a particular time, or the way feelings are expressed in public. Indigenous leadership is sufficient to allow the group to work with greater autonomy. Members can be rewarded through an appreciation for their ability to become independent and assume responsibility for carrying out the work of the group.

The positive qualities and high level functioning of the maturation stage sound ideal and perhaps even unrealistic. But we should understand that groups do not always move along at a steady and progressive pace in the manner described. Depending upon the nature of the group, its composition, goals, and the crises that may occur, groups reach varying levels of maturation.

Tuckman identifies this stage as *performing* (1965, 396), when interpersonal processes work in favor of accomplishing the group's set task. Enough security exists in the group for roles to be flexible and functionable, depending on current needs. Garland, Jones, and Kolodny call this phase *differentiation,* since persons are able to view themselves as "distinct individuals," free enough to be different and yet very much bonded with the group (1973, 52–57). Hartford continues to discuss this time as maturation and reminds us that the group can have "periodic reintegration phases if the group loses or adds members, if members face crises that are brought into the group content, if the group has failures or special successes in its operations, if some external factors change the group's status in the hierarchy of groups within which it exists" (1971, 87). During this time, the group can usually deal successfully with occasional setbacks.

Since the maturation stage presupposes an ability to work independently and a strong capacity for problem solving, Sarri and Galinsky believe that a treatment group requiring the services of a professional helper will usually not progress to this stage. Persons who seek remedial help would not need to continue in the group if the degree of autonomy that is suggested in maturation takes place (1985, 83).

Separation. Time-limited groups know when they will end, since the number of their meetings is often prescribed at the beginning. For other groups, termination will depend on the completion of a task, or, in the case of a treatment group, the accomplishment of personal or group goals. With open-ended groups, however, where membership is fluid, and members come and go all the time, there are continuous separations and beginnings for group members.

If the group has been able to progress to the maturation stage and achieve a high level of cohesion and personal satisfaction, the intensity of group members' feelings over separation is likely to be great. Members are continuously dealing with the dilemma of individuation/bonding or independence/dependence. Group members need to differentiate themselves as distinct individuals, and yet they need and want to depend on others. Thus, the most common characteristic of a separation stage is ambivalence. This reflects members' reluctance to give up the bonding and sources of gratification from others even as they anticipate pleasure from becoming more independent.

Group members express reluctance to give up the group in many ways, including denial or even anger at the formal leader for initiating the separation. Some members "flee"; toward the end, they do not attend meetings or withdraw when the group is together. Other members are less involved in expressing feelings or they may wind down their activities as they prepare themselves for leaving.

In the children's groups used in their study, Garland, Jones, and Kolodny discuss separation in terms of *regression* and *recapitulation* (1973, 57–64). Regression may be a way of saying that "we still need the club," and recapitulation serves a review purpose, where group members can integrate group experiences into their developing selves. Sarri and Galinsky view termination more as *task completion* and discuss the importance of evaluating goals related to the earlier contracting of a beginning phase (1985, 84–85). Hartford identifies three parts of a termination phase—the preparation, the ending itself, and plans beyond the group, including follow-up as needed (1971, 87).

Many persons who enter groups experience unresolved separations from former relationships. They may not have had an opportunity to discuss their feelings about leaving during these earlier experiences or to express the affection that they had for persons from whom they were parting. Thus for these group members, separation may be associated with pain and sorrow, and they may resist dealing with the new loss of relationships. The worker will need to spend time to bring out how group members are reacting to the upcoming separation and to point out how anticipating the pleasure of new experiences can help resolve ending the old one. This can help group members for new beginnings.

Within every group, persons take on various roles, many of which are learned from positions outside the group (female, male, student, parent, etc.). Roles may also be learned within the group, or behaviors associated with previously learned roles may be changed in the group, leading to new growth and change. This phase will be discussed in this next section.

Role Theory

By definition, a role is a "set of standards, descriptions, norms, or concepts held (by anyone) for the behaviors of a person or a position" (Biddle and Thomas, 1966, 11–12). Central to this definition is the notion of behavioral expectations determined by social norms. In this way, role theory provides some basis for predicting and explaining individual or group behavior.

In Caudill's study of the role of a patient in a psychiatric hospital, he found that there was a "patient role," which is ascribed to new arrivals through the value system of the patient (1958, 11). Parsons describes a "sick role"—a general category within which society defines a person in need of medical attention. The sick role includes social expectations of the sick person as well as the more obvious physical and emotional components. For instance, the sick person is exempted from normal social responsibilities, is obligated to get well, and has a moral obligation to seek technically competent help in trying to get well (1951, 452–460). For a person who gets sick, we can generally expect this kind of behavior. In the patient role, as described by Caudill, the patient is expected to be conforming. The complementary role to the patient is the more assertive and directive role of the doctor or nurse. The two types of behavior associated with these roles, taken in combination, make up a social system.

All persons have multiple roles, such as parent, child, worker, or learner. The sum of all these roles is considered a *role set*. *Role conflict* refers to the disparity which an individual experiences among competing roles. For instance, an adult who has been assertive as a parent or administrator returns to graduate school. The role of the student in our society usually involves conforming, following directions, and accepting the guidance of the teacher. The former administrator has found that the ability to take responsibility, express feelings and ideas, and generally assume an adult role has been rewarded in his former position, but this assertive behavior in the student role may not be appreciated. In fact, he may be discouraged from exhibiting this same type of behavior. When this happens the new graduate student is experiencing role conflict.

It takes a great deal of understanding and fairly sophisticated social awareness to function in an array of different roles and gain acceptance in all of these behaviors. One problem that sometimes occurs in a marriage is that one marital partner perceives the other as a parent figure and acts out toward the spouse prior conflicts with a parent. In this case, the husband and wife act in the roles of parent and child, which is inappropriate and creates problems in their relationship. In this type of situation, role conflict takes place because of unresolved childhood-related problems. Conflicts occur for virtually all of us occasionally. We are often both parent and child, leader and follower, friend and supervisor in different parts of our lives.

Groups and Role Behavior. A group in which personal growth is one of the purposes can provide an opportunity for members to gain greater awareness of their own role behaviors. In the sharing and feedback of reactions from group members, individuals can understand how they are using certain roles and can learn to modify behavior to gain more acceptance from others. Since role behavior is a response to a social situation or displayed within the context of an environment, changing the social situation or the environment often makes it possible to change the behavior. In a project at the Texas State Hospital (Smith and Ramsey, 1960), patients showed a marked decrease in symptoms during a one-week stay at a camp off the hospital grounds. The environment of the camp was therapeutic. Democratic forms of social control were encouraged; freedom of choice was permitted in as many situations as possible. The campers were made to feel that they had a real part in determining the organization and functioning of the camp, and appropriate behavior was expected of patients. The attitude of the staff was that the campers could be trusted to care for themselves and other campers. Patients temporarily assumed the character of campers—a shift from the patient-sick role to the camper-health role. This latter role was allowed to express itself because the nature of the setting was focused on normal social functioning and expectations.

Since role theory suggests that people can change their behavior by acting to fulfill a particular group or societal role, social workers can use this knowledge in activities that prescribe certain role behaviors. For instance, in role play situations, group members can be given roles that permit them to experience different ways of behaving, such as being more assertive or quiet or angry (Mayer, 1989). The experiencing of the new behavior provides opportunities for reflection on its meaning and can lead to expansion of the group member's role repertoire. The worker can also create new environments that have certain role expectations, in order to enable group members to demonstrate actions that are consistent with the role. The example used earlier of the Texas State Hospital camping project illustrates how an environment can influence behavior.

Social workers are paying more attention to social skills training in socioeducation groups. Role theory is a useful knowledge base in understanding the rationale for helping people learn social skills. Instead of "pathologizing" people who have limited or different experiences, group members learn behaviors associated with certain expectations in their lives, which they had not learned up until that time.

In this next section on learning theories, various aspects of learning will be considered that have a bearing on how people learn these roles.

Learning Theories

In the model of growth and change discussed in this book, the principles of learning theories are a foundation for understanding human development. Although no unified or comprehensive theory of learning exists, relevant principles can be identified and applied to work with groups. In fact, group work is essentially a learning process. It is no accident that many of the early group work thinkers, such as Dewey, Lindeman, Follett, and Slavson (see Chapter 2) were strong believers in progressive education and informal adult education,

education, which embody many of the principles outlined below. These principles include motivation, relevance, resistance, synthesis, participation, modeling, evaluation, and progression.

Motivation. Motivation is defined as a willingness, need, or interest in accomplishing a goal. Maslow (1970) proposes a theory of motivation in his hierarchy of common human needs (physiological needs, safety, belonging and love, esteem and self-actualization). He postulated that these needs are motivators of behavior. Usually, they act as multiple motivators. Those needs that are more basic to survival, such as meeting physiological needs, will be the strongest motivators. Self-actualization needs may seem less important if these other needs are not satisfied. Somers (1969) discusses several conditions that are related to increased motivation in a learning situation. These include becoming an active participant, setting specific goals and directions, and taking responsibility for what happens.

Most people have a natural curiosity and potential for learning. Unfortunately, however, childhood memories of teachers and parents may be associated with negative learning and perhaps even with punishment if the child did not perform according to a certain standard. Many group members have these negative associations with learning, which have contributed to lower feelings of self-esteem. The most important task of the worker is to create the conditions in the group that enhance motivation for problem solving and learning.

Relevance. Knowles (1972) proposes an andragogical approach—an adult-learning model—which emphasizes the individual's inherent potential for growth. He suggests that readiness to learn is related to the relevance of the material for the learner and the timing of the experience. In other words, people are more willing to be engaged in learning experiences that are applicable in carrying out their multiple roles (workers, parents, students, spouses, etc.). The content should be needed and perceived as useful. Persons are constantly dealing with life tasks, as proposed by Erikson (1963). When their new learning can help to resolve issues associated with these needs, it will be accepted more readily. In groups, relevance is often expressed in terms of importance to the group. It may be related to a stage of group development, such as the need for structure during an early group meeting or the need for reflection and review as the group is ready to terminate. Perhaps a group member has left the group suddenly. In this case, it would be relevant to discuss the meaning of loss.

Resistance. People develop a pattern of thinking and doing that has an internal consistency about it. In some ways, we are closed systems, looking for ways to support what we already believe. Hanson (1981, 28) refers to the frozen state, whereby people become set in their ways and are not open to new learning. Rogers (1969) discusses how changes in self-organization—in the perception of oneself—is threatening and tends to be resisted. The resistance may take many forms, including rebellion, attack, withdrawal or absence, confusion, irrelevance, and being overly intellectual (Hanson, 1981, 35). Change can be so frightening to some people that they will do almost anything to avoid it, even to the point of being self-destructive.

Some people fear the unknown and the lack of control in a new situation. In others, value conflict and role conflict may be the result of new knowledge and behavioral expectations. The bottom line is whether the change will still give them the acceptance and belonging that are basic needs. In order for people to overcome resistance to change, they will have to find acceptance, feel included, and maintain some continuity of their behavior and thinking patterns in the midst of change. If persons can make decisions about how they want to change, so that they are able to maintain control of their reorganization, it is less likely that there will be resistance.

Doing—Thinking—Feeling. Learning that involves the whole person is the kind most likely to succeed. Styles of learning vary. Some people are conceptual, other visual, and still others react more readily on a feeling level. When group members can take action, such as being assertive or engaging in a role play, the experience can help them reach an integration of ideas with behavior. Social work groups offer an excellent opportunity for a multitude of learning modalities. Experience is a basic ingredient of helping. A developmental learning design, whereby the content of the experience flows from the needs of the participants, has been part of the early tradition of social group work.

Participation and Involvement. Self-direction and being involved in a project promote a readiness to learn. This is a basic tenet of andragogy, as mentioned earlier by Knowles (1972). Education often involves an authoritarian atmosphere. The teacher is the expert, and the students are expected to learn what is planned for them. The notion of collaborative learning, where teacher and students design the curriculum together, creates a role change for the participants. The teacher, in this case, is also a student in the pursuit of knowledge. The student, recognizing his or her own rich reservoir of personal resources, is also a teacher at times. When students can become involved in the process of learning, it is more likely that they will be motivated to learn. The joint planning and self-direction enable students to achieve one of the highest levels of knowledge building—learning how to learn.

In social work with groups, participation and involvement contribute to the linkages of group members with one another and to mutual aid as a helping process. This kind of interaction also makes it possible for group members to assume leadership roles that can build group cohesiveness and increase motivation for learning and change.

Modeling. A type of learning is example setting by the worker or others involved in the teaching-learning transaction. If people find that someone's behavior is helpful to them or meets their particular needs, that person is likely to be imitated by them and his or her ideas adopted or followed. This is how we have all developed—imitating our parents, teachers, and other significant individuals in our lives. How persons act is more impressive than what they say. People have learned that nonverbal behavior is the truest indicator of a person's feelings or ideas, since actions cannot be disguised as easily as words. When there is congruence between the verbal and nonverbal modeling, the group member is most likely to incorporate the model's attitudes and behavior. There is constant modeling by the worker or other group members who have high status, and can therefore influence others.

Reflective Evaluation. An important element of learning is being able to reflect, question, evaluate, and examine what we do and how we think, so that it becomes possible to hone our skills and refine our thinking. When people are open to self-examination, their ability to solve problems is greatly enhanced. Reflective evaluation is essentially how persons are able to achieve awareness of their behavior and to advance their knowledge. If the group has an accepting climate, and persons are able to offer feedback to one another, evaluation can be a most enriching opportunity for growth.

Somers (1969) attempts to integrate what others have said about "reflective level learning and teaching."

> Essentially they mean that learners (and often teachers) are confronted with something which is problematic—that is, unclear or puzzling. The process may begin with some observed inadequacy, inconsistency, incompleteness, or irrelevance in substantive knowledge or in attitudes, beliefs, or values. In the reflective process, they center their thinking and research upon the problematic situation, carefully and critically examine facts and generalizations, in the light of testable evidence and in the light of conclusions and further questions. This type of learning and teaching requires of students major responsibility for their own learning, their active participation, their criticism of conventional thinking, their imagination and creativity. It requires of the teacher a clear grasp of the structure of substantive knowledge, an attitude of tentativeness and question about what exists, clarity of goals for the particular course, an openness to student goals of which the teacher himself has not previously thought, both support and expectation for rigorous and imaginative thinking on the part of students, and continuous demonstration of himself as a learner who strives to engage fully in such reflective learning and teaching. (p. 72)

This kind of thinking offers the rationale for reflective evaluation in the group. Since self-directive learning is a key goal in social work with groups, the worker will often create opportunities for members to examine and reflect on the meaning of individual and group behavior.

Sequencing and Progression. Learning involves knowing the relationship of parts to a whole. For instance, in examining a group or the linkage of physical and mental processes in human behavior, it helps to understand that there are stages in group development. It is difficult to comprehend a whole problem without recognizing the complexity of its elements and relationship to the larger picture. It is important at the outset to appreciate the significance of a large issue or problem. However, understanding of it will only come when we know what the parts are and how they fit together. For instance, in learning how to work with a group (the whole), it will be necessary to begin breaking down its component parts into the ways it functions at the beginning, in the middle, and at the end of its existence. We may also want to consider worker behavior according to the type of group, the group composition, the agency setting, the socioemotional and task dimension, and so on. A significant question for the worker is where to start, since there are obviously many ways to provide helping services. The answer lies in what is most relevant for the worker *and* group members. The extent to which the member is involved in identifying the component parts of the problem and selecting the point where the group should start is the extent to which he or she will be motivated to learn. Thus, the collaboration between worker and group members in partializing a problem is also related to involvement and motivation.

Ego psychology is closely related to learning theories also, since it permits us to examine the psychological and social needs and development of the individual in the learning process.

Ego Psychology

Psychoanalytic theory has enjoyed an esteemed position in the history of social work. Since the 1920s, social workers have embraced it to explain behavior, especially in difficult or resistant clients. It has also served to unify and legitimize the profession by providing a "scientific" body of knowledge as an underpinning for practice. However, in recent years many of Freud's original theories have been modified, particularly by ego psychologists.

Ego psychologists, such as Erikson, Hartmann, and White, place primary emphasis on the rational processes of the ego, rather than the instinctual drives of the id. Furthermore, they are concerned with how these conscious, rational processes mediate environmental demands and promote adaptive coping. This point of view takes into consideration the social development of the individual and the quality of his or her interaction with the environment as important determinants of psychological or personality development. The group is an excellent way to enhance social relationships and contribute to healthier ego functioning.

The concepts of readiness and growth, motivation, trust and closeness, self-esteem and identity, and resistance and defense are discussed briefly to highlight how change takes place so that the social worker will understand these aspects of personality in the growth process.

Readiness and Growth. Modern ego psychology provides a foundation for understanding the potential for growth and change. For example, Hartmann (1958) introduced the notion of the conflict-free sphere of the ego. He postulated that there are aspects of ego functioning which are not bound up in mediating the conflicting demands of id and superego. In other words, energy is available for mastery and achievement in relation to the external world. Such ego processes are engaged in adaptive functioning in relation to the "average expectable environment." This theory of adaptation embraces a positive outlook and emphasizes the individual's ability to grow with new experiences. The ego strengths are areas of conscious awareness in which the person feels competent. These abilities can be used to build the person's esteem and balance his or her negative concept of the self.

Group members bring their personal assets into the group so they can be used as resources for personal and group enhancement. It's important for the worker to know about the interests and competence of potential group members, especially during formation, so that a balance toward health can be kept in composing the group. Some group members who have special qualities to offer may become role models for others. When the social worker encourages indigenous leadership, he or she is making use of the ego strengths of the individuals who can help the group become more self-directed. The healthy parts of the group are fostered and nurtured, so that persons can use their strengths for more effective problem solving.

Motivation. Robert White (1960) proposed that the ego has functions related to seeking, learning, and discovery, in addition to its defensive functions. In particular, he identified competence as a principle of motivation. By this he means that the ego innately seeks to master the environment. An individual's need for a sense of competence motivates attempts at new and more complex activity. This sense of accomplishment and curiosity for its own sake has adaptive significance. It also fosters a belief that one can change his or her environment and, in turn, be open to changing.

In the following example, high school students were taught helping skills and encouraged to perform in the role of helper. They learned to be competent and had the opportunity to demonstrate their abilities, thus increasing their motivation for mastering more of their environment.

The Student Service Corps was a group of junior and senior high school students who volunteered to be peer leaders for incoming freshmen to the high school. They were trained in basic helping skills, such as listening, being responsive to ideas and feelings, nonjudgmental attitudes, and encouraging positive behavior. As peer leaders, they were able to ease the transition of the student from the middle school to the high school, while they themselves were strengthened in their positive role as helper. They were expected to be competent and acted accordingly. With increased self-assurance, they were able to take on more leadership in the high school and made recommendations to the administration about improving communication between students and faculty.

A self-concept of being worthy and capable can make the person more willing to experience close relationships. The helper, as in the case of the high school volunteers who assisted the incoming freshmen, was also helped. They were able to practice their competence and receive recognition and reinforcement for their abilities.

Trust and Closeness. Erikson's (1959, 1960, 1963) psychosocial stages of development focus on the inherent strengths of the human personality. The normative crises at each phase of the life cycle embody the potential for growth toward a higher level, as well as the opportunity to rework and resolve issues from an earlier stage.

The first stage in his schema is basic trust versus basic mistrust. In other words, the development of trust is the foundation upon which all other stages rests. He refers to a "reasonable trustfulness as far as others are concerned and a simple sense of trustworthiness as far as oneself is concerned" (1959, 56). This attitude toward oneself and the world reflects a mutuality and stresses the importance of interaction with others.

The resolution of the crisis of trust versus mistrust at this stage of development establishes enduring patterns, although the issue of trust is reactivated at each succeeding stage of development. In particular, a "sense of trust forms the basis for a sense of identity which will later combine a sense of being 'all right,' of being oneself and of becoming what other people trust one will become" (1963, 249).

One of the cornerstones of social work with groups is to create the conditions that lead to the establishment of trust. The genuineness, empathic understanding, and caring of the worker contribute to trust building. The values of self-determination and collaborative problem solving also set the stage for group members to participate in helping one another.

Self-esteem and Identity. The Eriksonian stage of identity versus role confusion emerges during adolescence. As with all other developmental crises, it rests on the relative mastery or resolution of earlier stages. The central issue at this time is the integration of various aspects of the self into a whole that has stability and continuity over time. Again, a mutuality is involved between the individual and the social environment. In other words, identity "connotes both a persistent sameness within oneself and a persistent sharing of some kind of essential character with others" (1959, 102).

A group experience may facilitate a sense of identity (given that identity develops in a social context and that there is always a potential for reworking issues from an earlier stage) through validation, feedback, clarification, and role definition. The struggle to resolve the issue of self-interest versus group interest is a continuing one that can be a source of growth through the creative tension in the group (see Chapter 1). The worker and group members enable one another to relate individual issues to the group as a whole, and vice versa. A primary purpose of group work is to help group members clarify their own identity in relation to the group. The maturation stage of group development, mentioned earlier in small-group theory, typifies the greater comfort of group members to express their individuality within the framework of group purpose.

Resistance and Defense. A major unconscious ego function is to defend against anxiety arising from conflict and instinctual drives. Anna Freud's classic work, *The Ego and the Mechanisms of Defense,* lists some of these defense mechanisms, such as projection, sublimation, reaction formation, and denial. In general, resistance to participation in a group experience may be a manifestation of these defensive functions. For example, the issue of authority, which arises in relation to the group worker, may evoke a group member's unresolved difficulties with earlier life figures and lead him or her to defensive behavior. However, defenses need to be respected, since they are often useful for the person during a period of stress.

On a conscious level, there are many possible reasons for resistance to manifest itself. It is important for the worker to establish a working relationship (or therapeutic alliance) with group members, based on warmth, empathy, and genuineness. Without these necessary conditions, leading to a sense of trust, defensive behavior may arise among group members, crippling the group's effectiveness. Also, there may be barriers related to sex, race, or social class, especially during the engagement or forming phase of a group. The need for inclusion may be thwarted if a group member perceives himself or herself to be unwelcome in the group. Finally, the degree of motivation and openness toward growth may be limited by a lack of hope (Compton and Galaway, 1984, 136–137).

VALUES

Values are the beliefs and principles that guide our actions, because they are considered desirable by persons or groups in our society. Each person's composite values are derived from a variety of associations, including family, friends, groups, and general societal expectations. Sometimes these values are at odds with one another and choices have to be made about which take precedence. Value conflict can be a major source of stress for individuals and is often an issue for groups, especially when the persons who enter groups share a diversity of attitudes and beliefs.

The values of the social work profession are identified in the National Association of Social Workers' Standards for the Classification of Social Work Practice (1982), as follows:

1. Commitment to the primary importance of the individual in society;
2. respect for the confidentiality of relationships with clients;
3. commitment to social change to meet socially recognized needs;
4. willingness to keep personal feelings and needs separate from professional relationships;
5. willingness to transmit knowledge and skills to others;
6. respect and appreciation for individual and group differences;
7. commitment to develop clients' ability to help themselves;
8. willingness to persist in efforts on behalf of clients despite frustration;
9. commitment to social justice and the economic, physical, and mental well being of all in society; and
10. commitment to a higher standard of personal and professional conduct.

The NASW has also described a Code of Ethics based on the values of the profession. It prescribes principles of behavior for the social worker, toward clients, with colleagues, to employers and employing organizations, in the profession, and to society (Barker, 1988, 197–205). Nevertheless, despite these outlines of ethical behavior, social workers are constantly facing value dilemmas. In a study of ethical conflicts for social workers, Conrad (1988) noted examples of pressing practice issues: whether to maintain confidentiality or report on client behavior when it may cause harm to the client or others; whether to maintain confidentiality with adolescents or disclose information to parents when the adolescent engages in questionable behavior. One of the most difficult quandaries for social workers is the conflict between professional and organizational values, where policies or procedures of the agency interfere with professional functions. For instance, considering the financial constraints under which most agencies operate, there may be pressure on workers to see as many paying clients as possible. If the priority is to collect fees, those clients who are unable to pay or who are not covered by insurance may not be served. There may also be less time devoted to home visits, involve significant others, and client advocacy. The worker is caught in the dilemma of wanting to spend more time in collateral contacts and feeling administrative pressures to confine social work activity to what happens within the group. When this takes place, workers need to discuss these issues with supervisors and administrators to seek some resolution, which may include a reordering of priorities, a different way of allocating agency resources, and appeal to funding sources about the need for a more thorough practice approach.

The concept of norms for group members is also mentioned in relation to values. Norms are approved ways of behaving that develop from values within the group. Rules may be introduced into the group, but they will not become norms unless they are generally accepted and practiced by the group. Since there could be a discrepancy between formal rules and evolving norms, this could be a source of conflict. The process of negotiating these differences is often part of the beginning stage of group development, and resolving them successfully may increase intimacy and cohesion in the group.

Some values that have particular relevance for group work are mentioned below. They are derived from the NASW's Standards for the Classification of Social Work Practice (see prior listing), Code of Ethics, and belief systems that underlie the professional development of social work with groups (see Chapter 2).

1. *Respect for human dignity and worth.* Each person in a group deserves respect and has worth. Unless the group worker can believe in the dignity of the individual, it is less likely that the group member will believe in his or her own potential for enrichment. Group members will be expressing feelings and ideas that may or may not be popular or accepted by those in the group. The worker needs to demonstrate approval of the person without necessarily accepting his or her thinking or actions.

2. *Interrelationship of individuals and their environment.* Social work operates within the context of "person in situation," always considering behavior in the totality of the person's life space. This type of thinking allows the social worker to focus on the individual and/or environment, depending on what the need is and how available the person is for social service. It shifts our thinking to multicausal reasons for behavior and establishes the need to work with social-change groups as well as those for treatment purposes.

3. *Collaborative process in problem solving.* There is a strong conviction in the social work profession that people are to be involved in making decisions and encouraged to take responsibility for their own actions. This value is based on the belief that people should be respected for their views and abilities. Besides the increasing evidence that cooperation yields more successful results in solving problems than does competition (Kohn, 1986), the participation of persons in joint decision making can build self-esteem and bonding within the group.

4. *Self-determination.* People who are seen for social services have a right to make their own decisions when they are able to do so. Professional or personal beliefs and attitudes are not imposed on others. Abramson (1985) discusses the "autonomy-paternalism dilemma" in self-determination. Can the professional allow the client to make his or her own decisions, even if they may lead to failure? When the client's rights for self-determination differ with what appear to be the client's needs, how is this resolved? Bernstein (1960) argues against self-determination in every kind of situation. When clients are making decisions

that are harmful to themselves or others, it is the responsibility of the worker to help them face the reality and consequences of these decisions.

5. *Mutual aid.* One of the essential beliefs in social work with groups is that group members are able to help one another. A primary task of the worker is to develop the conditions that will maximize a mutual-aid process. For persons to be able to share their ideas and feelings with others is a means of strengthening the giver and receiver. The collaborative problem solving that goes on during mutual aid can nurture group members, enhance decision making, and build more cohesiveness within the group.

6. *Constructive difference.* An effective group will have some commonality, whether it is an issue, problem, interest, or task. The common threads that bring the group together will help create the bond and affection between group members that provides support. The differences that present themselves offer the possibilities for growth of individuals and the group. We might think of differences as an opportunity for new ideas, alternatives to problem solving, and as expanding the creative potential of the group.

7. *Confidentiality.* One of the reasons why groups are difficult to form is the issue of confidentiality. Many persons are reluctant to share problems with peers, fearing that their admissions will be passed on to persons outside the group. The desire for privacy is very basic. Persons are sensitive about that right being violated, especially when so much information about people is now accessible through our new technology. Yet, the exchange of personal information, feelings, and attitudes is often necessary in a problem-solving process.

If group members can be seen separately before the group actually meets, it is desirable to discuss the boundaries of confidentiality with them. This kind of frank exchange may insure more willingness to participate in the group. With a treatment group, the role of confidentiality—or persons not discussing what happens in the group to those outside the group—should be discussed openly at the first meeting.

SUMMARY

Each of the theories described in the chapter has relevance for the person/group/environment constellation in social work with groups. Although the five knowledge areas are mentioned separately, in reality they are very much interrelated. When an event occurs in a group, it can be explained from a variety of theoretical perspectives. A goal of professional development is to seek greater integration of knowledge, values, and skills so that strategies and choices of intervention are made rationally and within a framework of ethical values. Social work practice is purposeful, disciplined, knowledge-based, and yet spontaneous and creative. A balance of science and art characterize the professional.

REFERENCES

Abramson, M. (1985). The autonomy-paternalism dilemma in social work practice. *Social Casework: The Journal of Contemporary Social Work, 66*(7), 387–393.

Anderson, R. E., & Carter, I. (1984). *Human behavior in the social environment: A social systems approach* (3rd ed.). New York: Aldine.

Barker, R. L. (1988). *The social work dictionary.* Silver Spring, MD: National Association of Social Workers.

Bernstein, S. (1960). Self-determination: King or citizen in the realm of values? *Social Work, 5*(1), 3–8.

Biddle, B. J., & Thomas, E. J. (1966). *Role theory: Concepts and research.* New York: John Wiley.

Caudill, W. (1958). *The psychiatric hospital as a small society.* Cambridge, MA: Harvard University Press.

Chin, R. (1961). The utility of system models and developmental models for practitioners. In W. G. Bennis, K. D. Benne, & R. Chin (Eds.), *The planning of change.* New York: Holt, Rinehart & Winston.

Compton, B., & Galaway, B. (1984). *Social work processes* (3rd ed.). Homewood, IL: Dorsey Press.

Conrad, A. P. (1988). Ethical considerations in the psychosocial process. *Social Casework: The Journal of Contemporary Social Work,* December, 603–610.

Erikson, E. (1959). *Identity and the life cycle.* New York: International Universities Press.

———. (1968). *Identity, youth and crisis.* New York: W. W. Norton.

———. (1963). *Childhood and society* (2nd ed.). New York: W. W. Norton.

Freud, A. (1966). *The ego and the mechanisms of defense.* New York: International Universities Press.

Garland, J. A., Jones, H. E., & Kolodny, R. L. (1973). A model for stages of group development in social work groups. In S. Bernstein (Ed.), *Explorations in group work* (pp. 17–71). Boston: Milford House.

Hanson, P. A. (1981). *Learning through groups: A trainer's basic guide.* San Diego, CA: University Associates.

Hartford, M. E. (1971). *Groups in social work.* New York: Columbia University Press.

———. (1976). Group methods and generic practice. In R. W. Roberts & H. Northen (Eds.), *Theories of social work with groups* (pp. 45–74). New York: Columbia University Press.

Hartmann, H. (1958). *Ego psychology and the problem of adaptation.* New York: International Universities Press.

Kohn, A. (1986). *No contest: The case against competition.* Boston: Houghton Mifflin.

Knowles, M. (1972). Innovations in teaching styles and approaches based upon adult learning. *Journal of Education for Social Work, 8* (2), 32–39.

Lippett, R., Watson, J., & Westley, B. (1958). *The dynamics of planned change.* New York: Harcourt, Brace & World, Inc.

Maslow, A. H. (1970). *Motivation and personality* (2nd ed.). New York: Harper & Row.

Mayer, H. W. (1989). Role playing: Structure & educational objectives. *Journal of Child & Youth Care, 4*(3), 41–47.

NASW standards for the classification of social work practice (1982). Silver Spring, MD: National Association of Social Workers.

Northen, H. (1988). *Social work with groups* (2nd ed.). New York: Columbia University Press.

Olsen, M. (1968). *The process of social organization.* New York: Holt, Rinehart & Winston.

Parsons, T. (1951). Illness and the role of the physician: A sociological perspective. *American Journal of Orthopsychiatry, 21,* 452–460.

Polsky, H. (1962). *Cottage six.* New York: John Wiley.

Rogers, J. (1969). *Freedom to learn.* Columbus, OH: Charles E. Merrill.

Sarri, R. C., & Galinsky, M. J. (1985). A conceptual framework for group development. In M. Sundel, P. Glasser, R. Sarri, & R. Vinter (Eds.), *Individual change through small groups* (2nd ed.). New York: Free Press.

Schutz, W. (1961). Interpersonal underworld. In W. G. Benns, K. D. Benne, R. Chin (Eds.), *The planning of change.* New York: Holt, Rinehart & Winston.

Smith, B. K., & Ramsey, G. V. (1960). *A view of the Texas State Hospital camping project.* Austin, TX: The Hogg Foundation for Mental Health.

Somers, M. L. (1969). Contributions of learning and teaching theories to the explication of the role of the teacher in social work education. *Journal of Education for Social Work* (Fall) 61–73.

Tuckman, B. (1965). Developmental sequence in small groups. *Psychological Bulletin, 63,* 384–399.

White, R. W. (1960). Competence and the psychosexual stages of development. In M. Jones, (Ed.), *Nebraska symposium on motivation.* Lincoln, NE: University of Nebraska Press.

———. (1960). Motivation reconsidered: The concept of competence, *Psychology Review, 66,* 297–334.

Zerin, E., & Zerin, M. (1986). *The Q model for the effective management of personal stress.* New York: Gardner Press.

TEACHING AND LEARNING IDEAS

When observing a role play, video tape, film, or record of a practice situation with a group, analyze the interaction according to the following knowledge areas and values that are described in the chapter.

Social Systems

1. How does the group define itself in relation to other groups or within the agency (boundary issues)? Is it closed or open in membership and what meaning does this have?

2. What are sources of energy from within the group? How does this energy work to help or hinder the group?

3. How are group members linked to one another and what is the meaning of the linkage? Is there evidence of the group forming linkages with persons outside the groups?

4. Who are the people in the group who exercise leverage toward change? What is the meaning and importance of their behavior?

5. What are signs of stress, distress, and eustress in the group? What might be sources of the stress and how is it being handled by the worker and group members? Is there also tension between the group and other systems in the agency or community?

Small Group Theory: Stages of Group Development

The following characteristics are often associated with certain stages of group development.

1. *Formation:*	ambivalence
	seeking commonality with others
	testing group members or workers
	seeking acceptance
	feeling different
	seeking structure
	maintaining distance
	appearing dependent
2. *Power & Control:*	subgroup forming
	seeking more focus
	reaching out to others
	expressing differences
	beginning indigenous leadership
	challenging worker
3. *Intimacy:*	willingness to become involved
	roles seem more clear
	and differentiated
	evidence of norms of behavior
	communication easier
	demonstration of support
	and liking for one another
	more focus on topics
4. *Maturation*	independence by group members
	constructive conflict
	willingness to assume responsibility
	decision making by group
	more risk taking
	evidence of cohesion
	willingness to share feelings and ideas
5. *Separation:*	ambivalence
	more distance
	anger
	denial
	some regression
	anticipation
	recapitulation

What is the group's stage of development? Are there any indications of the reasons for the group's particular stage? What would you suggest how the group might progress?

Role Theory

What are the roles taken by group members and the worker? Are task and socioemotional roles demonstrated in the group? How are these roles useful or not useful in helping the group fulfill its purposes? Is the worker able to shift in being task- or socioemotionally oriented, depending on the needs of the group? Does there seem to be any tension in the group caused by role confusion? Are there any indications of modifying role behavior when the environmental situation changes?

Learning Theories

What seem to be sources of motivation for change? Are areas of discussion and activity relevant for the purpose that brought the group together? Do people have much opportunity to control a part of their lives? Are the cognitive, affective, and experiential levels of learning all being used, and if not, which of these dimensions is favored? Are opportunities for involvement and participation maximized? What kind of model is the worker in terms of values and behavior? Do group members reflectively evaluate their process and goals in order to consider how and what they would like to change?

Ego Psychology

Are personal strengths utilized? Are there activities to enhance possibilities for competence and building self-esteem? What kinds of defenses are used by group members? Do they seem healthy or unhealthy for individuals and the group? Is there resistance to change and, if so, what might account for the resistance?

Values

What evidence of values are present in the group? Is there respect for group members and their cultural background? Are differences among group members appreciated, tolerated, or frowned upon? Is the environment considered part of the problem or is the group member the problem? Do group members exercise self-determination and is it appropriate to their level of functioning? Is mutual aid operating in the group? Is confidentiality respected?

CHAPTER 5

Practice Principles with Oppressed and Vulnerable Populations

The use of knowledge and values are now being translated into practice principles that are widely used in social work and particularly applicable to the oppressed and vulnerable. These practice guides take place within the context of a problem-solving approach. It is expected that during group interaction to solve problems, members will learn coping skills to increase their ability to function more effectively. A profile for any person who is considered oppressed or vulnerable will include a combination of relative strengths and deficits, as is true for the general population. Since these persons are often labeled as deviants and stereotyped as less than normal, the concept of a continuum of coping portrays them within a relative health framework.

Although the definition of who is oppressed and vulnerable and who is not will vary, depending on people's perceptions, some population groups fit this description more than others. Any person may be vulnerable when experiencing a crisis, such as a loss or a serious illness. Therefore, a distinction needs to be made about temporary vulnerability during the time of a crisis and longer-term vulnerability because of age, status, living situation, or mental/physical condition. A crisis or problematic event in one's life may also act to strengthen the person, offering new challenges for growth and stimulating an extra effort to overcome the obstacles.

DEFINITIONS

Persons who are *oppressed* are disadvantaged because of prejudicial attitudes, policies, and practices toward them. They usually experience emotional and physical pressure, which may inhibit personal and social development. The oppressed face societal restrictions in meeting basic needs and are limited in the use of available resources for growth. Ethnic and racial minorities, women, gays and lesbians are examples of these population groups.

Vulnerable persons, some of whom may also be oppressed, often lack the personal, financial, and community resources to satisfy common physical, emotional, and social needs. They may be neglected, abused, and at risk of further breakdown, because of the lower priority associated with their care. Pregnant teens and the physically and mentally handicapped are often considered vulnerable. So are persons who are very young or old, experiencing poverty and homelessness, abusing alcohol or drugs, having AIDS.

CONTINUUM OF BEHAVIOR

Obviously, not all persons who are identified as oppressed and/or vulnerable will exhibit similar behaviors. Besides the separate categories of oppressed or vulnerable, there may be wide individual differences in how people adapt to their circumstances or environment. The characteristics that are described below include *thinking, feeling,* and *acting* dimensions, and range from high to low coping behavior.

Thinking	Reasonable to unreasonable
	Inner-directed to other-directed
	Awareness to unawareness of behavior
Feeling	Focused to unfocused anger
	Optimistic to pessimistic
	Caring to uncaring
Acting	Resilient to submissive
	Reaching out to withdrawal
	Independent to dependent
	Assertive to nonassertive

These behaviors are associated with indices of mental health. They need to be understood in terms of the personal, neighborhood, and cultural contexts of behavior. For instance, being dependent may be a necessary condition during a crisis; it allows the person time to recover from a traumatic event. Being assertive may be frowned upon by certain ethnic groups, especially toward parents or older persons. Inner-directedness may not be an appropriate expectation for some ethnic groups, whose religious teachings dictate that life events are externally directed. Desirable patterns of thinking, feeling, and acting are discussed by the worker and group members in relation to the presenting need or problem. Behavior is viewed as functional or nonfunctional to solve problems.

Thinking: High to Low Functioning

1. *Reasonable to unreasonable*. Being reasonable means that the person is open to new ideas and is willing to weigh the consequences of certain alternatives in making decisions. The low-functioning person is apt to discuss new ideas as unworkable, threatening, or nonapplicable. Defensiveness and hostility may be the consequences of unreasonableness.

2. *Inner-directed to other-directed*. The inner-directed person is able to trust his or her judgment and rely on personal resources in making choices. The other-directed person is more of a fatalist, thinking there is little choice other than to accept the decisions or results of external events, and feeling more concerned about pleasing others than about doing what he or she wants.

3. *Awareness to unawareness of behaviors*. Being aware of behavior is associated with understanding the reasons for certain actions and willingness to explore further the meaning of thinking, feeling, and acting. The unaware person acts without understanding why he does what he does or what the consequences might be, and he or she has little interest in finding out. The unaware person may also use denial, avoidance, or a frame of reference that is unusual and may therefore seem like unawareness. Instead, the difference may be due to cultural, family, or neighborhood mores rather than to personal resistance.

Feelings: High to Low Coping

4. *Focused to unfocused anger*. Anger is a useful emotion if it is constructively channeled toward a person, policy, or procedure that has caused pain or injustice. When the anger is due to a misperception or poor communication (unfocused anger) it is more useful to direct it at a particular person or procedure (focused anger). When this happens it is more likely that clarification can take place, and the anger abated. Anger can be a source of energy, to stimulate the use of personal resources. If it is not understood or misdirected, it can cause harm to oneself and others, may become internalized toward self-destructiveness, or used to lash out at others in a hostile and punitive manner rather than for solving problems.

5. *Optimistic to pessimistic*. Optimism implies hope and a vision of solving problems. For oppressed and vulnerable populations, this optimistic outlook is a necessary mind-set in dealing with the frustrations in their lives, which often occur because of the insensitiveness of people or the restrictive policies of organizations. Hope does not mean false reassurance. It is the continued expectation of success, balanced by the realities of temporary setbacks in attaining one's goals. Pessimism is preparing for the worst of all possible outcomes.

6. *Caring to uncaring.* The caring person feels love and warmth for others. There is respect for the dignity of life and the human potential inherent in every person. Caring goes beyond self-interest to having an interest and regard for people. The uncaring person is consumed with self and has little interest or willingness to be empathic or explore another person's human condition. As a coping behavior, it is necessary to demonstrate caring in order to receive caring in return. It would be difficult to function effectively without the love and respect by others.

Action: High to Low Coping

7. *Resilient to submissive.* Resilience is the ability to recover from defeat. It implies a strength in being able to bounce back from discouraging events and still maintain some hope of success. Submission means giving up, either discounting the possibilities of personally overcoming failure or being unwilling to challenge the outside barriers that interfere with growth and development.

8. *Reaching out to withdrawal.* Being able to seek out others who may be helpful in providing needed resources is a strong indication of high coping ability. It is a recognition of the power of collective strength in overcoming obstacles. Withdrawal can become aloneness and isolation. The person who is a loner may be fearful of rejection and believe it is safer and less painful to withdraw from human contacts.

9. *Independent to dependent.* Being independent means being willing and able to assume responsibility for one's actions and act according to one's inner judgment. The dependent person relies on others to make decisions for him or her and to be responsible for his or her behavior.

10. *Assertive to nonassertive.* Assertion is a direct expression of a person's needs or desires without the hostile defensiveness that sometimes accompanies interactions with other people. Nonassertiveness implies a withholding or reluctance to declare one's needs or relate to another person in a direct and forthright way.

The guidelines for worker activity that follow are meant to improve conditions for high coping behavior. These principles are based upon an assessment of the person/group/environment situation and the worker applies them differentially according to the need.

PRACTICE PRINCIPLES

As part of the assessment, special knowledge is needed to understand and appreciate the background and values of the people being served. For instance, Asian cultural values emphasize family obligations, respect for authority, group over individual needs, and not showing off (Chu and Sue, 1984, 34). The influence of family values and ranking may also present itself within the group process. As an example:

> During the initial phase of a therapeutic group consisting of schizophrenic Asian men, considerable time was spent in recounting where each member had come from and what they had done during their lives. Each member shared different aspects of their personal history—some focused more on their education, others on their history of work, and still others on where and when they were born. The rank ordering of the group largely followed the order of age seniority and "expertise." When seen individually, each had been distant and withdrawn and within the group there developed a cheerful comraderie [*sic*]. Eventually, under the urging of the workers, each member agreed in turn to bring a snack for the group members to nibble on during their sessions. (Lee, Juan, and Hom, 1984, 41–42)

Prior work is necessary before seeing the client. Since an array of resources is often essential in providing basic needs and supportive services, the worker will want to be familiar with the availability of family, neighborhood, and government sources of help. The case manager role, where the worker initiates, coordinates, and evaluates services, is relevant for practice with persons facing environmental as well as interpersonal problems. Awareness of ethnic and social-class information (Devore and Schlesinger, 1987) is necessary so that the assessment can be processed within the framework of these cultural factors.

The principles are arranged in four categories: self-preparation, planning, intragroup process, and environmental support. The worker, group, and environment are used separately and together as major sources of helping the group members and group.

Self-preparation	Self-awareness
	Realistic expectations
Planning	Balanced group composition
	Activity and social action
	Clear guidelines
Intragroup process	Use of strengths
	Discussing differences
	Dealing with resistance
	Encouraging decision making
	Active intervention
	Structure and concrete needs
Environmental support	Significant others
	Advocate for change
	Indigenous leadership
	Outreach and neighborhood conditions

In some cases it is obvious how the principle is related to specific coping behavior. For instance, use of strengths should increase resilience and self-esteem. Encouraging decision making can foster independence and assertiveness.

Self-Preparation

Self-awareness.

Principle: *When the worker has experienced diversity and vulnerability in his or her own life, these impressions and feelings are drawn upon to increase empathy and responsiveness to the needs of group members.*

Social workers who are uncomfortable with the hurt of their own distressing life experiences are likely to avoid painful disclosures by others. During such times the worker may deny or minimize client feelings, present unrealistic expectations, or attempt to rescue the client. But pain must be recognized and consciously experienced for healing to occur, so, by giving appropriate support, the worker should allow the client to stay with the feelings associated with the discomfort. The client needs to understand that, even in the midst of traumatic events, there are choices. The worker not only helps the client to explore the pain fully but also to seek solutions, to muster latent strengths to help live with the situation or change it.

Social workers should explore their own attitudes and feelings about people who are oppressed and vulnerable. Although helping persons may have an intellectual understanding of diversity and discrimination, they often fail to recognize within themselves vestiges of emotional and cognitive prejudice remaining from early socialization experiences. Unless the professional can bring these thoughts and feelings to a greater level of awareness, he or she may unwittingly communicate these biases to clients. Hidalgo, Paterson, and Woodman (1985) underscore these ideas in writing about social work with gays and lesbians, stating that "we have all been socialized in a homophobic society" (p. 4) and therefore need to address our own prejudices. In training a group of volunteers to work with people with AIDS, the personal needs of the volunteers were explored. One of them admitted that his primary motivation for being a volunteer was to work out his feelings about homosexuality and fear of AIDS (Lopez and Getzel, 1987). Unless the volunteer can separate out personal feelings of this kind, it is unlikely that he or she will be able to respond empathically to the needs of the population being served.

Since community or organizational injustice often lies behind the problems of the oppressed and vulnerable, the worker risks having differences of opinion with influential persons in the community or organization. The worker is part of the agency system, and this makes it difficult to separate oneself from agency investments and to assume a mediator role. Actually, the tension caused by agencies' facing up to their own restrictive policies and practices can lead to creative solutions. Mutual-help staff groups, where practitioners solve problems in regard to work-related issues, is a way for staff to make constructive changes within the organization and simultaneously manage work stress (Brown, 1984; Brown, 1988).

Realistic Expectations.

Principle: *Worker expectations for individual and group accomplishments are realistic in terms of the strengths and deficits of group members.*

When there is understanding of what group members are capable of achieving, the worker can help them reach more of their potential. The worker has a vision for what they are able to accomplish. Oppressed and vulnerable populations, because they have experienced so much failure, may be regarded by others as limited in what they can achieve. But if hope is infused in them, creative challenges and the possibilities of success may generate the energy the group needs to seek solutions to their problems. Despite the practitioner's emphasis on positive accomplishments, there may be real deficits within the group that may limit the initial gains they seek. Unless the worker can respect the slow pace of change in such a situation, he or she may be discouraged early on, thus causing despair among the members. Patience and the appreciation of small gains are essential virtues. Temporary setbacks are common and need to be seen as part of the process of change.

Planning

Balanced Group Composition.

Principle: *Persons who are feeling different because of race, ethnicity, gender, or life experience should be in a group with other persons who share their characteristics or problems.*

The criteria for group composition should include a mix of homogeneity and heterogeneity of group members. The balance of diversity and commonality applies to oppressed and vulnerable populations as well. Since such groups may perceive themselves as different and often alone, it is especially necessary for them to have the support and closeness of those who are facing similar circumstances. However, within the same ethnic group there will be differences. Romero (1981), in writing about Puerto Ricans, discussed the danger of thinking about people in a minority group as all the same. Depending upon personality and subgroup affiliations, there will be a range of behavior and norms. With American Indians, for instance, among the 480 tribal groups in the United States, there are differences in closeness and structure among families, use of tribal language, and ties to their culture and Indian lands (Edwards and Edwards, 1984, 8).

As a general guideline, groups that are educational or task-oriented are able to withstand greater diversity in group composition. For groups that face oppression or seem vulnerable to the risk of further breakdown, the homogeneity factor is more strongly indicated. Similarity of interests and common problems increases the possibility of identification with others, enhances comfort through shared experiences (the belief that people will understand), and leads to feelings of safety in reaching out to others. As group members feel more connected, there is increased mutual aid and emotional caring. When persons demonstrate support and empathy, those who are the recipients of this nurturance are more willing to reciprocate benevolently.

In forming the group, persons should be included who have a range of different kinds of strengths. When it is feasible to bring into the group some members who demonstrate higher levels of coping, these persons may be able to influence others positively. The most likely gains for group members from a well-balanced group are increasing caring, optimism, and reasonableness—traits associated with indigenous leadership.

Activity and Social Action.

Principle: *The use of planned activities or social-action projects is especially helpful in releasing feelings, building relationships, increasing trust, and fostering cooperation and recognition through specific accomplishments.*

The use of activity does not negate verbal exchange. It simply means that the discussion is directed at a collaborative project, in which movement, affect, and the use of the senses are experienced individually and with others. It can be total interaction, since a combination of thinking, feeling, and acting comprises the activity. For oppressed and vulnerable populations, whose lives are often chaotic, an activity can offer the guidelines of needed structure. Activities can also help develop skills in dealing with interpersonal and community encounters. For children's groups, the use of activity is the usual means of interaction. It creates opportunities for socialization, the transmission of values, communication, recognition and self-esteem, release of feelings, and cooperative play.

Social-action projects can encourage independence and focus anger to achieve community or organizational change. It provides an outlet for the frustration that may build up in persons who face repeated rejection, failure, and disappointing experiences. Through the activity, anger can be channeled toward constructive outlets. Feelings can be released without destructiveness to oneself or others. Social action can also be a means of practicing assertiveness skills. Communicating thoughts and feelings is a way of taking responsibility for one's actions. Even as practiced within the group, this can be an empowering experience, but when carried over into community life, these skills can lead to increased control of one's life, feelings of personal competence, and sometimes to community change. For oppressed people in particular, it is suggested that the worker search for ways to help group members link concerns from within the group to the larger context of the environment (Breton, 1988).

For various cultural groups, the universality of activity can be a form of expression. Verbal exchange alone can lead to misperceptions, because of differences in the use of words and the various meanings of language. Even nonverbal communication contains different shades of meaning, depending on ethnicity and social class. In a review of the literature on Hispanics and group work, Delgado, and Humm-Delgado (1984) highlight activity as being particularly relevant with Hispanics. The expressiveness and interaction of the activity is compatible with communication patterns in Hispanic family and social groups. This may be one reason for the receptivity of nonverbal action as well as discussion in the group.

Clear Guidelines.

Principle: *Clarifying policies and procedures are necessary to enhance feelings of safety and security.*

The task of explaining and negotiating group purposes and worker/member roles (see Chapter 8) is most relevant to the guideline principle. For those who are facing personal, interpersonal, and community and/or organization problems, there are many issues to address. Establishing clear pathways for change, through a partialization of these varied concerns, will make the best use of the group members' energy and resources. Persons who face multiple problems of a personal and interpersonal nature, especially during a crisis, will feel scattered and at loose ends. The clarity of structure that is part of the contracting phase enables persons to find direction and security, a vital need when other parts of one's life are disorganized.

It is expected that the process whereby group members clarify their purposes and set directions for change will lead them to a state of reasonableness. Since being reasonable implies logical thinking, the negotiation of a workable group agenda, satisfying to members' needs and expectations, should contribute to reasonableness. It is also likely that self-awareness will begin to take place as problems are defined. Clarification of the nature of the problem is the first step toward increased self-awareness.

Intragroup Process

Use of Strengths.

Principle: *The identification and utilization of group member strengths can lead to increased feelings of competence and self-esteem.*

Those who are oppressed and vulnerable may be so preoccupied with their problems that they lose sight of personal resources. Their focus is often on what is wrong or what cannot be done. Without negating the importance of this problem, the worker helps members to define their positive qualities and interests. The emphasis is on exploring with the group members what *can* be done—the choices that *are* available. At first, the accomplishments may be small. However, even minimal signs of success can be a stimulus to further growth and feelings of competence. This view is similar to the strengths perspective advocated by Weick, Rapp, Sullivan, and Kisthardt (1988). They argue that a focus on strengths is consistent with social work values. People have a large measure of untapped resources that can be mobilized for growth and productivity. These personal strengths and interests, as well as previously untapped resources within the environment, can be used to support continued development.

In the following example, the strengths within the extended family are pointed out for a group member.

> Amy, a 16-year-old black teenager who was in a group focused on increasing independence and learning job skills, thought it would be difficult for her to ever live independently because she has not found a job and "could not do anything well." She indicated that she received a lot of negative feedback from her mother about being irresponsible. Although members responded by referring back to a session in which a speaker had discussed some of the external factors that could affect unemployment for Black teenagers (age and racial discrimination, etc.), they also pointed out that Amy had not completed any of the tasks related to improving her job search skills. When Amy noted that her failure to follow through was due to lack of confidence, the other members were able to point out an important strength they had noted: she was on the honor roll at school. They also helped her identify an aunt whom she felt close to, who often gave her positive feedback about herself. Members suggested that Amy talk with her aunt about her lack of self-confidence and about her fears regarding her ability to eventually become independent. The experience helped Amy and other members to think positively about the availability of extended family members for coping with separation issues. (Freeman and McRoy, 1986, 84)

Group work is a building process, starting with a foundation of trust and leading to increased personal and group achievements. These gains may stem from the abilities that group members bring to the group or may be acquired knowledge and skills learned within the group. When group members are able to make choices on the basis of their initiative, judgment, and responsibility, these actions should be supported by the workers and other members. Encouragement should be offered to group members for risking new behaviors or points of view that reflect personal ideas or feelings, thus reinforcing inner-directedness.

As feelings of competence and self-esteem grow, resilience should increase as well. Persons are able to withstand disappointments without considering them a personal defeat as long as they are comfortable about themselves. A person who feels secure can afford to be assertive about his or her needs. Using strengths in collaborative group activity can lead members toward feelings of greater self-worth, since there is continual positive reinforcement of group-member abilities.

Discussing Differences.

Principle: *When group members consider themselves to be treated differently from other people, these perceptions are brought out for discussion. The sharing of these feelings of difference, within a climate of mutual aid, is used in clarifying group member self-concept.*

The perceptions of group members about their identity may be based upon reality—certain past and present events—as well as on distortions in thinking. The group offers group members the opportunity to express their feelings of difference. In sharing their thinking and feelings, group members make an effort to understand the meaning of events and sort out what is based on reality and what on distortion. Since group members provide feedback to one another, thoughts and feelings are clarified, so that group members can correct misperceptions. The expectation that perceptions should be redefined and perhaps changed can be a source of stress within the group. The trust, collective support, and sharing of resources among the group members and with the worker provides encouragement and caring to balance the risk of change. In the first meeting of a group of mentally retarded young adults (see Chapter 6) the worker explores with the group their feelings and attitudes about mental retardation. It is evident that many of them have distorted notions about their own condition, associating it with being mentally ill and dangerous. Ted, one of the indigenous leaders, remarks that mental retardation is more like being a slow learner than like being "crazy." Other group members reach this conclusion on their own, through the unfolding group process.

Persons who have been oppressed and feel vulnerable are likely to feel a range of emotions, including anger toward the oppressor and self-blame. Through the encouragement of the worker and group members, underlying feelings are disclosed and there can be a focusing on what the feelings are and what they represent. The coping ability of assertiveness is supported, and the focused anger can lead to greater self-awareness, as well as action to deal with the anger constructively.

Workers sometimes face a dilemma when agencies resist facing controversial issues. For instance, public schools may find it difficult to help students deal with homosexuality. For gay and lesbian adolescents, there are many stressors, aside from the intense changes in their transition to adulthood. They are often socially isolated and may experience harassment and violence. There is a good possibility of rejection in the family. They face a greater risk of suicide (Hunter and Schaecher, 1987). Bringing out these feelings of difference can alleviate the stress, identify problems to be solved and provide sustenance through collective helping.

Dealing with Resistance.

Principle: *When group members are resistant to group participation and lack trust in relationships, the worker encourages the expression of common feelings and objectives, maximizes self-determination, and uses appropriate self-disclosure to build closeness and the receptivity to services.*

Being oppressed and vulnerable may cause persons to be wary of professionals, since these care givers, however well intentioned, are associated with the organizations and structures that are perceived as discriminating. The worker, under these circumstances, needs to form a relationship that can encourage trust and a willingness to enter into a change process. Establishing an agenda based upon the interests and problems of group members puts responsibility and control more directly in their hands. In order for group members to take more control of the group, assertiveness skills are necessary. The ability to communicate one's needs directly and without hostility is a means of letting others know the nature of the problem. Greater awareness can also come from dealing with resistance, since there is interaction in learning more about why the group member withholds cooperation. If the worker is regarded as part of a bureaucracy that is distant and ungiving, he or she will need to convey a personal warmth that indicates caring and respect. The worker's sharing of appropriate feelings or reactions may help the group members to see his or her human side, besides the professional role.

There may also be cultural resistances, such as the belief among some American Indians that to wish or plan for something may actually lessen the possibility of its happening (Edwards and Edwards, 1984, 14). Tsui and Sammons (1988) deal with the resistance of Vietnamese refugees to learning assertiveness by reframing the term as a "new language of action" (p. 92).

Resistance may also be expressed as negativism or as a way of finding out whether persons who exercise authority and power will be understanding. If the worker can accept anger, it is likely that it can be positively channeled. Anger is usually not meant as a personal attack on the worker, although it often seems that way. Hostile feelings may be directed at the kind of person the worker represents (role of professional) or the organization which provides services. If the practitioner becomes defensive because of the anger, group members may perceive the environment as a threat and shrink from expressing their feelings directly. In a multifamily group in a women's shelter, the initial complaints toward the shelter and its staff were an aspect of the ambivalence that women had about being in the shelter. After they were permitted to express negative feelings, they became more willing to seek constructive solutions (Rhodes and Zelman, 1986).

Encouraging Decision Making.

Principle: *The worker encourages group members to make decisions, however minor, that affect their lives. They are given any opportunity to assume some control for what happens in the group.*

One of the basic premises of social work with groups is that group members participate as actively as they possibly can in the planning and implementation of personal and group goals. The worker recognizes the need to share power and decision making. The give-and-take among group members and with the worker about the direction of the group is an experience in dealing with power, control, and authority.

Oppressed and vulnerable populations often feel that they have no control over their lives. This contributes to low self-esteem, and that in turn can lead to inaction, despair, and submission. As a means of contributing to empowerment, the worker encourages group members to make decisions that they identify as important. Assertiveness skills, increased independence, and more inner-direction are coping behaviors, and they can result from the active participation of group members in the decision-making process.

In writing about black empowerment, Solomon (1976) discusses the role of the worker as helping the client view himself or herself as causal agent in problem solving, or being capable of obtaining a change in the environment in response to his or her needs. What this may mean is that the worker shares expertise with group members as their partner and collaborator in the change effort. This function of the worker role is different from the usual helper-helpee relationship. Professional skill lies in creating a condition of mutuality, so that the client's power and opportunity for decision making are maintained.

Active Intervention.

Principle: *Active intervention may be necessary to provide the energy and leadership that will sustain persons who are feeling immobilized from oppression and vulnerability or expecting initial direction because of cultural values.*

When persons have had painful experiences with others, whether through rejection, loss, or discrimination, they may react by either withdrawing and becoming overly cautious in future relationships or lashing out in an attacking and hostile manner. In either case, they are sending a message they have been hurt. While these behaviors may be defenses to protect themselves from further personal injury, their continued use will be dysfunctional for social and emotional growth. Somehow trust needs to be reestablished, so that persons are open to the giving relationships of others. The pattern of isolation or aggression may be reversed through active, patient, consistent, and caring relationships. When personal energy is either lacking in a group member or misdirected, the forces for constructive change will have to come from the worker or from other group members. Active intervention may stimulate enough energy within the group to develop more caring relationships. It is hoped that resilience will be strengthened as support is maintained during adversity.

Examples from practice:

> Leroy is a member of a group for adults with problems of alcoholism—part of a Community Action Program in an urban area. The group members are all black and experiencing poverty. Leroy expresses an interest in going to an Alcoholics Anonymous meeting but is reluctant, because most of the people who will be attending are middle class and white. The worker goes with Leroy to the meeting and helps him make contact with some of the other participants who seem closest to his interests and background.

> A group of young adolescents are meeting because of social or learning problems in high school. An extremely active group member, Diane, is absent. The group members are unusually quiet and distant. The workers suggest that they act out a skit with prescribed roles. The group members respond to their story of the skit and act appropriately according to the assigned characters. The workers explore the meaning of the role play in connection with their real lives.

> A group of hospitalized mentally ill men are extremely withdrawn and are reluctant to talk to one another. The worker brings in a horse-racing game, where each member needs to roll the dice to move his horse on the board. There is some interaction as the race nears the finish line. After the game the worker serves coffee. There is some discussion about the game and life at the hospital.

In these examples the worker mobilizes action with a group member or with the group itself. The intervention takes the form of doing something to accomplish a goal (going to an AA meeting) or a structured activity to stimulate the process of interaction in the group (role play, horse-race game). In each situation the person or group seems stuck in place—unable to exercise leadership on their own. The active intervention is meant to infuse energy into the group, so that members can function and, if possible, assume more leadership on their own. The danger of active intervention is that it continues past the time when group members are able to take over and act independently. If this occurs, the worker's intervention will contribute to dependency in the group. Sometimes it's a fine line between active intervention and fostering dependency.

Some cultural groups, such as those from an Asian background, will expect the worker to initiate activities and become the active leader. They will see their role more passively at first (Chu and Sue, 1984, 30). There are also cultural aversions to sharing personal and family matters with outsiders. Admitting emotional distress is seen as personal failure. The educational role of the worker will be more acceptable when group members are being "educated" rather than "treated."

When working with abused and neglected children, the worker will let the group members know that he or she will protect them from injury from one another (Lynn, 1989, 85). Children who have been maltreated will often expect punitive measures from others and need to realize that adults can be nurturing and protective. The role of the worker in this kind of situation may present a dilemma. The children may provoke anger, to continue their pattern of getting attention in a negative way. The worker cannot permit destructive behavior, either personally inflicted or expressed. Yet, the practitioner wants to appear kind and loving in order to model the "good" parent. Thus, it is sometimes necessary to limit the negative behavior, find out its source, and to convey to the child that, although he or she is accepted as a person, the behavior should be discontinued.

Structure and Concrete Needs.

Principle: *During a crisis, the use of structure, attention to concrete needs and tasks, and emotional support often accompany the examination of the personal meaning of behavior.*

When persons are in the midst of change, they must relocate their energies and abandon behavior that is both familiar and unfamiliar. There may be a temporary fragmentation of thoughts and feelings, leading to immobilization or random activity. The organization of the person's life has changed. Dealing with the crisis can strengthen the person, through the use and confirmation of known strengths, or it can lead to the breakdown of fragile defenses. If the person's usual pattern of response is not useful for the new situation, he must find new and more functional ways of reacting. During this time of personal disintegration and reintegration, the worker can help the person achieve some stability and sense of wholeness by focusing on specific, concrete needs and tasks. Attention to the organization of behavior will alleviate the client's feelings of dislocation and assist him or her in performing activities that can be useful for the crisis. Berman-Rossi and Cohen (1988) discuss the Dinner Group, female residents of a single-occupancy hotel, who meet out of a common need to plan, prepare, and eat an evening meal. The women all had a history of homelessness and mental illness, yet they were all survivors, and these strengths were supported. The clear purpose of preparing dinner and eating together had all the ingredients of mutual aid, decision making, and socialization, and it led to increased feelings of self-esteem and empowerment. The structure of the activity provided support and safety, and the subtasks of menu planning, shopping, and cooking required specific behaviors which would either be reinforced if used before or learned from the socialization experiences within the group.

Martin and Nayowitz (1988) cite the Shower Group as another example of a men's group that was formed by a street outreach team who were escorting homeless men for showers, clean clothes, and medical/psychiatric treatment.

> The group members were Jim, a mildly retarded overweight white male in his late thirties, Philip, in his early sixties, a self-detoxified recovering alcoholic with alcohol hallucinosis, and Kevin, a young white paranoid schizophrenic suffering from feelings of persecution. Their initial contact with staff in the van formed the basis for developing relationships and interactions among themselves which in time carried over to relationships independent of the team workers. The men began to show concern for others by asking for individuals who were not at their usual pick-up spots at the specified time. Their concern for others served to remind them of the possibilities they faced themselves.
>
> Over time when the opportunity arose for the three men to be placed in housing their connection with a structured task-centered program played a significant role in helping them to become oriented to the new environment. Jim, Philip, and Kevin were able to address issues among themselves about moving into a new residence at first in the van, and thereafter in the hotel. Jim's enthusiasm about the move did not assuage his concern about Philip. He worried that Philip would not keep his room clean enough to remain in the hotel and offered to help when needed. The ability of the two men to plan support for one another in the new environment demonstrated to the workers their capacity for relationship in supportive and concrete ways. (p. 84)

In this situation, the group process leads to increased caring among the group members. They are more willing to be optimistic, since the nurturing relationships give them reason to be hopeful. When there is a focus on partialization of a problem and attention to specific tasks, the coping behavior of reasonableness is more likely to develop and be useful in solving problems.

Environmental Support

Significant Others.

Principle: *Receptive and accessible persons in the environment of the group members are encouraged to provide emotional and resource support.*

To counteract the destructive effects of the oppressive part of an environment, it is necessary to locate those other parts that can be sustaining. The role of the worker is to help the group members reach out to persons and use constructive resources that will be an impetus for growth. It is necessary to assist the oppressed and vulnerable person to be assertive about his or her needs. Whether group members make contact singly or collectively, the experience of involving significant others can model reaching out as a coping behavior.

Group members may be hesitant in taking the necessary steps to involve others in helping relationships, considering the experiences of past disappointments. The worker will need to recognize and appreciate this resistance. If therapeutic ingredients are strong within the group, they should involve sufficient trust for members to initiate environmental contacts, and that should lead to the needed enrichment.

Family members are the most obvious significant others to be considered in creating a more supportive environment. For some ethnic populations, such as Hispanics (Acosta and Yamamoto, 1984), Asians (Ho, 1984), and blacks (Ward, 1981), contact with key members of the client's family will often increase his or her receptivity to social work intervention. For many cultural groups, the extended family is a major helping network to call upon as an important resource in time of need.

Advocate for Change.

Principle: *It is often necessary for the worker to be an advocate for group members or to influence systems to be more accessible to their needs.*

It is best, when possible, for group members to be their own advocates, making use of their assertiveness skills and increasing their feelings of independence. However, when the circumstances do not permit group members to take the initiative, the worker will assume this responsibility. Besides using his or her professional influence to affect changes, the worker can be a role model for the group members, so they can borrow some of these skills at a future time. Just as social action can be a vehicle for channeling angry feelings, advocacy can also help in focusing the anger in a positive change direction.

Indigenous Leadership.

Principle: *Involving natural leaders from oppressed and vulnerable populations as helping persons can be effective in stimulating further leadership, resourcefulness, and improvement from within these groups.*

Within every group or neighborhood, there are persons who are capable of some leadership—an ability to influence others in a positive or negative way. Since persons who are oppressed or vulnerable may be cautious or resistant to professional intervention, the natural leaders can be a powerful factor in effecting change. Since they are peers, it is more likely that group members will identify with them and trust their judgment. The role of the worker is to locate and support indigenous leadership when that leadership is helpful to the group. It may be possible to train such leaders in techniques that will add to their abilities in reaching their peers. Besides the benefits of increasing the leadership potential within the group or neighborhood, empowerment is increased and with it feelings of being able to function on one's own. Indigenous leadership in self-help groups exemplifies the effectiveness of peer-led groups. The group member in these groups is more apt to take on an independent role than the dependent role that sometimes occurs when professional intervention is present.

Outreach and Neighborhood Locations.

Principle: *Outreach and meeting with people in familiar neighborhood locations can increase receptivity to services.*

For many reasons, persons who are oppressed or vulnerable are reluctant to make use of community services. They may feel alienated from the official arrangements in the community or perhaps associate professionals with their plight of discrimination. When professionals can reach out to these population groups in their local surroundings, such as places of worship, schools, community centers, or housing complexes, it is more likely that they will have a favorable response. It is comfortable and reassuring to meet in familiar surroundings with friends. The norms of the neighborhood provide a known structure and relatively clear expectations. Persons who are meeting on their own turf generally feel more in control of their personal situation. Another advantage of outreach into the community is the greater likelihood that local lay and professional persons will be involved in the helping effort. In planning a strategy of intervention, it would be desirable to do so jointly with local people, including indigenous leaders and professionals.

In the Whole Life Program described by Brown (1986), over a hundred minority adolescents participated in evening recreational activities at a local high school, as an introduction to social, health, job, and family services that are offered by professionals during the evening program. This informal arrangement was less threatening to the mostly black adolescents. With professionals coming to their neighborhood, the youths were more in control of the interpersonal encounter, and the interaction with the service providers encouraged independence, since the teenagers could make use of their own norms and leadership.

A teen pregnancy-prevention program at a public school relied on self-referrals or referrals from friends. The local setting and the belief of the adolescents that there would be confidentiality were the cornerstones of its success (Doty and King, 1985).

SUMMARY

Practice principles are applied differentially to those receiving social work services, depending on the assessment of the person/group/environment. The aim is to increase coping strategies and skills of group members, making use of existing strengths and creating opportunities for learning and practicing problem-solving skills. Of utmost importance in the helping relationship is the worker's ability to communicate hope, empathy, and compassion. While this is true for all clients, it is especially necessary for those who are experiencing oppression and vulnerability. Such persons have often been exposed to the insensitiveness of others and may be wary of people who profess to help them. Patience and understanding are necessary virtues for the care giver.

Social group work, with its broad range of modalities, is well suited to this population. The use of activity can often bridge cultural differences. Diversity within the group can be appreciated and useful as mutual interests are pursued. The multiple levels of intervention with person, group, and environment provide a holistic and integrative approach to helping. The social work principle of "starting where the client is" may take the form of meeting a concrete need, such as the Dinner Group and Shower Group that were given as practice examples. The common needs that bring people together are a beginning—a way to build trust, communicate, nurture, and eventually meet other personal and social needs that may be more resistant in an initial encounter. Persons who think of themselves as being alone can learn to work, play, and help one another. The group becomes an instrument of power and vitality, since its eventual purpose is the empowerment of its members. The coping skills that are learned and experienced as part of group development can also be applied to situational problems outside the group. Since the source of oppression and vulnerability is often in the environment, the group at some point may take on a social-action or system-development direction and assume more control and responsibility for community or organizational change.

If the profession of social work is to be true to its mission of helping the poor, oppressed, and ethnically diverse, its professionals need to be prepared with knowledge, values, and skills. To be effective practitioners, trainers, and researchers for those in most need, they must also ally themselves with other care givers and service providers: teachers, clergy, police, hospital personnel, and so on. The team effort has a greater impact on resolving the problem than a singular approach.

The role of the social group worker as resource and consultant will take on even more importance in the years ahead. This is especially true with self-help groups, which include a vast array of people who are vulnerable because of the specific problems that bring them together. Involving and training indigenous leaders and paraprofessionals will not only help with social treatment but move in the direction of prevention as well. The problems associated with the oppressed and vulnerable are extremely costly in both human and financial terms. Developing social programs that are effective will require research and evaluation. With limited staff and monetary resources, communities want to know what works best. Social work, in cooperation with other helping professions, needs to monitor services and use the technical research methodology that is available in designing strategies for evaluation. Lastly, the holistic approach should include involvement with government officials and key persons in the community who have the power to make policy decisions. Coalitions with persons from these varied and influential interest groups can provide a unified and united front to combat social problems. The practice principles are general guidelines of appropriate social worker activity for the oppressed and vulnerable. In the next chapter, specific techniques will be described to implement these principles. These techniques offer another framework for understanding what the worker can do in the group.

REFERENCES

Acosta, F. X., & Yamamoto, I. (1984). The utility of group work practice for Hispanic Americans. *Social Work with Groups, 7* (3), 63–73.

Berman-Rossi, T., & Cohen, M. B. (1988). Group development and shared decision-making working with homeless mentally ill women. *Social Work with Groups, 11* (4), 63–78.

Breton, M. (1988). The need for mutual-aid groups in a drop-in for homeless women: The sistering case. *Social Work with Groups, 11* (4), 47–61.

Brown, L. N. (1984). Mutual help staff groups to manage work stress. *Social Work with Groups, 7* (2), 55–66.

———. (1986). Mobilizing community service for adolescents in trouble. *Social Work with Groups, 9* (1), 107–119.

———. (1988). Staff groups: Creative problem-solving in the workplace. In M. Leiderman, M. L. Brinbaum, & B. Dazzo (Eds.). *Roots and new frontiers in social group work.* New York: Haworth Press.

Chu, J., & Sue, S. (1984). Asian/Pacific–Americans and group practice. *Social Work with Groups, 7* (3), 23–36.

Delgado, M., & Humm-Delgado, D. (1984). Hispanics and group work: A review of the literature. *Social Work with Groups, 7* (3), 85–95.

Devore, W., & Schlesinger, E. G. (1987). *Ethnic-sensitive social work practice* (2nd ed.). Columbus, OH: Merrill Publishing.

Doty, M. B., & King, M. (1985). Pregnancy prevention: A private agency's program in public schools. *Social Work in Education, 7* (2), 90–99.

Edwards, E. D., & Edwards, M. E. (1984). Group work practice with American Indians. *Social Work with Groups, 7* (3), 7–21.

Freeman, E. M., & McRoy, R. (1986). Group counseling program for unemployed black teenagers. *Social Work with Groups, 9* (1), 73–89.

Hidalgo, H., Peterson, T. L., & Woodman, N. I. (Eds.), (1985). *Lesbian and gay issues: A resource manual for social workers.* Silver Springs, MD: National Association of Social Workers.

Ho, M. K. (1984). Social group work with Asian/Pacific Americans. *Social Work with Groups, 7* (3), 49–61.

Hunter, J., & Schaecher, R. (1987). Stresses on lesbian and gay adolescents in schools. *Social Work in Education, 9* (3), 180–188.

Lee, P. C., Juan, G., & Hom, A. B. (1984). Group work practice with Asian clients: A sociocultural approach. *Social Work with Groups, 7* (3), 37–48.

Lopez, D., & Getzel, G. S. (1987). Group work with teams of volunteers serving people with AIDS. *Social Work with Groups, 10* (4), 33–48.

Lynn, M. (1989). Group treatment. In S. M. Ehrenkranz, E. G. Goldstein, L. Goodman, J. Seinfeld, (Eds.). *Clinical social work with maltreated children and their families.* New York: New York University Press.

Martin, M. A., & Nayowitz, S. A. (1988). Creative community: groupwork to develop social support networks with homeless mentally ill. *Social Work with Groups, 11* (4), 79–93.

Rhodes, R. M., & Zelman, A. B. (1986). An ongoing multi-family group in a women's shelter. *American Journal of Orthopsychiatry, 56* (1), 120–130.

Romero, S. (1981). Counseling Puerto Rican families. In E. Mizio & A. I. Delaney, *Training for service delivery to minority clients.* New York: Family Service Association.

Solomon, B. B. (1976). *Black empowerment: Social work in oppressed communities.* New York: Columbia University Press.

Tsui, A. M., & Sammons, M. T. (1988). Group intervention with adolescent vietnamese refugees. *Journal for Specialists in Group Work, 13,* 90–95.

Ward, N. T. (1981). Counseling from a black perspective. In E. Mizio & A. I. Delaney (Eds.). *Training for service delivery to minority clients.* New York: Family Service Association.

Weick, A., Rapp, C., Sullivan, W. P., & Kisthardt, W. (1988). A strengths perspective for social work practice. *Social Work, 34* (4), 350–354.

TEACHING AND LEARNING IDEAS

1. Write a process recording (a narrative account) of group worker activity in relation to the interaction within the group. Identify the practice principles that illustrate worker actions or plans. Explain how the use of certain principles is related to the type of group, its purpose, and composition.

2. Develop a beginning profile of coping behaviors for one or more group members by identifying a place along a continuum for each of the thinking, feeling, and acting behaviors. Continue these profiles at periodic intervals to measure any changes in coping behavior. Consider how the use of specific practice principles may have accounted for some of the behavior change.

3. Do a role play of an incident in a group that illustrates the use of one or more practice principles. Evaluate the use of the principle(s) with the worker and group members.

CHAPTER 6

Use of Techniques

There are many terms to define what workers do in groups. It might be called a procedure, a technique, a skill, a task, or an intervention according to various writers in group work: Middleman and Goldberg, 1974; Bertcher, 1979; Henry, 1981; Shulman, 1981; Balgopal and Vassil, 1983; Toseland and Rivas, 1984; Glassman and Kates, 1986; Garvin, 1987; Northen, 1988. Northen (1988) clarifies the distinctions among a procedure, a technique and a skill: "*procedure* refers to a particular course of action or manner of intervening in some process. A technique is a set of specific interrelated actions that carries out the intent of a procedure. Skill denotes proficiency or expertness in the use of procedures" (p. 56). This author uses technique and task to communicate group worker actions. Eleven techniques are listed, each with a number of behaviors.

Tasks are broader activities, related to helping the group accomplish its purposes during stages of group development. For instance, one task is to help group members clarify their reasons for being in the group, so that a contract (usually verbal) can be formulated. In completing this task, the worker may use a combination of techniques, especially in the areas of information sharing and support/involvement. There will be a full explanation of tasks in Chapters 8–10.

The techniques that will be discussed have been organized by the author in their present form. Some of them are similar to what other writers have identified as techniques or skills (see above). The explanation of each technique includes a variety of behaviors that are described later. Some of these techniques are also performed by group members as a way of demonstrating indigenous leadership. The group worker is always a model for behavior that may be adopted by group members. When group members incorporate helping techniques into their behavior repertoire, it enhances their ability to deal with interpersonal situations. The techniques will be explained and discussed in relation to a short-term group that meets for eight sessions. The analysis of the group will include the rationale for using the techniques.

TECHNIQUES

There are three sections of techniques—information sharing, support and involvement, and self-awareness and task accomplishment. All these dimensions of worker activity are necessary for the many different types of groups in social work. The use of techniques will depend on the group purpose, composition of members, and situation in the group. When the group purpose is oriented toward personal change, the self-awareness and task accomplishment techniques will be used more often than when the group is focused on community or organizational change. The socioeducation group will probably use more of the support and involvement techniques, since the element of support is a major ingredient for this type of group. When information is required to clarify group purposes, understand an issue, or solve a problem, the information-sharing techniques will be used. Techniques are used differentially to enhance individual and group growth or to complete a project, and need to be responsive to the kinds of situations that occur in groups.

The techniques are listed as follows:

Information Sharing
1. Giving information, advice, or suggestions; directing
2. Seeking information or reactions about (a) individual, group, or significant others, or (b) agency policies and procedures

Support and Involvement
1. Accepting and reassuring, showing interest
2. Encouraging the expression of ideas and feelings
3. Involving the individuals or group in activity or discussion

Self-awareness and Task Accomplishment
1. Exploring with the individual or group the meaning of individual or group behavior, as well as life experiences
2. Reflecting on individual or group behavior
3. Reframing an issue or problem
4. Partializing and prioritizing an issue or problem
5. Clarifying or interpreting individual or group behavior, as well as life experiences
6. Confronting an individual or the group

Information Sharing

The giving and seeking of information is used to identify a need or problem and clarify its meaning. Information sharing is especially important during the beginning stage of a group when structure is necessary to the continued development of the group. Information about agency policies and procedures, expectations for behavior in the group, and available resources offer guidelines of security for the new member.

In order for problem solving to occur, the group will need to collect relevant data that defines the problem, establishes its boundary, and suggests alternative solutions. The exchanging of information is also a means of reality testing, whereby ideas and feelings are elicited to support or refute perceptions of the participants.

1. Giving Information, Advice, or Suggestions; Directing. The giving of information provides necessary knowledge to the group or is a response to a question. It is also used to maintain a focus on a topic being discussed in the group. Self-disclosure by the group worker may be used as a means of making him or her more accessible and genuine as a person. When this kind of personal sharing is appropriate and not used to meet the personal needs of the worker, it can enrich relationship building in the group. Setting limits are those words or actions to prevent or discontinue behavior that is detrimental to members of the group. The group worker uses understandable language and avoids professional jargon.

2. Seeking Information or Reactions about (a) Individual, Group, or Significant Others, or (b) Agency or Community Policies and Procedures. Seeking information about group members, the group or significant others can assist in making an assessment about individual or group behavior. It can also help those in the group to learn about one another and gain access to data which can be used in problem-solving.

Seeking information about how group members think or feel about agency or community policies and procedures can help clarify expectations and enable group members to use agency or community resources more productively.

Support and Involvement

This is the socioemotional component of worker activity that helps group members feel more comfortable in the group and become involved in problem solving and self-awareness. For many group members, especially when starting a group, there may be fears, disorientation, and ambivalence about being in the group. The techniques of support and involvement could foster the kind of affectional ties that will balance the stresses of an uncertain beginning.

Encouraging group members to express pent-up feelings is often necessary, to release the damaging effects of anger or other emotions that distort thinking or create adverse bodily reactions. However, the discharge of feelings needs to be preceded or followed by an exploration of its meaning. Group members should be encouraged to take action in a constructive way to communicate these feelings to others, such as offering feedback to another person or being assertive about a personal need or belief.

1. Accepting and Reassuring, Showing Interest. Being responsive to ideas and feelings expressed by group members conveys interest and caring. Validation of issues, needs, and problems can demonstrate respect for individual differences. While the group worker may show liking for the group member as a person, he or she should not accept behavior that will be harmful to oneself or others. Normalizing concerns can be reassuring. Helping group members discover common areas of need, interest, or problem is a means of support and can lead to the mobilization of energies for joint problem solving. Use of humor, when appropriate, can be reassuring, contribute to closeness in the group, and relieve tension.

2. Encouraging the Expression of Ideas and Feelings. Cognitive and feeling dimensions of expression are both important. The group worker encourages elaboration of ideas and feelings when this seems desirable. There is awareness of latent and manifest levels of communication and, if it seems appropriate, to help the latent idea or feeling become more apparent and accessible to the group. There may be attention to nonverbal messages (part of the latent content) to find out whether group members want to disucss its meaning. Self-disclosure by the worker may be used to model the expression of feelings.

3. Involving Individuals or the Group in Activity or Discussion. Involvement is a key ingredient in the development of cohesion and group maturity. Wherever possible, group members are encouraged to become engaged in activity or discussion. They are expected to communicate with the group worker and other group members in the sharing of ideas and feelings. However, there is respect for the distance which some group members need at particular times in the life of the group. Involvement may take the form of introducing group members to each other to foster relationship building, relating individual issues to wider group themes, creating a structure to enhance communication (seating arrangement, prescribed roles in an activity, etc.) and presenting choices for decision making. Scanning by the worker to establish periodic eye contact with all members can nonverbally invite participation. Allowing brief silences is another way of expecting group members to assume responsibility in the life of the group.

Self-Awareness and Task Accomplishment

The purposes of all social work groups includes a combination of self-awareness and completion of certain tasks, either prearranged or developed once the group forms. In the extreme situation where the group is solely self-awareness- or task-oriented, there may be limited success, because the other component of group life is missing. This section includes some of the steps of problem solving and those techniques that help group members consider the meaning of their behavior and its impact on other people. Group members also need to understand how other people influence them.

1. Exploring the Meaning of Behavior and Life Experiences. Encourage the individuals or group to think about what has happened or is happening in their lives, especially in the here-and-now of the group. These are activities which attempt to engage the individuals or group in examining their own behavior and feelings, and the behavior and feelings of others who influence them. The worker may raise questions about whether there are similarities or differences in their manner of solving problems.

2. Reflecting on Individual or Group Behavior. Identify, accent, or paraphrase what is taking place in the group, or what other group members are saying. It is a way of mirroring individual or group interactions. The reflecting activity is a way of demonstrating active listening and can offer encouragement for persons to continue speaking. It may also provide the opportunity for the correction of perceptions if the reflection does not accurately express the meaning of a statement or situation.

3. Reframing an Issue or Problem. Suggest reframing an issue or problem so it is viewed more positively and with hope for change. It is a way of cognitively restructuring how a problem is initially presented. The new meaning of the problem may be perceived as more accessible for resolution.

4. Partializing and Prioritizing an Issue or Problem. Engage the group in considering the various aspects or parts of an issue or problem. The areas that are defined should be clear and specific. A further step might be to set priorities with the group for those areas that seem most accessible and manageable for resolution. Usually partialization leads to selecting a smaller area that is more within the control of the person or group for solution and leads to greater receptivity and motivation for problem solving.

5. Clarifying or Interpreting Individual or Group Behavior or Feelings, as well as Life Experiences. The clarifying activity attempts to explain or connect certain happenings that have taken place or been shared by the group members.

While clarification may attempt to explain or help group members become more aware of conscious needs, problems, or interests, interpretation is an activity that brings into their awareness a feeling or wish that may be consciously unacceptable to them. Interpretation is only used when group members might be able to accept and understand the meaning and implications of this type of intervention.

6. Confronting an Individual or the Group. When there is avoidance or resistance to work related to group purposes, the worker may point this out to discuss its meaning. The resistance in a beginning session could be a need to maintain distance and should be respected. When this continues, the resistance is addressed. Confrontation is a statement that defines how thoughts, feelings, or actions by group members seem to be self-defeating for the person as well as the group. It may also be proposed as a question for further exploration. In either case, it should be stated in a way that encourages further elaboration and explanation for increased self-understanding. It is especially important to challenge thoughts, feelings, or actions when they are a pattern of dysfunctional behavior, or when there is a discrepancy between what a person says and the accompanying actions. Confrontation is also a form of giving feedback.

TECHNIQUES APPLIED TO A GROUP

The use of helping techniques in a socioeducation group of mentally retarded young men are described and illustrated during eight meetings of this group at a YMCA. This community agency, which represents normal growth and belonging in a community, is used in the transition from residential to community living. The concept of a continuum of social experiences toward more independent functioning is demonstrated.

Elements of group process are shown throughout the life of this short-term group. The group develops its own goals toward more independence. Formal leadership, represented by the techniques of the group worker, are used to accomplish the tasks within the group. However, group members also exhibit leadership, especially Bob (task-oriented leader) and Ted (socioemotional-oriented leader) who are able to influence the group toward more independence.

The close relationship of activity and discussion is important in helping to develop individual and group growth. Community resources are used as a means of reality testing with persons in the wider community.

The techniques are related to stages of group development and contribute to the empowerment of the group members. The group worker does not come to the group with an arranged agenda. He attempts to be responsive to what is uppermost in the minds of the group members. The group worker is active when necessary but also tries to share power and control with the group members.

Description of the Group

The group being described is composed of mildly retarded young men (ages 17 to 22) living at a school for people who are mentally retarded. They all have varying degrees of social and emotional problems. The school, Davidson, has an academic and vocational program, including on-campus and off-campus vocational training. There is a full range of other services, such as recreation, social services, speech and hearing therapy, and psychological testing and counseling. These students are returned to the community as soon as they seem able to make a satisfactory adjustment with their family, in foster placement, or in independent living. They are the older students, all working in the community and preparing to leave the residential school. The group was organized to help them become more capable of functioning independently in the community. Each of the young men was seen individually by the group worker and invited to participate in the group. They were all coming voluntarily.

In order to fulfill their purpose, the group met at a local YMCA for an eight-week period. The excerpts that follow were taken from a one-hour tape-recorded group discussion, which was only part of a four-hour period. Their earlier time together was essentially experiential—eating suppers together, using the swimming pool and Ping-Pong and pool tables. The worker was with them during this entire time, except in the last few weeks of the group when some of them went shopping in town for about an hour by themselves. This was done to contribute to their independence. Their experiences of using activities together and mingling with other Y members was just as important as their formal meeting. The combination of the Y experiences and group discussion was instrumental in fostering their individual and group growth.

Group Members. Two of the boys will be highlighted—John and Bob—both of whom were meeting at the agency for the first time.

John is twenty-one years of age, white, and Catholic. He has always exhibited behavior problems, being described in infancy as "unusually hyperactive, erratic and unpredictable." Both parents are living. He has never been able to get along with his father, who is very domineering and has high expectations. He entered public school at six years but was expelled because of behavior problems. He has been in institutions since the age of ten. His behavior has improved somewhat. Earlier, he would refuse to bathe or wear clean clothes. He is still very stubborn, easily excited, and inclined to become abusive if he is thwarted. His adjustment on job placements has been poor, since he complains constantly and is not amenable to directions. His I.Q. is 62.

Bob is twenty years of age, black, and Protestant. Little is known of his actual parents, except that his mother had been sent to an institution for the retarded. He was raised by a foster mother from the time he was one year old. For a brief time he attended school in the community. However, he demonstrated undesirable behavior, such as stealing, bullying other children, and molesting young girls. A description of his behavior at the age of ten characterized Bob as being a "quiet, obedient child who speaks only when spoken to and prefers to shake his head rather than talk." He was institutionalized at the age of eleven years. More recently he has shown progress at the school, getting along well with other students and employees, and rated highly on his job placements. His I.Q. is 64.

Other group members include

Ned,	age 18,	I.Q. 71,	white,	institutionalized 8 years.
Gene,	age 22,	I.Q. 64,	white,	institutionalized 8 years.
Steve,	age 17,	I.Q. 76,	white,	institutionalized 8 years.
Ted,	age 20,	I.Q. 70,	white,	institutionalized 8 years.
Bill,	age 20,	I.Q. 70,	white,	institutionalized 5 years.
Jack,	age 19,	I.Q. 65,	white,	institutionalized 5 years.

Group Worker. The group worker was educated as a social worker with a group work specialization. He worked at the school during the summer when these meetings were held. Throughout the regular academic year, he was a social work field instructor at the school and had known the boys casually from contacts with them on the school grounds.

Preparation for the Group

The idea for the group was originally conceived at a meeting of the social services department when the staff were discussing plans to prepare students to leave the school. The group was meant to ease the transition to community living. Key persons at the school were contacted, such as the vocational counselor and cottage staff where the students lived. It was necessary to inform them about the plans, ask for suggestions, and enlist their cooperation in supporting this type of off-campus activity. If these persons had not been involved in the planning phase, they might have demonstrated resistance to the idea and possibly undermined its implementation. (For a fuller discussion of staff resistance to group formation, see Chapter 7.)

When the students were contacted about the idea for the group, they were extremely receptive. They had all known one another from common living arrangements and, in some cases, similar work situations in the community.

The other major part of preparation was with the YMCA itself. The director was seen first, and he was very favorable to the plan that was presented. Besides the director, an associate administrator was apprised of the group and could lend his support. The Y staff knew that the students would eat supper in the agency cafeteria, use their swimming pool and Ping-Pong and pool room at the end of the evening session. The young men used the money that they earned on their jobs to buy Y memberships.

First Meeting. Before the group discussion, John became upset because he was inadvertently separated from the rest of the group. Feeling rather lost, he left the agency and sat in the station wagon by himself. He had to be persuaded to join the group. In the ensuing discussion the boys examine their feelings of how persons in the community, represented by the YMCA, may regard them. Their need for trust and support by others is brought out as they describe their reactions to the lifeguard. It is a way of asking for the same kind of acceptance from the worker and the group members. They reveal their concept of mental retardation, which is at first quite distorted. Through exploration in the group, a more accurate description of mental retardation emerges. The group worker helps them express their feelings in an accepting atmosphere and guides the discussion, through participation by the members, to a more accurate understanding of mental retardation and themselves.

> WORKER: What about any of the people that you've met tonight? What did you think they thought of you?
>
> EXPLORATION: Seeks to help group members identify feelings about meeting new people in order to deal with any inclusion issues.
>
> JOHN: That's the way I felt out there in the car.
>
> (*Several group members talking at once*)
>
> WORKER: Let's hear from John.
>
> ENCOURAGING EXPRESSION OF IDEAS AND FEELINGS: Gives John an opportunity to respond further.
>
> JOHN: That's the way I felt out there in car.
> WORKER: How's that?
>
> ENCOURAGING EXPRESSION OF IDEAS AND FEELINGS: Enables John to elaborate more on what has been said.
>
> JOHN: I wondered about how they felt about me.
> TED: What do you mean?
> BOB: In your opinion, what do you mean about how they felt about you?
> NED: What is your—proposition—reaction?
> BOB: Express yourself.
> JOHN: In other words, I wondered how they were thinking about me. I was just wondering about how that lifeguard was thinking about my actions in the pool.
> WORKER: Ah-heh.
>
> ACCEPTING, SHOWING INTEREST: Demonstrates listening and encouragement to continue.

NED: Did you think inside you that he liked you, that he helped you, and been nice to you and showed you?

JOHN: Plus, you can even tell the way he was nice to you when he went down there and didn't holler.

TED: Did he holler at you?

JOHN: No.

WORKER: How did you think they might have felt toward you?

ENCOURAGING EXPRESSION OF IDEAS AND FEELINGS: Continues attempt to bring out feelings about acceptance or rejection. (If there are unexpressed feelings of rejection, it could contribute to resistance of agency experience.)

JOHN: That I'm a pretty good guy.

WORKER: Did you wonder if they thought that you were from Davidson—that you were mentally retarded, or what did you think about that?

EXPLORATION: Seeks to bring attitudes about mental retardation and themselves out into open.

NED: No, I don't think that he thought that we were mentally retarded. That's for sure.

JOHN: I don't think so either.

NED: Because we sure don't show it.

JOHN: We don't show it down there.

NED: Because, the main thing—if we were mentally retarded, we'd be jumping around crazy—

WORKER: Is that what somebody is who is mentally retarded?

EXPLORATION: Focuses on their perceptions of mental retardation and self-concept.

BOB: In my opinion, a retarded student, the way that I feel, what they mean by retarded student, that if we were retarded like some of these people think we are, that a retarded person is like you don't trust them. Like you figure if I was retarded, now in your opinion, if I jumped in that pool, probably you might think I would try to hurt myself or something—try to jump in the pool and try to kill myself. Something like that. That's what I feel a retarded kid is—don't care what happens to them.

WORKER: You mean that if they thought you were retarded, they wouldn't trust you.

REFLECTION: Indicates listening and wanting to understand their intended communication.

BOB: They wouldn't trust us in the pool. Because the lifeguard would be right there all the time. He would probably get in the pool and stand around watching to make sure, because the man would figure that we were off.

NED: And there's another reason that would make you show that you were mentally retarded.

WORKER: What's that?

SEEKING INFORMATION: Inviting Ned to bring out reasons and contribute further to the discussion.

NED: That, for instance, like the man tried to tell you nice and then you come like a tornado . . . and curse him out.

WORKER: Control yourself—is that the idea?

REFLECTION: Wants to see whether control is an accurate perception, possibly for further discussion as an issue.

NED: Yeah, you have a fast temper.

TED: I don't think retarded is that. I think retarded is a slow learner.

JACK: Slow learner.

TED: That's what I think retarded is. It's a slow learner.

WORKER: A slow learner.

REFLECTION: Repeats "slow learner" as a way of emphasizing what Ted was saying.

TED: That's right, a slow learner.

Second Meeting. Some of John's problems in getting along with others are brought out by Bob, the indigenous leader. John is able to find out how others perceive his behavior. In this way, he evaluates his actions and prepares himself for constructive changes. The boys reveal their attitudes toward authority, both on the job and with their parents. Some of them are able to express the way they have adjusted to employers and parents. The group worker helps John to clarify his feelings.

BOB: I figured that Ted should have been one of the boys that had a choice to stay down there [working at the hospital]. Because, just like you said about when you first work and you've got to get yelled at once in a while. Right? John's actually the only one that needs talking to about something like that. He'll jump up in your face, and say, Ah, darnit, first you tell me to do this and then you tell me to do that, and then he'll get to using obscene language and all that, so the man just walks away from him.

[Comment: Bob resents the fact that John was chosen for the hospital job rather than his closer friend, Ted.]

WORKER: I guess John has a hard time sometimes in getting along with other people.

REFLECTION: Identifies possible problem of John that may lead to problem-solving.

JOHN: I'll tell you, Mr. Rogers, you ain't done with one job down there, and then they shove you on another one. They don't even give you a chance to get one job done.

BOB: Excuse me, that's the only way that they can actually find out you are ready—are you fully trained to take orders. Because any job that you get on the outside you're going to be changed around.

JOHN: I mean they don't give you a chance to get it finished.

JACK: And just like this afternoon, as soon as I got done eating, I was sitting on the bench and Mike come over and he wanted me to get two rakes and a shovel. . . . I was to fix up by the hill. So I went over there and then after that there was only about five or ten minutes after that he told us to go over and help them guys, so I didn't say nothing. I just did it, and that was all.

JOHN: And then he told us three guys to go over and start loading up the truck and report back to Bill [an employee at the hospital]. We kept on loading it up.

WORKER: You think it is hard for you sometimes to take orders from other people?

EXPLORATION: Engages John in considering feelings about authority.

JOHN: Yeah, the way they push orders around there.

WORKER: They're a little too hard on you?

REFLECTION: Expresses empathy in putting into words what John is feeling.

(*Later in the meeting*)

STEVE: Like my mother, she'll tell me to do something and I'll do it. Then my father will tell me something to do. So I'll do a little for my mom and a little for my father. Then they both can't say I didn't do nothing for both of them. That's the way I feel.

WORKER: You're trying to please both of them.

REFLECTION: Identifies how Steve is attempting to solve his problem.

Third Meeting. The social worker enables some of the group members to elaborate on their attitudes toward authority, especially being told what to do by their employers and staff and the school. The discussion about authority leads to the continued expression of feelings toward their parents. There is the realization that they will need to do things for themselves. Although they express their desire intellectually, it is doubtful whether they are yet about to accept this responsibility. It is through the collective group support, perhaps representing the family that they would like to depend upon, that they are able to develop a greater feeling of self-sufficiency. As they begin to evaluate their behavior, the group worker helps them to think more about behavioral changes and how they view some of these changes.

WORKER: Some of the fellows are saying they like the idea of being told what to do when they're out, and here Steve and Bill don't like to be told what to do.

REFLECTION: Poses a dilemma of being told what to do for the group to consider.

STEVE: I don't mean like that. I mean, he'll tell you to do two or three things at one time, doing it at the same time that you're doing the other one.

WORKER: I see.

ACCEPTANCE: Demonstrates understanding and validation of Steve's concern.

STEVE: That's what I don't like. And then he'll get mad, say somebody broke a couple of windows, and he got the report down, and they said they want him to fix some windows and he got the job and has something else to do. He'll get mad and take it out on the students [the group members].

BILL: When I work in Mr. Walter's shop up at the school, he kept telling me to do this and do that, do a lot of things at one time, Mr. Rogers, and I had to do the one job at one time and then five minutes later here he is, put this glass in. Comes along, put this glass in. He pushes the work. He has too much work for you to do.

GENE: You got to do that. He keeps you busy.

BOB: You should be the same way that Steve is . . . his mother would tell him to do something and his father would tell him to do something. You should do like he said. You should do a little of what one persons tells you and a little of what the other person tells you.

STEVE: Yeah.

BOB: Then by the same thing you're doing the same work, you're doing two jobs at one time so the man figures that you are trying to learn to do two things at one time. So the man can give you credit.

WORKER: You were saying something last week about wanting to do one thing for your mother and another thing for your father. Does it seem like the same kind of thing is happening now with the people that you are working with? Is there anything similar about the way you get along with your parents and the way that you get along with some of the people on the job?

EXPLORATION: Attempts to develop self-understanding about relationships with persons in authority at work.

STEVE: The way you get along with them is to do a little something for each one.

NED: Your parents are—in some cases your parents are kinder and more important to you than any other person. Because don't forget, your parents take good care of you.

BOB: Excuse me, there was one mistake that you made, man. You said, yes, your mother and father is important to you. But there's one mistake that you made. Your mother is not important more than any person in the world because your mother is not going to be the one to get you out and get a job. You got to learn some day to get out and do it yourself so your mother can't be running behind you all the time saying I want you to do this and I want you to do that. Because one of these days you got to grow up some day and go out and take care of your own self.

(*Later in the meeting*)

NED: I was a little bad, see, and I was doing this, being bad and getting out of bounds, getting punches, getting wrote up and all that. Then I had to think, you know, I was thinking to myself. I'd say to myself I'd better be good and get gold cards and go out and get jobs.

["Punches" were punches on a card. The school had a behavior-modification program, whereby a boy with a minimum number of punches would be entitled to a gold card, which meant extra privileges.]

WORKER: Well, let me just ask you this. You were saying that for a while you were bad, you were doing things, and then you started getting better—

REFLECTION: States what he had heard in order to foster communication.

NED: —and better and better, each time.

WORKER: And I think this is probably true with some of the rest of you, too, isn't it?

SEEKING INFORMATION: Attempts to involve others in discussion.

NED: That's right.

WORKER: Sometimes you do things that are bad and then you do things that are good.

GIVING INFORMATION: Maintains focus of discussion from Ned's comments.

BOB: That's the way I was, Mr. Rogers.

WORKER: Why do you think you make this change from being bad to being good?

EXPLORATION: Seeks self-understanding but expectation for level of conceptualization is too high.

STEVE: I give Eugene credit when he says that when he got wrote up being at Ford Hall and lost some of his gold cards. The first thing you figure, he's going to stay out of trouble. He ain't like the other boys. Some other boys like me, once in a while, somebody writes me up, I'll get mad and don't care about it, I'll mess up the rest of the month. But he figures that if he stays out of trouble and doesn't get caught out of bounds and stays not out of bounds and does what the people tell him, he gets a gold card, he figures he did right then. He figures before you did anything wrong or right.

WORKER: So you respect him for being able to do the right thing and know what to do and how to—

REFLECTION: Validates what Steve is saying and recognizes Gene's positive behavior.

GENE: That's right.

WORKER: —straighten out, heh?

Fourth Meeting. John wants to quit the group. The boys consider his wanting to leave as a rejection of them. The worker brings out that at the very first meeting John was upset because of something that had happened. Mention was also made of other instances when John had become upset because something did not go his way. The worker wonders if John was always going to "drop out of things" or run away when something doesn't go his way. In this case—confronting John with his behavior but not wanting to threaten him—the worker focused on how others in the group might act in a similar situation. Actually, John was attempting to withdraw from the rejection he felt in the group. The worker brings to the surface some of John's feelings and hopes that the group will be able to offer him the necessary support. As he was able to feel acceptance by the others, he was more comfortable about staying in the group.

> WORKER: I can remember the first meeting when we left you, and you came out, and you didn't see anybody, and you went to the car, and you were kind of down in the dumps and didn't feel like talking. And then I think something happened even last week when you felt like we didn't care about you. Does this happen over and over again? And what's going to happen if something goes against you or you can't do exactly the same thing that you would like to do? If you are always going to do this, aren't you always going to have these troubles and problems? You'll run away from it?

CONFRONTATION: Challenges John to address his pattern of behavior and consider consequences.

> JOHN: I just want to drop out.
>
> BOB: The way we kind of figure it, if you're dropping out because there is a reason for one of us, it's no use in telling us in front of our faces because Mr. Rogers can correct it. What's wrong, if it's between us, between the group, Mr. Rogers can correct it.
>
> JOHN: It's not between none of you guys, so there.
>
> BOB: Spill it right here.
>
> JOHN: It's not between you guys.
>
> TED: It must be between us, otherwise you wouldn't be dropping out.
>
> BOB: Mr. Rogers, that don't make no sense . . . he figures he wanted to join the YMCA. Why was he so hasty to join? Now he's so anxious to get out, and he was so anxious to get in it. He was one of the boys who actually agreed with me that we should come from the hospital to the YMCA. He's one of the boys that agreed with me that night.
>
> TED: He's the one that was so anxious to go.
>
> WORKER: Maybe we can help John out a little bit here.

ACCEPTANCE: Seeks mutual aid for John's concerns.

> TED: Why don't he tell us what's really wrong with him? We know it must be us.
>
> WORKER: Yes, but sometimes you just feel like you don't like to talk about something. Maybe we can help him in this way. Here is something that happened, something happened, and I don't know exactly what it was. But it wasn't the way he wanted it. He was disappointed, and he decides that he wants to get away from it or drop out. How would you fellows handle this? Has this ever happened to you?

EXPLORATION: Focuses on group so John can learn from group member experiences.

> BOB: It happened to me tonight.
>
> WORKER: You've been disappointed about something. Something didn't go exactly the way you wanted it. What did you do about it?

SEEKING INFORMATION: Misses opportunity to bring out Bob's concerns—elicits ideas and feelings from group to enhance further exploration.

STEVE: But he shouldn't take it out on the club. He shouldn't quit the club because something happened.

GENE: He should take it out on himself.

STEVE: He should take it out on himself, go some place and try to forget it, figure it never happened.

WORKER: Maybe he's trying to forget it by just—

BOB: Dropping out.

WORKER: —dropping out of the club.

CLARIFICATION: Explains that John has flight response when he feels rejected.

STEVE: After a while when he quits, then he may want to come back, and it'll be too late.

GENE: It'll be too late.

STEVE: Then he'll wonder why. He might get all mixed up and try to say that we threw him out, or he'll forget about how he got out of the club. Say about four months go by, he might figure we threw him out, that we didn't want him.

WORKER: Maybe that's the way he feels, that we don't want him.

CLARIFICATION: Explains John's actions in relation to his feelings.

STEVE: He's all right in this club with me.

NED: He's all right with me, too.

BOB: He's okay with me.

JACK: He's okay with me.

BOB: Now you figure, Mr. Rogers.

WORKER: It looks like the fellows want you, John.

REFLECTION: States feelings of acceptance by group members toward John.

Fifth Meeting. The group is developing a greater feeling of independence. John is less secure. When the group wants to try a different place to eat, he resists. Although the group worker attempts to offer support to John, he recognizes the group's need to gain greater independence through new experiences. He relates some of John's present attitudes to his earlier feelings around the adjustment to the YMCA. In this way there is the opportunity for John to recognize that he was able to make a prior adjustment in coming to the YMCA and that he might be able to make other modifications when it became necessary. The group members are able to risk themselves in these new situations because they have the support of the group worker and each other.

WORKER: I'd like to talk more about what you were saying—the feeling that you have in coming to the Y, the feeling of freedom that you have and the kinds of things that you would like to do more on your own.

INVOLVEMENT: Invites more participation about planning for greater independence.

BOB: If we're going to eat out, don't you think we should talk a little bit more?

WORKER: Anything you want to . . .

BOB: Make it two or make it three.

GENE: What?

BOB: If we're going to eat out, how do you know how much the food is going to cost?

GENE: That's right.

BOB: It might cost different here. Yeah, I don't mind the five dollars for the YMCA, because when we come here we know what is expected of us, but we might go out to another restaurant, we may want spaghetti, it might not cost what it costs here.

GENE AND TED: That's right.

BOB: We'd wind up spending all our money.

WORKER: Is it agreed with everybody that we want to eat out?

INVOLVEMENT: Seeks consensus or indications of resistance as a basis for further planning.

TED: It's agreed with me.

WORKER: Outside next week.

SEEKING INFORMATION: Continues focus on participation in planning.

BOB: If it's agreed with you, raise your hand.

MOST OF THE BOYS: I.

BOB: Do you agree with all of us (*focusing on John*), do you agree?

[John does not want to eat out.]

JACK: Why not?

BOB: Even if he didn't agree, we'd still win because—how many, one-two-three-four-five.

JACK: How about you, Mr. Rogers?

BOB: What do you agree, Mr. Rogers? It's actually your idea. It's up to you.

WORKER: It's up to you fellows.

ACCEPTANCE: Demonstrate belief in their self-determination.

BOB: It's okay then.

WORKER: Would you like to eat out (*referring to John*), what do you think?

SEEKING INFORMATION: Wants to know John's thinking so he could discuss his feelings of resistance within group.

JOHN: I'm used to eating here.

JACK: Oh, man.

BOB: Wait a minute. One can't mess up the whole bunch. You forget it takes one apple to spoil everything so we can't actually let . . .

WORKER: Don't you think we might want to let John tell us . . .

ENCOURAGING IDEAS AND FEELINGS: Gives John an opportunity to respond so issue of resistance could be discussed in group.

BOB: Wait a minute. Let John explain why he don't want to eat out.

JOHN: I'll tell you why. Because I'm used to the prices here, and I like coming right from work to here.

WORKER: I guess you're used to the Y, you know people here and you know what to expect. If you go to a different place, everything is going to be new to you.

ACCEPTANCE: Expresses empathy for what John may be feeling—joins with resistance.

TED: It's going to be new to us, too.

BOB: It's going to be new to us, too, Mr. Rogers, but that's the only way you can make friends. How do you expect to make friends?

WORKER: You figure this is the way of learning.

REFRAMING: Puts desire for new experiences in positive context of learning.

BOB: That's the only way, Mr. Rogers. You said it yourself. You got to meet friends some day, don't you? So this is only one way . . . Oh, yes, probably there are a couple of more people here that we ain't met, but it will take time and time for us to meet them. That's like you said, as we get together and be a group next year, what we leave off from the summer we can catch up in the winter time. I figure that while there's good weather now, why can't we get out into the community and meet people because some day that we might be in a little trouble and then people will probably say, we knew these kids when they come to this diner, and they act like gentlemen and everything, so people are going to try to back us up and try to help us from getting into trouble. Now you answer your question (*referring to John*) why you don't want to go to other diners.

JOHN: I've got quite a few friends around here.

TED: Go ahead, keep going.

JOHN: Why should I keep on eating some place else when I can eat here?

WORKERS: You think that you'd be wondering if you went to a different place what they'd think of us just as you wondered the first time that you came here what they thought of us. Remember the first time you came here, what did you do? You went to the station wagon.

EXPLORATION: Fosters cognitive awareness and recognition of having overcome earlier discomforts.

JOHN: That's right. When I couldn't find nobody.

WORKER: And then you got used to it here, and you like it.

CLARIFICATION: Points out reality of John's ability in adjusting to Y.

TED: But, Mr. Rogers, you got to figure this way—it's all right to stick with the Y, but I mean you can't make a regular habit out of it (*Bob and Jack join in*), you know. I mean, I ain't saying the Y ain't good but I mean you can't like depend on the Y all the rest of your life.

Sixth Meeting. John is ready to quit the group again. The worker encourages John and the others to express their feelings about why John wants to quit. Some of the boys, especially Bob, uncover John's defenses. Bob identifies the problems that John is facing in the group as the same kinds of problems he has at work. After Bob makes the comment that John also acts the same way at work, the worker emphasizes the association with the hope that John might become more aware of this pattern of social behavior. The worker continues to focus on John, but it is questionable whether this was wise. It might have been better to focus on the problems that the other boys are facing, as Bob suggests, lifting the pressure off John and "giving" to the rest of the group.

> WORKER: Just before, John was out in the hall saying he wasn't coming in. He says he doesn't want to be here. He's quitting. He doesn't want to have anything to do with the group any more. Do you want to tell the fellows what your beefs are (*referring to John*)?

GIVING INFORMATION: Brings out problem for group to consider.

ENCOURAGING IDEAS AND FEELINGS: Seeks to engage John in problem solving.

> JOHN: Monday's it.
> GENE: He wants to quit.
> WORKER: Monday's it!

REFLECTION: Restates for emphasis, confirmation, and validation of John's wishes.

> JOHN: That's right. For good this time. Nobody ain't going to force me back in, either.
> WORKER: Would you like to tell the fellows what's bothering you—what's the problem?

ENCOURAGING EXPRESSION OF IDEAS AND FEELINGS: Continues engagement in identifying issues for problem solving.

(*Long pause*)

> WORKER: What do you think, would you rather not—

INVOLVEMENT: Encourages expression and yet respects right not to discuss it.

> BOB: —discuss it.
> WORKER: This is the place to talk about it. This is what we're here for. Isn't that right?

GIVING INFORMATION: Emphasizes appropriateness of group to discuss problems.

> TED: I'd like to . . .
> BOB: I'd like to hear what your troubles are. You're always one of the crew that always wants to get out. You're always the one that's got the complaints. Nobody else has got complaints but him. If it ain't one week, it's the following week. He always has some excuse to get out of the group and then after you explain it to him, what and everything, then he changes his mind. He is staying in the group.

JOHN: I mean it. This week—the following Monday I ain't going to be here.

BOB: The only thing the matter with him is that he always wants somebody to baby him up. He always wants somebody to sweet-talk him.

(*Some side comments*)

He can't learn to take care of himself. That's the same way he is at the hospital. He gets mad and says I don't want to do this. The next week, two weeks ago, he told my boss—our boss—I ain't coming to work no more. After Monday, I quit. That Monday coming he was the first one out of bed, ready to leave.

WORKER: What he's doing here at the meeting he's also doing at work.

CLARIFICATION: Points out pattern of behavior for increased self-awareness.

BOB: It's the same way, Mr. Rogers, honest.

WORKER: Same thing.

REFLECTION: Confirms what has been said for increased emphasis.

BOB: Same thing, he just wants somebody to pay attention to him. He wants you to take your mind off everybody else in the group and put it on him. He forgets that there are other boys in the group that got problems besides him. Gene's got problems, I've got problems, everybody else has got problems. By you paying your attention to him its holding the other boys back from getting a chance to tell what's the matter with them, that's what he wants.

GENE: He wants you to baby him.

(*Later in the meeting*)

JACK: And then, after that, he went back up on the ladder, he took his own can of paint, he spilled it. So I figure he probably did that just to get a full can, but me, I don't know, see. I don't read his mind or anybody else's mind.

WORKER: Do you think we've been jumping on John a little bit too much? After all, last week we had something to say and now we have something to say. It seems that a lot of the times he's being teased by the other boys, and we're sort of on his back—we're jumping on him a lot.

CONFRONTATION: Raises issue with group of John being put on the spot by group members, in hopes of encouraging more mutual aid and increased support for John.

BOB: Mr. Rogers, it can't be our fault, it can't be ours. He's bringing it on himself by starting it and then taking it out here.

Seventh Meeting. On the way to the YMCA, the boys who work at the hospital almost had an automobile accident. They are edgy, as Ted explains. Bob is especially negative. It may be that some of their hostility is related to the fact that there is only one more meeting at the agency. Earlier in the meeting the group worker helped them to express their feelings about separation, and at this time centers on the meaning of the social climate and how the behavior of some boys can affect others in the group. Ted, sensing the need to stabilize the destructive influence of Bob, supports the worker.

WORKER: We're in a pretty messy state tonight. Everybody is jumping on everybody else. What do you think is behind all this? . . . And then you think that because of what happened before the meeting that some of the guys are edgy.

CONFRONTATION: Points out conflict for problem resolution.

TED: Yeah, it could be that there. But I've got one thing to say. I'm not mad now at what happened tonight. I was mad before, but I'm not mad now.
BOB: Mad about what, what was you mad about? What?
TED: About what happened tonight.
BOB: Oh.
TED: I forgot all about it, but I'm like that there, you know. I think the trouble wrong with me, man, I don't stay mad long enough to hate anybody.
WORKER: Do you think that's bad?

EXPLORATION: Encourages self-awareness.

TED: No. It's good. Do you know why? Because I'm not quick tempered. It takes me a long time to get mad. I mean a real long time, it has to pile up on me. And then once I get started, boy!
BOB: I'll smack you in the mouth with a shovel (*in background to another boy*).
JACK: It's hot in here.
WORKER: Do you know what's happening tonight? Maybe I can explain a little bit and see what you think about it.

EXPLORATION: Combines exploratory statement with intent to clarify meaning.

TED: Yes, I wish you would.
WORKER: I think this happens so often, maybe one or two fellows feel irritable about something, maybe something went wrong at work or somewhere else, and they come in, and they start barking at somebody else.

CLARIFICATION: Brings out possible meaning of behavior for increased self-aware-ness.

TED: That's right.
WORKER: Start bawling somebody else out.
TED: You got the right impression.
WORKER: And then somebody feels what's he bothering me for, and I'm going to take it out on somebody else.
TED: That's right, you got the right impression.
WORKER: And before you know it, everybody is jumping on everybody else.
TED: And the only one we haven't been jumping on is you.
BOB: I'm anxious to do that.
TED: If anybody jumps on you (*referring to social worker*), then I'll have to jump on them.
JACK: Oh, yeah.

BOB: Oh, now listen to this.

WORKER: Som..times you might want to jump on me, too.

ENCOURAGING IDEAS AND FEELINGS: Gives permission to express anger toward worker.

BOB: Listen to the big bad wolf (*referring to Ted*).

TED: I don't have to jump on you. You know why? I don't see you that long.

WORKER: Fellows, what do you think about what I've said?

SEEKING INFORMATION: Encourages reactions to increase participation in problem solving.

TED: That's the truth.

BOB: I don't agree with you.

TED: I agree, I disagree with you (*referring to Bob*) but I agree with him (*referring to social worker*).

WORKER: What do some of the other boys think?

INVOLVEMENT: Continues to seek broader participation.

(*Speaking out to the group*)

BOB: What do you think?

TED: I'm getting hot underneath the collar.

BOB: I'm getting hot. Ain't you getting hot?

GENE: No, I'm getting cold.

BOB: Come on, Mr. Rogers, let's quit. It's getting hot.

TED: Well, actually, wait a minute, I want to get this off my chest.

JACK: Come on, Mr. Rogers, I had a bad cold for one week, and I still got it, and also it's too hot.

BOB: Mr. Rogers, I've been in heat all day, and I don't want any more of it.

GENE: Me, too, man.

WORKER: Well, Ted says he wants to get something off his chest. I think we should give him a chance.

MAKING SUGGESTION, DIRECTING: Monitors group discussion to involve group members.

BOB: Do you have something on your chest? Move it, let me see it. Where is it at?

JACK: Let me get my torch. I'll burn it off for him.

JOHN: Get the acetylene torch and burn it off.

TED: Wait a minute, on the suggestion that you were talking, you were right. On that there, about you know, getting mad. That's the same thing at the job—happens at the job, too. One guy gets mad at another guy so that guy goes and takes it out on somebody else cause he can't take it out on the other guy.

WORKER: Sometimes a guy wonders why am I getting so mad, why am I yelling at somebody else, not really knowing or understanding that maybe it's because somebody was yelling at him.

CLARIFICATION: Makes connection of how people displace their anger to increase self-awareness of group members.

TED: Right.

Eighth Meeting. The group worker deals with what the group experience has meant to the boys. They are able to evaluate their progress to some extent and recognize that the group has helped them. John now feels that he belongs. He makes a suggestion which is accepted by the group—buying YMCA T-shirts. Buying clothing from the agency symbolizes their desire to be a part of the community. Bob expresses what most of the boys are thinking—that they can "join things just like anybody else can." The worker emphasizes what Bob is saying as a way of strengthening their concept about themselves as being able to function with the more normal population. They are feeling more accepted in the community and consider their membership cards and T-shirts as tangible evidence to that effect.

WORKER: This would be a good time for us to look back on what happened this summer. You've been coming here now for two months. Well, what did it seem like to you, what kinds of things have you learned, how do you feel about being out on your own more?

EXPLORATION: Invites review of group to enhance integration of prior and present experience, leading to more positive self-concept.

NED: I really feel good about it. Even if we had a couple of arguments, I still feel good about it. As long as the guys, as long as the boys liked you and tried to help you in case you made a mistake—including you (*referring to worker*), but the fellows are all my friends, no matter what.

BOB: I miss poor Ted for not being here the last night.

JOHN: Yeah, the last night. Too bad all the guys didn't chip in and get shirts.

WORKER: You think it would have been good if everybody wore shirts?

REFLECTION: Encourages increased discussion of association with Y.

(*Several boys talking at the same time*)

GENE: I got a briefcase.

NED (*speaking to Gene*): Let me see that.

BOB: If I thought about that in the middle of the time of this meeting started, I would have brought up that question. Why couldn't everybody chip in and buy shirts?

NED (*examining Gene's briefcase*): That's a plastic one.

WORKER: That would have been a good idea.

ACCEPTANCE, SHOWING INTEREST: Supports feelings of closeness with Y.

JOHN: I thought about mine.

NED (*still examining the briefcase*): How do you open this thing?

BOB: Well, Mr. Rogers, anyway, since it cost him five dollars for that, three dollars for that, so Saturday when I come down here, I'm going to ask to give me a little bit more money. Enough money so I can get me a shirt and that.

WORKER: Are you going to get one of those, too?

SEEKING INFORMATION: Continues to demonstrate interest in group discussion and supports independence.

BOB: I'm going to get both of them. I'll take five dollars out of my own money. I've got some money down at the hospital for a briefcase and three dollars ain't nothing so I'll have everything to remember the Y. It proved to the people that at least I joined something that's got some sense to it. It proves to the people on the outside that Davidson just don't sit around and do nothing for us. It proves that we can join clubs just like anybody else can.

NED (*speaking to another member*): Do you know how much that costs? That costs seven dollars?

JACK: Four.

BOB: Four, four, and three for that.

WORKER: Bob is saying that by belonging to the YMCA . . .

BOB: We should have something . . . we should actually have something . . .

WORKER: . . . you are able to take part in things just like any other guy your age.

REFLECTION: Emphasizes Bob's statement to reinforce their concept of self-sufficiency.

BOB: Mr. Rogers, see what I mean. If somebody walks up to you and says you boys belong, did you ever belong, what kind of club are you at, you say you belong to the YMCA club. Somebody might come up and say do you have something to prove that you belong to the YMCA. If you don't have nothing to prove, people ain't going to believe it. Somebody walks up to you and says, You ever been in any type of club? You say sure, I've been in the YMCA club. So you got something to prove it, to show it to him.

JOHN: All you got to do is show him that or show him the shirt . . .

BOB: . . . or show him the shirt or show him the card.

ANALYSIS OF GROUP AND WORKER ACTIVITY

Within these short episodes of the eight meetings, the worker used ten of the eleven techniques that were described earlier. The only one not identified was partializing and prioritizing an issue or problem.

Besides demonstrating some elements of stages of group development, the group illustrates the issues of inclusion, intimacy, and conflict resolution. The tension of group members dealing with their own personal needs and yet making an accommodation to the group is illustrated in the socialization of John and his struggle for acceptance. The most widely used techniques of exploration, reflection, and clarification point up the group worker's intent to help the group members search for meaning in their personal and group encounter.

Several of the practice principles for vulnerable populations are a basis for intervention. In the first meeting, the worker makes use of "discussing differences" when he asks group members whether agency staff might have thought they were mentally retarded. Since this is a first meeting, it is expected that group members will have a range of emotions and perceptions of what is happening to them. The worker uses this occasion to explore these feelings, especially how they might feel different in the strange setting. The use of activity is clearly a major focus in this group, as members make use of the Y facilities and meet people from the agency. The worker is active in guiding group members but takes every opportunity to involve them in decision making in order to bolster self-esteem, make use of strengths, and increase feelings of independence.

Stages of Group Development

The eight meetings depict elements of the stages of group development. The use of techniques is related to the needs of the individuals and group. For instance, clarifying and confronting techniques are not used until the fourth meeting, presumably after the group has advanced to the point where they could accept these kinds of intervention. The four involvement techniques are in the last half of the group sessions when the group was struggling to resolve conflict and facing separation. It was especially important during this time to maximize participation since there is the tendency for members to withdraw from the tension of the conflict.

The themes of the group meetings are mentioned below according to the stages of group development and some characteristics of the stages as identified in Chapter 4.

STAGE	MEETING NUMBER	THEME
Formation		
Seeking acceptance	1	Avoidance (John staying in car
Appearing dependent		when he couldn't find anyone)
Feeling different	1	Need for trust (reactions to life
Maintaining distance		guard)
Seeking structure		
Power and Control		
Expressing differences	2	Continued interpersonal conflict
Reaching out to others		(members in relation to John)
Beginning indigenous	2	Reactions to authority (jobs,
leadership		parents)

	3	Continued attitudes toward authority (staff at school, employers)
	3	Desire for independence (more on intellectual level)
	3	Beginning evaluation of behavior (at school, not yet in group)

Intimacy

Willingness to become more involved	4	Recurrence and intensification of conflict (in regard to John)
Communication easier	4	Increased support (group in relation to John)
Demonstration of support and liking one another	5	Increased feelings of independence (wanting to eat out)
	5	Willingness to risk new situations

Maturation

Constructive conflict	6	Increased support and willingness to challenge behavior and defenses (toward John)
More risk taking		
Evidence of cohesion		

Separation

Anger	7	Hostility in regard to separation
Anticipation	7	Some awareness of interpersonal behavior
Recapitulation		
	8	Increased cohesion (wanting to continue group)
	8	Plans for continued involvement at YMCA (buying Y materials, discussion of Y card)

Worker Collaboration with Staff

During all of these meetings with the group, the worker was maintaining contact with staff at the school and Y. This is an example of using the practice principle of involving significant others. It was necessary to keep school staff informed of the progress of the young men in the group so there could continue to be a team effort in their behalf. He also met several times with the Y director to discuss the activities in the group and handle any problems that might occur. The environment of the residential school and community agency supported the risks for new experiences by the group members. Persons in these two systems were part of the important helping network that contributed to their increased independence. Unless staff who had contact with these young men felt invested in this project, they could demonstrate resistance to its continuance. When persons are not involved, there is always the danger of misunderstandings that can occur from poor communication.

SUMMARY

The use of helping techniques in social work with groups is demonstrated with a group of mildly retarded young men. Since there were excerpts of eight continuous meetings, the chapter illustrates worker activity during stages of group development. Only one of the eleven techniques was not shown— "partializing and prioritizing an issue or problem."

This particular group is considered vulnerable to reduced social and emotional functioning because of their lack of cognitive, emotional, and environmental resources. Several practice principles for vulnerable populations, as discussed in Chapter 5, are illustrated in the group. The profile of the worker is someone who is relatively active, hopeful, and yet not unrealistic about what group members can accomplish, and prepared to mobilize resources in a community (the YMCA) in order to help group members fulfill their purposes of more independent living. Furthermore, he makes use of group member strengths, encourages them to discuss their differences, and involves them in decision making to increase indigenous leadership and possibilities of mutual aid. There is ongoing contact with important people in their lives, both at the Y and at the residential school, in order to foster a healthy environment for growth and change.

The next section, "Phases of Work," starts with the chapter "Pregroup Forming." It includes all the aspects of preparing for the group, which were mentioned briefly in Chapter 1.

REFERENCES

Balgopal, P. R., & Vassil, T. V. (1983). *Groups in social work: An ecological perspective*. New York: Macmillan.
Bertcher, H. J. (1979). *Group participation: techniques for leaders and members*. Beverly Hills, CA: Sage.
Garvin, C. (1987). *Contemporary group work*. Englewood Cliffs, NJ: Prentice-Hall.
Glassman, V., & Kates, L. (1986). Techniques of social group work. *Social Work with Groups, 9*(1), 9–38.

Henry, S. (1981). *Group skills in social work.* Itasca, IL: F. E. Peacock.

Middleman, R. R., & Goldberg, G. (1974). *Social service delivery: A structural approach to social work practice.* New York: Columbia University Press.

Northen, H. (1988). *Social Work with Groups* (2nd ed.). New York: Columbia University Press.

Shulman, L. (1981). *Identifying, measuring, and teaching helping skills.* New York and Ottawa, Canada: Council on Social Work Education and Canadian Association of Schools of Social Work.

Toseland, R. W., & Rivas, R. F. (1984). *An introduction to group work practice.* New York: Macmillan.

TEACHING AND LEARNING IDEAS

1. Write a narrative of what the worker does during the interaction with the group. After each worker action, attempt to identify the technique that was used by putting the techniques or its number in brackets after the description of what was done. Analyze the record according to the number of different techniques used. Note which ones were used most often and least often. Explain the reason for this occurrence.

2. Listen to an audio tape, see a video tape, or observe a role play of two different kinds of groups. Identify the worker techniques in each group and compare the similarities and differences. Explain the reasons for your findings.

PART III
Phases of Work

CHAPTER 7

Pregroup Planning

There are many factors to consider when forming groups, including preparation of potential group members, staff, and oneself as group worker. The agency should decide whether groups are the most ideal choice for providing a service or contributing to a change effort. Groups should be used when it is the most appropriate way to meet a particular need, problem, or interest that is shared by clients or others served by the agency. It is more likely that groups will be successful if there is attention to the forming phase.

Kurland, Getzel, and Salmon offer a model to conceptualize the planning process before the group starts. It contains seven components to consider:

- *Agency Context:* conditions existing in the agency or host setting that may have an impact on worker action and on the group that is being formed.
- *Need:* individual and social wants, drives, problems, issues, and/or areas of concern that can be expected to exist universally for people in the target population as they function socially and, more specifically, that exist among persons in the particular target population the worker has in mind as potential members of the group s/he is planning.
- *Purpose:* the ends toward which the group is formed, encompassing both the ends and objectives that the group will pursue collectively (i.e., the group purpose) and the hopes, expectations, and objectives that each group member holds for what s/he will gain from participating in the group (i.e., individual goals).
- *Composition:* the number and characteristics of both members and workers who will participate in the group.

- *Structure:* the concrete arrangements the worker makes to facilitate the actual conduct of the group.
- *Content:* the means that will be used to achieve the purpose for which the group is formed, encompassing what is done in the group, how it is done and why it is done.
- *Pregroup Contact:* the securing of appropriate members for the group that is being planned and the preparation of them for their participation in the group. (1986, 61–62)

When group composition is not already specified, the authors identify need as the place to start in group formation. For instance, persons who are homeless have a common need to find housing. Persons living in shelters might be brought together as a group to offer each other support, share information, or learn about ways to deal with landlords. Need is considered from the various views of agency staff, potential clients, and community persons, but it is a need that is within the agency context for service delivery. From an assessment of need, the purpose of the group is formulated—first by agency and worker and then jointly with group members. The other four components—composition, structure, content, and pregroup contact—become ways of implementing the process of group formation and are considered together. When group composition is predetermined, such as parents who register for a family-life education group, need is determined from those in the group. The other parts, as described above, follow as it was when the group composition was not predetermined (Kurland, Getzel, and Salmon 1986, 62–64).

REASONS TO FORM GROUPS

Before planning for a specific group, agencies should think through their rationale for using groups generally. Staff attitudes about the group's values and limitations should be considered. If staff do not have adequate group-work training and feel ill at ease at the prospect of leading a group, they may find reasons not to have them at all. When this happens, it may be desirable to bring in a group consultant to offer the necessary knowledge and skills for working with groups. The consultant can also work with staff to develop a more receptive attitude toward groups (Birnbaum, Catalina, Nisinzweig, and Abrams, 1989). Unless staff believe in groups and can learn to trust their possibilities for mutual aid, the group will start out at a disadvantage.

It is not enough for the agency simply to believe that groups can provide a beneficial service. Its organizational policies and practices should also support the formation of groups. Intake procedures and decisions about a preferred client service need to include groups as a possibility. Adequate time should be considered to prepare for the group, for meeting times, and recording. Credit should be given for the additional workload of a group (Gitterman and Shulman, 1986, 54–55). Resources must be available, so that the agency can offer groups the physical facilities and program materials they need.

Sometimes the conditions within the community put excessive strain on agencies to provide services that they are not prepared to handle. For instance, in the wake of deinstitutionalization of the mentally ill from psychiatric hospitals, community mental health centers had to limit groups for outreach and prevention in order to serve the flood of discharged patients. At a women's resource center, which began as a small-scale self-help organization for women in transitional roles, the burgeoning women's movement plus support of the discharged mentally ill created a waiting list for group services of 200 women. The agency was faced with such decisions as who should facilitate the groups, who should get preference for groups (most-in-need or first-come first-served) and what group is most appropriate for those registering for groups. The organizational structure that had served them well, such as the use of peer leaders, was now inadequate to meet the demands of an increased population of women in need of socioeducation groups. It became clear that the organizational structure had to be reassessed and changed in order to keep pace with the requests for group services.

WHO SHOULD BE IN GROUPS

Agencies are sometimes uncertain about who should participate in groups and who shouldn't. This is especially true when there is a long tradition of seeing clients individually. Those who share a common experience or life event often benefit most from groups (Tropp, 1976, 198–201; Napier and Gershenfeld, 1985, 79–82). Their mutuality enables them to be more empathic since they can identify with one another's situation and appreciate its meaning. The sharing of experiences also increases the possibilities of bonding. Yalom identifies motivation as being the most important factor for inclusion in a group (1975, 235). In describing a client group, Schwartz and Zalba (1971) speak of "a collection of people who need each other in order to work on certain common tasks, in an agency that is hospitable to those tasks" (p. 7).

The decision about who should be in a group will also depend on the type of group. Persons who cannot tolerate the intimacy and self-disclosure that is part of a treatment group may nevertheless do well in a socioeducation group, where social skills training is the focus (Gazda, 1986, 205). The educational nature of the group would presumably have less demands for introspection and behavioral changes. Sometimes activity groups are encouraged when clients are fearful of close relationships or are unwilling to share in the verbal interaction that is necessary in the traditional treatment group. The activity can provide a structure that is relatively safe, often with prescribed roles, so that interaction is predictable and less overwhelming. As personal problems come up in these groups, it is easier to keep the discussion on a cognitive level, perhaps picking up on common themes rather than dealing more exclusively with the disclosure of feelings.

The socioeducation group, with its primary features of education, socialization, and support, can be an ego-building experience, and that may be sufficient for some individuals. For others, it can be a preparation for the greater demands of self-revelation and expected change that are part of the treatment group.

Among prospective clients, there are generally accepted indications and contraindications for group treatment. Toseland and Siporin (1986, 172), citing Yalom (1975), state that persons "who are socially and psychologically isolated, shy, and inhibited are good candidates for group psychotherapy." Persons who are having problems with interpersonal relationships can benefit from the groups' combined nurturance and challenge to change maladaptive behavior. The emotional safeguards by the group worker and others in the group can increase a willingness to risk socialization and intimacy. Contraindications for group treatment are for those individuals who are so absorbed in a personal crisis or need that they cannot give to others. Also, persons who exhibit extreme personality traits—domineering, hostile, aggressive, or self-centered—may cause others to withdraw from the group and would therefore not be appropriate (Toseland and Siporin, 1986, 174).

Various approaches are used to screen applicants for groups and explore with them the most desirable form of helping. The intake procedure, which usually includes a formal interview to discuss the reasons for social service, can be a means of determining whether a group should be considered. Besides the interview, psychological testing and diagnostic groups may be used during planning (Balgopal and Vassil, 1983, 129). The diagnostic group will usually meet for a few sessions to assess individual functioning and for treatment planning.

Depending upon the function of the agency, various kinds of groups might be formed. For instance, a neighborhood house or community center may offer a wide range of educational, counseling, and community activities for persons of all ages. An agency with a narrower range of functions would be more limited in the kinds of groups it would sponsor. Once the agency is clear about what it wants to do, it needs to define the purpose of the group from an agency point of view. This description should be clear, concise, and feasible within a time period that can be identified. For instance, an elementary school recognized that many of the children were experiencing stress as a result of parents being separated or divorced. The turmoil that they faced was interfering with their learning. The school decided to offer a short-term educational group for the students to help them articulate their needs, give and receive support from others, and learn ways of becoming assertive to take more control in their lives. The stated purpose assertion. It is easier to evaluate group progress when there are specific and identifiable objectives. However, the purposes may be modified once the group members meet to present their expectations. With funding sources demanding greater accountability of agencies, the need for measurable criteria in work with clients is increasingly important.

GROUP COMPOSITION

Groups are composed with a combination of similarity and differences. The similarity part—or what is considered homogeneous features—is the commonality of problem, interest, need, or task. It may also include what Bertcher and Maple (1985, 181) call descriptive attributes: common socioeconomic background, age, sex, type of occupation, neighborhood, and any other factor that would create closeness because members are familiar with what the other people are like. The differences, or heterogeneity, would be the way that people respond to problems or accomplishing tasks. These are considered behavioral attributes— the range of feelings, attitudes, or amounts of knowledge that people have in solving problems (Bertcher and Maple, 1985, 181).

There should be variation in these personal characteristics, but the differences should not be so great that group members will feel isolated or out of step with the other persons. The commonality in groups offers security to members, since they know what to expect, whether because of like background or like experience. There is also an expectation that persons who have shared similar life events will be able to understand one another and contribute to mutual aid in the group. Whereas homogeneity increases possibilities for closeness and cohesiveness, heterogeneity introduces the differences that foster a wider assortment of choices and creativity in problem solving. Both similarity and differences are important, and there needs to be a balance of the two. If the group is overly homogeneous, persons will be content and socialize well together. However, there will be little challenge to view a problem from a new perspective, and thus a minimum of growth. On the other hand, a group that is overly heterogeneous may have a difficult time developing cohesiveness, and the dropout danger is high. In planning for a group, this combination should be kept in mind. Feldman and Caplinger (1977) cite research to indicate that adolescents who exhibit antisocial behavior show more favorable outcome in groups with prosocial youth than when they were in groups by themselves (pp. 5–33). The element of heterogeneity present in the mixed group contributed toward group norms that supported prosocial behavior. There were also more choices available in the wider range of behavioral alternatives in the mixed group of prosocial and antisocial youth.

Under ideal circumstances, staff will be able to select persons for a group who range along a continuum of behaviors and coping skills, while at the same time having sufficient sameness to enable them to coalesce. In many agencies there are not enough persons who either want to be in a group or have the desirable differences for creative problem solving. An absence of sufficient heterogeneity will increase the need for the worker to introduce differences, in order to challenge group members to think more broadly.

What about persons who are not selected for groups, either because they are not appropriate candidates or the group is at the maximum limit in size? Since some persons who are seeking an agency group may be vulnerable to rejection, wouldn't their nonacceptance for a group confirm these inadequate feelings? This raises the question of how well the agency plans for a range of ways to meet the variety of needs, interests, and problems of its clientele. If persons are not suitable for a group, individual services might be offered. It has already been mentioned that some persons who may not be successful in a treatment group may do well in a socioeducation group. When the presenting problem is not within the function of the agency, then a referral to a more appropriate agency is necessary.

DEALING WITH RESISTANCES

The formation of a client group at an agency is sometimes met with resistance by the staff. Professionals who are seeing clients individually and are asked to refer them to a group may consider it a threat: They are expected to "give up" or at least "share" a client. Sensitive issues about professional competence may emerge. This is especially likely to take place if the staff person has little understanding of the group's purpose and the gains that are envisioned for the participants.

To reduce or preclude resistance, staff should be prepared for the group and its potential advantages for the client. They should be encouraged to share their thinking about the group, its values and limitations for the client; thus they will have made some investment in its shape and purpose. The purpose of the group should be made clear so that staff will feel freer about making referrals. Shulman, (1984, 191–192) found that a referral workshop was useful in helping colleagues work through resistance issues. The workshop was organized for staff of different agencies to discuss problems and strategies for dealing with referrals. Some staff are basically afraid of groups and allow these feelings to interfere with making or accepting referrals. If the professional has misgivings about the beneficial effects of a group, he or she may attempt to protect the client from participation. It may take repeated interpretations of the meaning and purpose of the group to induce staff to cooperate in encouraging clients to request group work. Coven reports on attempts to start a group among severely disturbed outpatients in a mental hospital. Staff were unwilling to cooperate, so she started the group with just two patients. Once the group was established, she used it to demonstrate its positive results. When the group became a tangible reality, rather than an abstraction, it was easier to get referrals (Coven, 1981, 99–116). The kind of disturbed patients in the Coven article are usually not put in groups, because they are very needy and preoccupied with self. But by starting out with a very small number, it is possible to cater to their individual needs as a preparation for focusing on group-related issues at a later time.

REFERRALS AND RECRUITMENT

Screening and selecting members of the group are based upon the combination of homogeneous and heterogeneous factors mentioned earlier. During pregroup contact the worker explains to prospective members the reasons for the group, and encourages a sharing of their interests. They are given an opportunity to express any apprehension about joining, and further clarification about the agency's expectations may take place.

The means of getting referrals and recruiting for a group will depend on the type of group. For a treatment group, there should be some face-to-face contact with prospective clients as part of assessment, so that their eligibility can be determined. For socioeducation and social-action groups, the interview is desirable but not essential. However, it is necessary to have at least telephone contact with the applicant, so that persons who are ambivalent about participation will at least be able to raise questions, perhaps share their concerns, and learn whether the group is appropriate for their needs. The worker can also use this occasion to screen applicants who are obviously not suitable for the group. In this case, he or she may be referred to another part of the agency's program or to another resource in the community.

In the discussion above of staff resistance to forming groups and making referrals, it was pointed out that when colleagues understand the reasons for the group and can have some input into the planning process, they are more likely to make referrals. This is also true for professionals in the community who may be in a position to refer clients to the agency. The prospective group worker should visit the community agency most likely to work with potential clients and talk personally with staff to discuss possibilities for the group. At the very least, a phone call is in order.

When trying to reach a particular population, such as children in a school, tenants from a housing complex, or patients in a hospital, it is advisable to visit the site where potential group members are located. This kind of personal contact will add greatly to the readiness of prospective members to participate in a group. It indicates a willingness in the worker to reach out to meet their needs and demonstrate support. In addition, persons who are considering the group will gain needed information to help them decide whether or not to participate.

In the recruitment effort, the agency can prepare a brochure or poster with a description of the type of group to be formed, and use the media, such as newspapers and radio, to publicize it. Advertising in this way often reaches a large number of people. With a sizable pool of potential candidates to choose from, the agency is more likely to have a group of adequate size and varied composition.

CONDITIONS FOR THE GROUP MEETINGS

In preparing the groundwork for the group, many factors must be considered. Frequency and length of meetings, as well as size, will depend on the group purpose and characteristics of group members. For treatment groups, it is usually expected that they will meet at least once a week. This is also true for support, socialization, and educational groups in general, but there is more variability with these groups. For instance, certain educational or skill-development groups that use a workshop format, might meet only for one or two sessions but of half-day or all-day length. Task groups will meet until their goals have been accomplished. Length of meetings will also vary, from one to two hours. However, with persons whose attention span is short, such as hyperactive children, the meeting time would be even less.

The trend is for groups to be more time-limited, with a specified number of meetings designated beforehand (usually six to twelve). Presumably, this kind of an arrangement creates more focus and direction for goal accomplishment. However, it can also put pressure on the group to deal with issues prematurely, and some persons who are not as assertive may be shortchanged in favor of those who are more articulate. Alissi and Casper (1985) point out that there is little hard data to compare the success rates of short-term groups with those of longer, ongoing ones. However, many of the advantages of short-term groups are cited, such as being cost-effective, establishing clear boundaries, specifying goals, and reducing dependency on groups (pp. 3–16). It is more likely that time-limited groups are closed after the initial session, whereas long-term groups are open-ended. The closed group has the advantage of stability in being able to progress through stages of group development without the disruptive influence of new members. The open-ended group, while needing to create new beginnings for persons entering late, which may slow down its development, sometimes can profit from the fresh perspective of a new member.

The place of the meeting, time, space, arrangements of the room, size, and needed supplies for activities are other aspects of planning. In most cases the group will meet at the agency, but there may be good reasons to consider another facility that is more accessible to the prospective group members. The place and time of the group will be good for some persons and inconvenient for others. It is recognized that certain meeting times will exclude certain persons. The space and attractiveness of the room will add to the comfort of group members and introduce a dimension of caring. The way the room is arranged and where the group worker or co-worker sits will also convey a message of how much the leader wants to share responsibility and power with the group. A circle arrangement usually implies an egalitarian structure, whereas if the worker sits facing the entire group, it will mean that he or she wants to maintain control. A circular pattern means that there will be more verbal and nonverbal communication among the members, leading to group cohesion. Eye contact is maintained in this arrangement.

The size of the group will also vary. An ideal size for a problem-solving task group is about five (Hare, 1976, 214), whereas a treatment group should have about six to eight persons, with an outer limit of ten (Yalom, 1975, 284). When starting a treatment group, it is suggested that the group begin with one to three more persons than the ideal size, since it is expected that there will be some dropout during the early meetings. With socioeducation groups, the size can often be larger. The educational nature of the group reduces the intensity of relationships and allows group members to withdraw more comfortably and acceptably if they have concerns about closeness. In a larger group "the most active participants become more active, while the least active become less active and may even become silent" (Hartford, 1971, 165). When this happens, the worker usually takes on more of a discussion-leader role to encourage balanced participation.

When the group increases in size, it becomes difficult to attend to the socioemotional components of group life. There could be an exaggerated conflict period, which may be the group members' way of vying for attention or expressing hostility indirectly to the group worker, because their needs are not being met. If the larger group is more structured, it often helps to reduce the hostility, since there are clear guidelines about roles and expectations. Again, this might be more appropriate for a socioeducation group but not for a treatment group.

The preplanning phase should allow time to think about rules and beliefs for the group. The worker should consider what is acceptable and unacceptable behavior and what aspects of behavior are negotiable. For instance, in a treatment group, confidentiality is one of the hard-and-fast rules. Smoking, however, if the agency does not have a firm smoking policy, can be decided on beforehand or negotiated within the group. As the worker expects to share power and responsibility with the group, some areas of the group's functioning should be open for joint decision making.

The group worker identifies topics of activities that may be especially appropriate for the type of group, its purposes, level of individual or group development, and member characteristics. These ideas provide a source of input into the direction the group will take. In preparing for what the group might need and want in being together, the worker anticipates what they—or persons facing similar experiences—might feel or think about their situation: for example, the meaning of loss for older persons or discrimination for blacks. This is what Schwartz refers to as "tuning in"—the preparation that allows the group worker to be sensitive to the subtle meanings of behavior (1976, 186–188). Shulman (1984) has refined the tuning-in concept to include the "client's sense of urgency," the "worker's own feelings," and the "meaning of the client's struggle" (pp. 53–56).

PREPARING GROUP MEMBERS

In screening potential group members and preparing those selected, it is helpful to orient them to the group. They may feel ambivalent about participating or even negative, so, a premeeting interview is advisable to explore feelings and expectations. Pregroup interviews enable clients to be more clear and realistic about what to expect from the group, as well as more understanding of group purposes (Meadow, 1988). In a study of client notions about group therapy, Slocum (1987, 39) found that many felt group therapy was unpredictable, less effective than individual therapy, and sometimes detrimental to participants. Even while they anticipated pleasure about joining with others in a group— meeting the inclusion needs—they feared losing autonomy and personal control under the dominance of the group worker and group. There may also be a fear of rejection and uneasiness about sharing personal material.

Manor (1986, 38) suggests that in the preliminary interview, the social worker can initially focus on the client's anxieties. By discussing these uncertainties and eliciting personal expectations, he or she can relate the prospective member's goals to how they might be achieved in the group. The preliminary interview can also begin to establish some trust and liking between worker and prospective group member. It will be easier to face the uncertainty or acceptance in the group if the person has established a positive relationship with the worker.

Outreach

Breton (1985) describes the hard-to-reach as "the socially isolated and alienated: newly arrived immigrants, the increasingly ghettoized poor, teenage single parents, and the dependent elderly, among others" (p. 7). Especially for this population, it is necessary to recognize the possible reasons why they are not participating in agency services. It is not a question of whether persons are motivated. They simply are not motivated to become involved in the way that the social worker would like. Breton (1985) suggests practice principles: meeting people where they are—in terms of their needs and even on their turf; helping with concrete services, as necessary; creating challenging experiences to build or restore feelings of competence; and helping people to use natural support networks (pp. 7–21). Maslow's (1970) hierarchy of needs can explain the rationale for helping with specific environmental or survival needs before attempting to change behavior. Persons who are considered unmotivated or hard-to-reach may have experienced excessive failure or disappointments in relationships with others or have cultural values that make them appear less accessible. In this situation, the building of trust is essential, especially in relation to helping persons achieve their goals. There must be some common ground between client goals and agency goals; otherwise the client may not be suitable for the services the agency has to offer. When this happens, the client should be referred to another agency that may be more appropriate for his or her needs.

The Involuntary Client

With the involuntary client who is required to attend a group, perhaps because of alcoholism, drug abuse, or another court-related offense, resistance may seem to be an insurmountable obstacle. What can be done to prepare this kind of person for a group? For one thing, both worker and client must have realistic expectations about what can be achieved. An involuntary client can be helped only to the extent that he or she is willing to be helped.

If the principle of "starting where the client is" has validity, the worker should first attempt to find out the meaning of the client's behavior from his or her own frame of reference. This is the client's reality. However, there is another reality—the structure imposed by another authority. Together with recognizing the expressed feelings and attitudes of the client, the social worker can explore with the client the choices that are available: not participating and facing other consequences; being present but not being involved; participating in a way that the client feels is helpful.

One of the reasons for resistance is the client's reaction to loss of control imposed by an outside authority. But in addition to the nonnegotiable parts of the contract, there are negotiable ones. With an involuntary client, the worker should emphasize these. When it is possible to restore some control by assisting the client to make a decision, it will engage him or her more fully in an effort to learn or change patterns of behavior. The social worker treats the person with respect and dignity, even though his or her behavior is unacceptable to societal values.

Pregroup Training

Piper and Perrault (1989) examined twenty studies on pretherapy preparation over a twenty-year period, and found results that were only suggestive of its value. The one conclusive finding was that attendance by group members improved. Nevertheless, despite mixed evidence about its usefulness, the authors were optimistic about the benefits of pretherapy preparation.

Workers often mistakenly assume that group members will understand the unwritten rules of the game once they are in the group. Since strong inclusion needs are part of any new group experience, inexperienced group members can become anxious about being accepted if they do not adhere to group norms. Specific skill training can demonstrate to group members proper helping behaviors toward others, which should improve the effectiveness of the group and reduce premature termination.

Kivlighan, Corazzini, and McGovern (1985, 500–503) report on a number of studies that list areas of pregroup training for group members. These include role clarification, skills in expressing feelings, interpersonal feedback, self-disclosure, here-and-now interactions, anxiety management, and information about group processes, especially developmental stages.

LEADERSHIP PREPARATION

Messages, conveyed through the verbal and nonverbal communication within the group, influence interactions between group members and the development of behavioral norms. Since the worker is in such a prominent position, his or her attitudes and feelings will have a powerful effect in shaping the group. The group worker can represent all forms of authority figures in the lives of the group members. Early in the group, members may test out the worker as a way of finding out what he or she is really like. They may actually try certain behaviors from past experiences to see whether the worker will abuse the position of authority.

In preparing for the group, the worker should anticipate what some of these feelings and actions might be. Having some knowledge of the background of the participants, group purpose, composition, and the beginning stage of group development, he or she can foresee what members may be thinking and feeling. This type of preparatory empathy, as described by Gitterman and Shulman, (1986, 26), may help to sensitize the group worker to the cues of member behavior and enable him or her to be more responsive when these behaviors occur. It will also help obviate defensiveness in the worker when group members act in a hostile manner because of prior negative experiences with authority figures. But—a cautionary note: The worker should respond to *actual* behavior. If preparation causes the worker to "program" his or her behavior so that he or she responds to anticipated behavior rather than what the group actually does, the ultimate result could be inappropriate actions. What the worker should provide is spontaneous and genuine responses that can be most helpful.

Workers may have fears and anxieties about their upcoming role in the group. There could be questions about being liked or accepted, either by group members or a co-worker (Manor, 1986, 27). Certain types of group members, such as aggressive teenagers, may raise questions about whether the group worker is competent enough to work with them. Emotions could be stirred up in the worker, such as dependency feelings in working with a sickly group of elderly clients. Personal explorations and recognition of these thoughts and feelings could have the effect of normalizing them, so that the worker is not overwhelmed by their presence during the group sessions. It is also worthwhile to discuss anticipated concerns with a supervisor or colleague. In this way it becomes possible to understand the anxiety and prepare oneself to manage it successfully. Just as stage fright for an actor can increase spontaneity, so the worker can make the fears work for him or her. In some cases it may be useful to share these feelings with the group, but only when the sharing can benefit the group through modeling self-disclosure. Group members must not be used as a therapeutic experience for the worker.

With a co-worker, it is essential to discuss how both persons will work together, sharing beliefs about human behavior, styles of leadership, strengths, and limitations in the worker role. All that has been said about anticipating group member behavior and dealing with issues of the work are now the subject of mutual exploration and exchange. The openness of the relationship between the co-workers is a model and source of strength for group members in experiencing how two persons work together.

PREGROUP PLANNING ILLUSTRATION

The framework on pregroup planning that was mentioned by Kurland, Getzel, and Salmon (1986) in the beginning of the chapter is being used to illustrate planning for a group at an agency.

Children of Alcoholics Group

A privately funded family service agency has a contract with the state child protective agency to provide a variety of services for adolescents and families who are at risk of further family breakdown. Many of the families have problems of alcoholism, and the state agency has referred many teenagers to be in a group for children of alcoholics.

Need. Adolescents usually respond favorably to groups. It is an age when youth naturally seek out peers to strengthen their own identity and to separate from parents. From what we know, children of alcoholics generally do not discuss their problems outside the home. They spend a great deal of energy in covering up their secret. They need to share their common concerns and feel connected to their peers. There may also be a lack of sufficient knowledge about the disease of alcoholism. Their self-esteem has probably been shaken, since children in an alcoholic family may feel guilty for thinking that they have contributed to problems within the family. There is also a need for a stable structure in which expectations are clear and consistent, since life in an alcoholic family can be chaotic. For many of these reasons, a group seems desirable, since it would help them deal directly with these needs.

Purpose. Assuming that what is discussed is kept confidential, the group offers an opportunity to release feelings in an accepting atmosphere. The group members can feel emotional support and empathic responses, since others are experiencing a similar situation. There would be some presentation of information about alcoholism, so that the youth would gain more understanding of the disease and feel less responsible for contributing to the family problem. They would also learn about how they can make choices that will allow them to take more control of their lives. Through the appropriate expression of feelings, added knowledge, group support, and good decision making, it is expected that the adolescents will gain more self-esteem, experience less guilt, and learn to separate themselves from the self-destructiveness within the family.

Composition. In this case fourteen adolescents were referred, ranging in age from eleven to eighteen. However, it is desirable to limit the size of such a group to about eight members, so that, if one or two drop out during the early meetings, there would still be six or seven. The age range should not exceed three years, preferably at the younger end of the scale—eleven to thirteen—to be consistent with the need for homogeneity in groups. The closeness in age enables group members to communicate with one another more easily. Admission of a given youngster would also depend on his or her maturity level; an immature fourteen-year-old might be considered. Besides age level, homogeneity would include the common situation of being children of alcoholics. Heterogeneity should also be built into the group, such as school achievement, gender (boys and girls), ability to express feelings, leadership traits in some, including the capacity for support and empathy. These characteristics would ideally range along a continuum, so that the young people would have different degrees of these qualities. In this way those who have more personal resources would be helpful to others who had less to offer. The group would be voluntary, and group members would be selected who have access to transportation.

For those group members who are not selected for the group, the agency considered six options: individual sessions with a staff person; an activity group to build self-esteem through the successful completion of group projects; an educational group that primarily deals with information about alcoholism; family treatment; placement on a waiting list to participate in another group when one becomes available; and referral to another agency that is prepared to work with the adolescent immediately.

Structure. It is planned that the group will meet weekly for one and a half hours at the agency. A tentative time is set for early evening, from 7:30 to 9:00 P.M., which should not interfere with any after-school activities and will make it possible for a parent or friend to drive the child to the agency. Transportation may be a problem for some of the families. Perhaps car pools can be arranged for some. Others may be able to take public transportation.

The only space available is a fairly small room, suitable for discussion but more limited for an activity that requires a great deal of movement. It is important that sound not carry beyond the room, since confidentiality is essential. There are chairs in the room, which can be arranged in a circle for a discussion. However, it is also suggested that soft cushions be brought in, so the teens can sit on the floor and spread out if they like. This will make the atmosphere seem less formal and rigid.

The group will meet for twelve weeks and not be open to new members unless the size drops below five. There will be co-workers—a man and a woman. The workers will decide how certain behavior will be handled, like group members wanting to walk out of the room during the session, smoking, cursing, fighting, or arriving late. As much as possible, the group members themselves should be involved in deciding what should be done about behaviors like these, which may interfere with the group's function. Since the composition of the group was balanced toward prosocial behavior, the group should be capable of decisions that enhance group development and the best interests of group members.

Content. Some of the content will be educational, emphasizing information about alcoholism. The first couple of meetings will be devoted to clarifying the expectations of the group, including what group members would like to do and what the agency is prepared to offer. The roles of the co-workers will be explained as helping the group members to achieve their goals and enabling the group to work together. The group members will be expected to bring in issues and problems for discussion. They may also suggest activities that interest them and can be performed as a group. Where it is possible, group members will make decisions for what happens, as long as these fit within the purposes of the group. If it is feasible and the group wants to, they may take some trips outside the agency.

Pregroup Contact. The potential group members should be seen for interviews as a means of assessment of their individual and family situation. During this time the agency expectations and the purpose of the group are explained, and the adolescents' expectations are shared with the social worker. They should be encouraged to express their questions about the group, including both positives and negatives. The social worker tries to get to know them as persons who may be needy but have strengths and abilities that can contribute to the group. This initial relationship is important and may be the deciding factor in whether the adolescent will want to participate in the group.

The parents need to be apprised of the intention to include their child in a group and how the purpose of the group is meant to improve the family situation.

Since family members are aware of the planning and can offer their reactions, the workers have an opportunity to interpret the needs of the adolescent and deal with parental ambivalence. The parents must give their permission.

The social workers who will be working with the group will want to prepare themselves for the group experience. This may mean an exploration of their personal attitudes toward adolescents and an anticipation of what may happen in the group. It is essential that the co-workers communicate with one another about their feelings and ideas in working with this population. They should also discuss their leadership styles and roles that may be similar or different in the group.

Finally, other staff persons should be aware that such a group is being planned, so that they can contribute their input, perhaps on the basis of previous contacts with alcoholic clients. The receptionist, or the person who will have the first contact with the adolescents, should know about the group and be prepared to welcome them to the agency.

SUMMARY

Attention to the preforming phase ensures greater possibility of success with groups. Many groups fail because there has been insufficient groundwork in preparing staff, group members, or the group worker. Sometimes organizational shortcomings, such as poor group composition, will contribute to failure. Even though this preparation time may seem lengthy and nonproductive (since the group members haven't yet met), it is well worth the time. If the group members terminate prematurely or get locked into a power and control struggle that persists, this is most costly for the agency.

REFERENCES

Alissi, A. S., & Casper, M. (1985). Time as a factor in social groupwork. *Social Work with Groups, 8* (2), 3–16.

Balgopal, P. R., & Vassil, T. V. (1983). *Groups in social work: An ecological perspective*. New York: Macmillan.

Bertcher, H. J., & Maple, F. (1985). Elements and issues in group composition. In Sundel, Glasser, Sarri, & Vinter (Eds.). *Individual change through small groups* (2nd ed.). New York: Free Press.

Breton, M. (1985). Reaching and engaging people: Issues and practice principles. *Social Work with Groups, 8* (3), 7–22.

Birnbaum, M. L., Catalina, J., Nisinzweig, S., & Abrams, V. (1989). Institutionalization of a group service in an individual-oriented agency. *Social Case Work, 70* (8), 495–501.

Coven, C. R. (1981). Ongoing group treatment with severely disturbed medical outpatients: The group formation process. *International Journal of Group Psychotherapy, 31* (1), 99–116.

Feldman, R. A., & Caplinger, T. E. (1977). Social work experience and client behavioral change: A multivariate analysis of process and outcome. *Journal of Social Service Research, 1* (1), 5–33.

Gazda, G. M. (1986). Discussion of "When to recommend group treatment: A review of the clinical and research literature." *International Journal of Group Psychotherapy, 36* (2).

Gitterman, A., & Shulman, L. (1986). *Mutual aid groups and the life cycle.* Itasca, IL: F. E. Peacock.

Hare, A. P. (1976). *Handbook of small group research* (2nd ed.). New York: Free Press.

Hartford, M. E. (1971). *Groups in social work.* New York: Columbia University Press.

Kivlighan, D. M., Corazzini, J. G., & McGovern, T. V. (1985). Pregroup training, *Small Group Behavior, 16* (4), 500–514.

Kurland, R., Getzel, G., & Salmon, R. (1986). Sowing groups in infertile fields: Curriculum and other strategies to overcome resistance to the formation of new groups. In M. Parnes (Ed.), *Innovations in social group work: Feedback from practice to theory.* New York: Haworth Press.

Manor, O. (1986). The preliminary interview in social groupwork: Finding the spiral steps. *Social Work with Groups, 9* (2), 21–40.

Maslow, A. H. (1970). *Motivation and personality* (2nd ed.). New York: Harper & Row.

Meadow, D. (1988). Preparation of individuals for participation in a treatment group: Development and empirical testing of a model. *International Journal of Group Psychotherapy, 38*(3), 367–384.

Napier, R. W., & Gershenfeld, M. K. (1985). *Groups: Theory and experiences* (3rd ed.). Boston: Houghton Mifflin.

Piper, W. E., & Perrault, E. L. (1989). Pretherapy preparation for group members. *International Journal of Group Psychotherapy, 39* (1), 17–34.

Schwartz, W. (1976). Between client and system: The mediating function. In R. W. Roberts & H. Northen (Eds.), *Theories of social work with groups.* New York: Columbia University Press.

Schwartz, W., & Zalba, S. R. (1971). *The practice of group work.* New York: Columbia University Press.

Shulman, L. (1984). *The skills of helping* (2nd ed.). Itasca, IL: F. E. Peacock.

Slocum, Y. D. (1987). A survey of expectations about group therapy among clinical and nonclinical populations. *International Journal of Group Psychotherapy, 37* (1), 39–54.

Toseland, R. W., & Siporin, M. (1986). When to recommend group treatment: A review of the clinical and the research literature. *International Journal of Group Psychotherapy, 36* (2), 171–201.

Tropp, E. (1976). A developmental theory. In R. W. Roberts & H. Northen (Eds.), *Theories of social work with groups.* New York: Columbia University Press.

Yalom, I. D. (1975). *The theory and practice of group psychotherapy* (2nd ed.). New York: Basic Books.

TEACHING AND LEARNING IDEAS

1. Using the Kurland, Getzel, and Salmon model described in the chapter and used in the illustration, write a projected plan to form a group at an agency.

2. Consider how you would use the practice principles on working with oppressed and

vulnerable populations (see Chapter 5) in planning to work with a group that is oppressed or vulnerable.

3. Do a role play of a social worker who is having a pregroup interview with a prospective group member. What do you think would be important to consider with the person before the interview? Try it and get feedback about how you presented the notion of group purpose and other ways of preparing the person for the group.

4. When preparing to work with involuntary clients, what are three techniques (see Chapter 6) that could be most useful? Give a rationale for your thinking.

CHAPTER 8

The Beginning

The beginning phase will vary, depending on the expected duration of the group. It can be as brief as the early part of a single session (Alissi and Casper 1985), but usually the beginning is considered to be the first few meetings of the group (Brown, 1971). The first session, in particular, is crucial in determining whether the group will get off to a good start. Unless group members are able to satisfy some of the basic needs of inclusion, control, and affection (Schutz 1961), they may perceive the group as a threat to their well-being and not return. The interventions of the worker during this time are designed to help persons feel included (inclusion), make decisions about what happens in the group (control), and feel respected and cared about (affection).

EMERGENCE OF GROUP STRUCTURE

This early period includes the group-development stages of formation and power and control (see Chapter 4). Group members may feel ambivalent about being in the group, anticipating the possibilities for personal and task accomplishment but also wary about participation. They may question whether their concerns and interests will be met. These feelings are usually present in some form for any type of group.

Some of the hesitation about involvement and the closeness that may result from liking and being liked by others is that such involvement may be accompanied by discomfort when the group ends. If prior separations have been emotionally draining or if the person had no opportunity to share his or her feelings about the meaning of a relationship, a separation could be associated with incompleteness. Members may bring these unresolved feelings of loss into the beginnings of new groups, which could partially explain the avoidance behavior that is often present.

Subgroups

Group members will use other group experiences as a frame of reference by which to shape their actions. The norms and values of these prior associations will be the standard for what is considered acceptable behavior (Garland, Jones, and Kolodny, 1973, 36). An informal group structure will develop as persons with common interests communicate more with one another than with others. The apparent commonality of values and backgrounds of group members will be the basis for the formation of subgroups within the larger group. These connections among group members will be noticeable from the increased communication with one another, agreement with the other person's views, and greater physical closeness. The bonding that takes place at this early stage is the way group members attempt to find acceptance and security in their newness to the group.

Indigenous Leadership

Members who are consistent in being able to assist the group in satisfying socioemotional or task needs are perceived as indigenous leaders. They are able to contribute personal resources (knowledge, expertise), achieve influence in the group, and exercise control of the interpersonal situation. The extent to which leadership from within the group will emerge depends on whether the group worker truly encourages self-determination.

Group members will react to indigenous leadership with mixed emotions. It is comforting for members to know that others in the group are taking responsibility for raising questions, seeking clarity about group purposes, and making suggestions for the group's direction. However, if indigenous leaders talk too much during a first meeting, they may be seen as "taking over" the group, thus diminishing the importance of the others. If the indigenous leader(s) can be responsive to the socioemotional needs of group members, such as offering support and modeling the expression of feelings, it is more likely that they will be accepted. More than likely leadership will be demonstrated by several persons in the group besides the group worker. Some persons are better in the socioemotional area, others in the task accomplishment side of group life.

Use of Conflict

Conflict is a natural part of the group's development, since group members are expected to have a range of views from their varied backgrounds. These differences can be used constructively to help the group accomplish its purposes.

In order for the group to develop, at least two conditions must be met: The group members will have to find sufficient commonality of purpose and motivation to work together in pursuit of their goals; they will also need to negotiate their differences successfully. This does not mean that group members must all agree with one another. It does mean that persons should be able to communicate with one another well enough about differing values, interests, and problems that there is increased understanding of these beliefs and respect for persons who may differ. In the early meetings, since there is a strong need to be liked and accepted, the presence of conflict may be denied or avoided by some participants. The worker needs to introduce the idea that differences and controversy are acceptable and useful in the group.

The group's range of experiences, attitudes, and coping strategies will provide the needed resources to help members in solving problems. Opposing views are almost certain to raise some controversy, but when group members are able to recognize and communicate over this controversy, it can lead to increased closeness and respect. Group members may find that differences—at first so apparent—are less important after discussion. As the group progresses in its development, members will be freer to express their differences and still feel accepted as valued persons in the group. It is when conflict is experienced as destructive to others that it will lead to rejection.

INTERRELATIONSHIP OF THE PERSON, GROUP AND ENVIRONMENT

In the integrative, holistic approach to social work with groups that is presented in this book, the person, group, and environment are interrelated and interdependent. When two or more persons interact face-to-face, they influence one another through the exchange of ideas, values, and feelings. These transactions are part of the socialization and growth process. We constantly learn from others and teach them in return. The physical environment, with its significant persons, will also be a factor in shaping behavior. Similarly, if there is enough collective strength in a group, the group can affect the environment, either positively or negatively.

The basis for social work intervention with clients is that the worker will be able to influence change. The relationship between the social worker and clients becomes an interactional system, affecting both clients and worker. This is what Chin (1961, 207–208) refers to as an intersystem model where both systems—the social worker as a system and the client(s) as a system—are developing into a single system with a defined purpose of accomplishing one or more goals.

In conceptualizing social work practice, we often discuss how the client is changing. There is relatively little consideration of how the social worker is affected by the unity of the relationship. And yet the notion of professional self-awareness is at the very core of the helping process. Siporin (1975) refers to it as

> an accurate perception of one's own actions and feelings, and of the effects of one's behavior on others. It means a third ear and a third eye, which one can use to view oneself in action and also to view the innermost recesses of oneself. (p. 78)

In practicing social work with groups, the group worker needs to have tripartite vision, keeping in mind the person in the group, the group as an interacting unit, and the environment in the lives of the group members. However, it is also essential that the group worker consistently examine how his or her own feelings, attitudes, and values affect or are affected by those in the group or environment.

This may seem like a juggling act. How can you be aware of yourself as well as the dimensions of person, group, and environment? A place to start is simple recognition that all these factors are worthy of consideration. It is the holistic nature of problem solving. Once aware of this, the worker is more able to relate personal issues to the group as a whole and involve, where appropriate, persons from the environment to influence the direction of the group toward its defined purposes.

TASKS OF THE GROUP WORKER

The term "task" has different shades of meaning. Studt (1968) discusses how "task" is used in social work practice—as something to do (behavioral), as part of a sequence of actions (process), or in relation to a specific problem (situation). Here, it is used to mean an activity that is expected or assigned to a person in a particular role or work situation. The collective tasks in the next three chapters are meant to describe what a social worker might do in working with groups. It is likely that *not* all of these tasks will be attempted for every group. The selection will depend on the type of group, its purposes, the stage of group development, and the needs of the individuals or group. The tasks are outlined into beginning, middle, and ending stages of groups (see Figure 8.1). The timing of when they occur is not always confined to a particular stage of development. Although the tasks are described in relation to work with individuals, the group, or the environment, these three are interrelated, so a task will affect all these three dimensions. However, there may be an emphasis on helping individuals, helping the group, or involving people in the environment at one particular time in the group's development.

The social worker will usually take responsibility for these tasks, but there are times when they will be initiated and performed by one or more of the group

	PERSON	GROUP	ENVIRONMENT
Beginning Stage	1. Help group members get acquainted, form relationships. 2. Deal with feelings and attitudes about being in the group. 3. Identify and clarify group member, group worker, and agency expectations. 4. Assess psycho-social and cultural factors.	5. Explain and negotiate group purposes and worker/member roles. 6. Recognize and deal with resistance in the group. 7. Introduce structure in the group. 8. Plan with the group to accomplish its purposes.	9. Arrange physical structure. 10. Act as broker for needed services/resources. 11. Identify and involve potentially support-ive persons.
Middle Stage	12. Enhance group member self-esteem. 13. Encourage group member self-understanding. 14. Relate individual issues to the group as a whole. 15. Encourage responsibility for action.	16. Recognize and negotiate conflict. 17. Redefine purposes. 18. Build relationships and group cohe-sion. 19. Clarify norms and roles. 20. Continue problem solving to complete personal and group objectives.	21. Mediate differences between group and environment. 22. Advocate for change or addi-tional services. 23. Collaborate with other professionals.
Ending Stage	24. Review and summarize individual and group progress.	25. Deal with feelings and attitudes about separating from the group.	26. Plan for the future. 27. Refer group members to other services.

Figure 8.1. Tasks of the Group Worker

members. As the group develops, group members, encouraged to share leader-ship, will take an increasing responsibility for helping roles within the group.

Tasks: The Person

Persons enter groups with their individual needs, interests, and problems. The group worker should keep in mind that, even when people participate in groups, they still see themselves as separate and distinct. They do not want to be consumed by the group. There may be a fear of losing one's individuality by what has been referred to as "groupthink" (Janis, 1982). In groupthink, the person feels pressure to conform to a way of thinking that will protect the group. Persons may be fearful about expressing their differences.

The worker takes into account the group member's ambivalence about involvement in the group. At this early stage, the balance that must be maintained between group member separateness and togetherness is slightly tipped toward separateness. In this way there will be the time for those who are slower to participate to find a place for themselves in the group.

In the following explanation of the various tasks, usually with practice illustrations, the techniques of the group worker will be mentioned. A combination of techniques is ordinarily employed in each of the tasks.

1. Help Group Members Get Acquainted and Form Relationships.

WORKER ACTIVITY: *Introduce yourself and group members to one another. In addition to giving their names, persons might share something about themselves. The giving and receiving of information by group members might eventually help persons to connect with one another in the discovery of their common bonds.*

Recognizing the importance of inclusion, mentioned earlier, the getting-acquainted activity begins to satisfy that need. The initial self-disclosure by the group worker, which may include some personal information if it seems appropriate, can help to overcome fears and stereotypes of the professional as being distant or detached. Besides actually making the rounds of introductions, there are activities that can be an innovative and creative opportunity for sharing about oneself.

☐ *Example of the Task.* At the first meeting of a stress-management group of child-protective social workers, the group worker asked the group members to use blank newsprint to illustrate something about themselves, such as interests and abilities, as well as sources of job stress. They could use pictures, designs, or words to convey their meaning. The colors of the pens or crayons could be used to portray emotions. The group worker also participated in the activity. After about fifteen minutes, they were asked to hold their paper up and discuss it with the others. Group members and the worker could comment and ask questions about the drawing. Names were put on the paper for everyone to see.

This activity was fun for the participants, different and interesting. It enabled group members to identify commonalities and differences in one another, so that mutual aid could begin to develop in the group. Since the group worker also participated in the activity, there was more acceptance of him as someone who was open and accessible to the others. The activity had value in locating themes for later discussion. It could also be used for further assessment of group members, as they shared information and feelings about themselves.

What group members chose to share and the nature of the disclosure revealed more about their characteristics. This could be taken into account in meeting their needs in the group. The focus on interests and abilities indicated areas in which persons had strengths. These healthy parts of themselves would be called upon throughout the group to deal constructively with job stress.

2. Deal with Feelings and Attitudes about Being in the Group.

WORKER ACTIVITY: *Ask what it is like for persons to be in the group. You might ask if persons have been in other groups like this one, recognizing there may be some unresolved feelings of loss from prior separations that may create anxiety about starting a new group. Encourage both the positive and negative expression of feelings and attitudes toward the group. Validate their concerns. Normalize their fears. Recognize the ambivalence. Express your own feelings if it seems appropriate.*

It is common for persons to have some anxiety about starting a new group. Actually, feelings are probably mixed—joy, anticipation, fear, caution—so often identified as ambivalence about participating in a group. If previous group experiences have been successful and self-fulfilling, it is likely that the emotions will be balanced on the positive side. However, if participation in groups has been negative, there will be additional caution and fear that the group will be a repeat performance. Just being aware of the range of feelings enables the group worker to be more sensitive to the subtle signs of distress, such as body language, that signal a closed or withholding position.

Some group members may want to bring out past experiences with similar groups, especially if there are unresolved feelings of loss associated with their separation from the group. These feelings should be encouraged and used as a springboard to discussing their presence in the existing group.

☐ *Example of the Task.* In an older adult group that is meeting in a Family Service Agency to discuss personal problems, Group Member B is attending the group after a period of time in a casework relationship. The group worker is aware that the change from an individual to a group experience is strange and unsettling for her.

WORKER: Let's get back to being here.

MEMBER A: Yeah, that's right.

WORKER: How are you all feeling today? Some of you are relatively new. Some of you have been here for a while. There are three group members who are not here today. How are you all doing? What are you feeling like being here? It's really a new experience. *(Addressing comment to Group Member B)* You had a very close contact with your worker.

MEMBER B: Yes, I did, I really did.

WORKER: You really did.

MEMBER B: Yes, very much.

WORKER: This is a new experience. You're with people who have, by the way, many of the same problems that you have, you will discover.

MEMBER B: I shall.

WORKER: But it's hard, I think, making the change from a one-to-one relationship.

MEMBER B: It is very hard.

WORKER: All of a sudden you're with a whole group. How are you feeling today. You're talking about names and origins—let's talk about us—what we're doing here, how we're feeling right now.

MEMBER A: We come here to pour our heart out. To have a little help. To see if we can be helped.

The group worker centers on their present feelings in the group. She encourages the expression of these feelings and attempts to involve group members in discussing them. By providing the information that other persons in the group have similar problems, she is offering support and fostering a climate of mutual helping. The group worker validates the difficult transition for Member B. As Member B experiences caring and concern for what she is going through, and she expresses some of the pain associated with the loss of the casework relationship, it becomes easier to "let go" and join with the others to "pour our heart out."

3. Identify and Clarify Group Member, Group Worker, and Agency Expectations.

WORKER ACTIVITY: *Ask what group members hope to gain from the group. Bring out your own expectations. Share any pertinent information about the agency (procedures, rules, etc.). Acknowledge areas of agreement and disagreement among group members and with yourself. Define appropriate boundaries (confidentiality, etc.). Explore other needed rules or guidelines of behavior to facilitate the accomplishment of the group's objectives. Involve group members in decision making about these rules, where appropriate.*

Even though the group purpose may seem clear, the diversity among the group members will often lead to varying expectations of what they hope to gain from the group. The group worker, partly reflecting agency interests for the group, may or may not share all the member expectations. As the group members and worker discuss their views, norms begin to form for the group, and a foundation is laid for the group structure. The expectations and rules offer guidelines about appropriate role behavior. Group member participation in shaping these norms increases their motivation for involvement in the group. The expression of differences in regard to expectations provides a forum for defining what is appropriate to expect in regard to the purposes of the group. Some expectations of group members may not be realistic. The clarification will address itself to what is feasible, considering the potential and limitations of the group. Being able to accommodate some diversity reinforces the value of individual differences and self-determination.

☐ *Example of the Task.* In this illustration of a parents' group, we see a blend of the social worker helping the group to continue their focus on the topic of expectation, involving more than one person in the group, and reaching for feelings. The emphasis is on engagement of the group members in a discussion of what the group is for, especially in relation to whether Mrs. F should deal with her personal problems in the group. The social worker is able to help Member A through the support of others in the group in encouraging the mother to bring out her individual and family concerns.

MRS. F: All I can think about are my own problems so I really don't think that's what this group is for.

WORKER: Are you saying that you don't really feel that the group can in any way solve the problem for you?

MRS. F: No, I'm not saying that. I'm just saying that I don't think that my problems are the reason we're here.

WORKER: Well, how does the rest of the group feel about it. Should Mrs. F bring out her personal problems because she isn't really sure that this is what the group is for? And I think that's really where we stumbled again. And maybe we ought to redefine what everybody feels the group is for.

MRS. W: Actually, I'm here to find out what I can do for my son. That's all I'm concerned about—my son, period. Nobody else but my son.

WORKER: Then how do you feel about Mrs. F's question.

MRS. W: That's all right. Whatever she feels inside her, she should let out. That's how I feel. The worst thing you can do is keep it inside.

MRS. T: . . . We are at an age when our physical well-being is not at its best. Your nerves are not at their best. And you work full-time. I work full-time so that you have many, many things that try your patience besides the fact that you are trying to calmly handle a child who has emotional problems. If you don't get it out in the open—I don't think it's so wrong to talk about your problems—I really don't.

WORKER: Mrs. W didn't feel it was wrong, if I understood you correctly.

MRS. W: She should let everything out that's bothering her.

WORKER: Mrs. T actually said it would be good if you could. . . . A group such as this is for the discussion of problems, whether they are related directly or indirectly to the one child attending the clinic. Or whether they are related to the child not attending the clinic. It really doesn't matter. What matters is, as Mrs. W points out, that you are concerned about your child or children and that's what matters. If you weren't concerned, I suppose you wouldn't be here.

The initial expectations of group members were that they discuss the problems of their children. There is obviously a relationship between what they are personally experiencing as adults, mothers, wives, or employees and what is happening with their children. The group worker, with input from the group members, redefines the expectations to include a broader focus.

4. Assess Psychosocial and Cultural Factors.

WORKER ACTIVITY: *Observe how group members are relating to you and other group members. Be aware of both the content and feeling level of communication. What does their communication mean? How do they perceive of issues or problems? What particular interests and strengths do they exhibit that can be reinforced and used constructively in the group? Be aware of the cultural meaning of behavior that accounts for ethnic differences. Character-istics of social class should also be considered. The analysis of this data should assist you in making an assessment of the level of group functioning and your strategy of intervention.*

In addition to the assessment of members during the preforming period, the beginning phase is used for continued assessment in relation to group member participation in the group. Being aware of nonverbal communication will contribute toward the overall understanding of behavior since some persons may withhold verbal comments because they are still uncertain about being involved with the group. It is particularly useful to notice interests and strengths among group members. These should be reinforced to maximize self-esteem. Since indigenous leadership is such a valuable resource, persons who exhibit leader-ship qualities should be encouraged to continue their contributions.

Those from ethnic minorities will reflect their background, and their behavior should be assessed in its cultural context. Persons are sometimes labeled as socially or psychologically deviant when the reasons for their differences may be cultural. The meaning of time, formal authority, space, intimacy, family, religion or spirituality, seeking help, independence, age, sex roles, expression or withholding of feelings, language, and community involve-ment are all influenced by cultural background. Unless social workers are sensitive to the meaning of these differences, they will find it difficult to demonstrate the kind of acceptance that comes from understanding. Professional self-awareness is also essential, since the practitioner may unwittingly present negative messages to clients about their values and behavior.

Social class considerations must also be taken into account. There is a tendency among workers to evaluate behavior from a middle-class perspective, since most professionals come from this stratem of society. But socioeconomic position, like ethnic origin, reflects a wide range of values and responses to life situations. For instance, persons from a lower social class may seem more present-oriented than those from a middle class, who are willing to look more to the future. The worker listens to what people are saying and observes how they act. The place to start the helping relationship is where persons perceive the need to be the greatest. Some may be overwhelmingly concerned with basic survival—not having enough food to eat or being unable to pay the bills. Others will focus on the difficulty of an interpersonal relationship.

Working with people in regard to their initial request for services may be only a first step toward other ways of helping. Resolving a concrete need, such as finding a place to live, could lead to a reevaluation of one's marital situation or feelings about being a parent. The issues of race, ethnic background, gender, or social class are considered with all their implications in regard to these presenting needs and problems. The worker should be aware of the possibility of preconceived stereotypes that could limit the understanding of behavior.

The assessment could provide additional understanding of the meaning of behavior, which should prove useful in clarifying group purposes. Being able to estimate the level of group functioning will give the worker some guidelines for his or her own activity. If the group members are perceived to have little capacity for leadership, the worker needs to be more active in developing the initial structure in the group. However, if group members display a high level of ability, the worker may be less directive in formulating structure, since the group will probably be able to take on the responsibilities of group life and become involved in developing the structure as a collaborative activity.

Tasks: The Group

On the level of the group, the group worker needs to be aware of all the factors that shape the development of the group—the group composition, agency and group member expectations, group size, pregroup planning, physical conditions of the room, and presence of the worker as an authority figure. All these and perhaps other factors contribute to the development of the group in a unique way. However, from what we know about groups, certain occurrences must be expected in every group. In order for the group worker to adhere to the values of self-determination and maximize the groups' capacities for growth, he or she must take on certain tasks that will facilitate these conditions. These tasks are the subject of this section.

5. Explain and Negotiate Group Purposes and Worker/Member Roles.

WORKER ACTIVITY: *In a short, clear statement, describe your idea of the group's purpose and invite the group's response. Describe how you envision your role, also asking for the group's response. Group members should also be encouraged to share their ideas of group purpose and their perception of what they will do in the group. Identify similarities and differences of how those in the group understand group purposes and the roles of group members and worker. Negotiate differences by locating areas of commonality that will provide direction for the group while not neglecting the fact that there are differences which should be respected.*

In order to begin the work that brought the group together, all the participants will want to determine their reasons for being in the group. Each person has some piece to contribute to the whole, but the group purpose is more than a collection of individual interests. Through sharing ideas and feelings, becoming more aware of values and beliefs, and examining a range of purposes, it can become clear how the expectations of group members will fit within the boundary of what the agency is prepared to offer.

Expectations are also shared about the roles of group members and worker. However, it is more than an intellectual exchange. In their discussion, the social worker talks about what he or she is doing—the explanation and reasons for certain behaviors that are part of the professional role. The client will also be encouraged to discuss the expectations of his or her role as they move toward a working relationship. Unless there is clarity about the ''contract'' between social worker and group members, which is a mutual agreement about purposes and roles in the group, it is likely that there will be dissatisfaction in the group (Maluccio and Marlow, 1974). For instance, let's say that parents join a Parent Effectiveness Group to learn more about their parenting role. The worker has a belief that the marital relationship is most important in providing security to the child and brings this out for the group to consider. The parents will perceive the lack of congruence between what they want from the group and what the worker is prepared to offer.

The negotiation that takes place in the clarification of multiple purposes and roles is a beginning task of the group. It provides an arena for communication and the emergence of indigenous leadership. It is the beginning of a collaborative relationship where joint problem solving is valued. The structure that is introduced at this time—smoking or not, confidentiality, how people can participate, responsibilities—provide some security in group members knowing what they can expect.

☐ *Example of the Task.* The following excerpt illustrates how the social worker begins to clarify purposes and roles. The group is called Joining Together—a women's group that was formed when a Family Service Agency determined a need for a socioeducation group from among its clientele.

The agency purpose in forming the group was to provide an opportunity for women who were facing common issues, such as life transitions (divorce, separations, etc.) and seeking greater autonomy as women, to discuss these concerns in a supportive atmosphere with others and work toward some resolution for themselves. In this first session of the ten week group, the worker's goals were to help members know something about the others, to determine individual needs and to clarify group purposes on the basis of the expectations of the individuals and group worker. It was also important for group members to recognize similar needs and issues in developing possibilities for enriching one another.

WORKER: What I'd like to do now is talk a little bit about the group. We call it Joining Together because we saw it as having two parts—the working part and the together part. The working part is the group members bringing into the group concerns that they have, issues that they are needing to discuss, wanting to discuss, feelings that they want to share. The group can work at developing ideas—suggestions to other group members. We feel that in being a working group, we spend time and energy on developing relationships in the group and on sharing knowledge, resources, that we each may have because we are all very different people. And when you pool all that in working together, then it can enrich all of us. . . . And especially in the area of feelings, we'll offer feedback to the individual group members. That's a really important part of working—that we will *offer feedback* to one another. You will be offering feedback to us that this group is meeting your expectations and that these are the things that you are looking for in this kind of a group experience. When we work, we really mean work. You come to the group, you are committed to the group, you are committed to not only being here, but being here and sharing—opening to the group members and really offering interest, caring, support to the group itself. . . . I guess what we'd like to do now is have us begin to meet each other. So what I'd like you to do is to pick someone that you don't know and to talk with them about what your expectations for this group experience are.

(Group members meet in twosomes for about fifteen minutes.)

WORKER: I'm glad you had an opportunity to meet one other person. I was really lucky because there was an odd number and I got to meet two people. I think what I'd like to do now is see if we can go around and talk together about what our expectations for the group might be. And also to introduce ourselves so that we can begin to know each other.

JEAN: I'm Jean, and I have no expectations, because I don't know if I really want to be here, but I received a phone call, and I decided I would try it out. I teach school. And I am separated. And I live on the shore. I don't know what else to say.

WORKER: But you're not sure you want to be here?

JEAN: The last two months have been very difficult. I've been separated a year and the first six months were great. They really were—it was full of relief, as I prepared for it for many years. And the last few months have been hell. And now I'm like the guy who became a hermit and I've just stayed away from a lot of people. I've been very selective of the people I want to see and talk to, and there have been about three, I would say. And I've just resigned from a lot of physical activities that took up a lot of time and space, but which meant nothing. And I'm kind of working my way back to things that I really want to do; not just to take up time and space. So, I'm in the middle of that and that's why I really don't know if I want to be here right now, but I'm here. And I'm not gonna leave until it's over. It's your turn . . . *(Laughter)*

LAURA: My name is Laura and I'm about to—no I expect to become separated very shortly and to me it's quite traumatic, because I had one other separation in my life. I lost my husband, my first husband, in death and this one I'll be losing in life. So, I'm just looking for strength.

WORKER: Do you see the group as offering you this support?

LAURA: I hope it can.

PAULEEN: I'm Pauleen, I've been separated for six months and I have an eighteen-month-old daughter. My life has changed so much in the last six months that I just would like to meet new people and share with them all the difficulties in bringing up a child by myself and returning to work; and just having a life that's changing so much. It's just so different than what I've had before that I'd like to find a different approach to the problem by joining and participating.

BETTY: I'm here because I am very hopeful that there will be a positive experience and also I am going through a lot of changes in my life and I also am separated recently and I want to make the most of what I have and I want to come into contact with other people's attitudes . . . other women's attitudes of how they cope with their problems and how they manage by themselves in a rather sexist society that we live in. And I'm just really glad to be here.

ESTELLE: Perhaps by coming to this group we are saying that we will not judge each other and that's one of the hardest things to find is people that don't judge you. And that is what I think we are all sort of saying, no matter how bad you feel, or how awful you think you are, or ashamed, or humiliated, or weak, or horrible, that we are not sitting in judgment of you. That's what I hope you think of me and that's what I think about all of you.

WORKER: That's a very important thing.

ESTELLE: That's very, very, very important.

WORKER: It's a really important part about working together.

ESTELLE: If you can dare to risk who you are without being entirely wrong.

In the beginning of this first session, several events have taken place. The group worker discusses how she understands the purpose of the group. There is an expectation of sharing ideas and feelings in the common pursuit of group problem solving. She brings out the notion of offering feedback to one another for greater self-understanding. There is an implicit suggestion of collaboration, building trust, openness, and a faith in the group process for them to be able to join together as a helping network.

There are mixed feelings about group members being there. Jean is uncertain about continuing and yet is open about her feelings. The worker acknowledges her wariness, using the technique of reflection to demonstrate understanding. As a reuslt of having her feelings recognized, Jean is able to elaborate more about the reasons for being so unsettled. The comment by the worker, "But you're not sure you want to be here?" was also a way of giving her permission to continue. Other persons bring out more favorable feelings and expectations. The hopes and fears are all present. The acceptance of these varying expressions of attitudes, feelings, and ideas will provide the climate for acceptance of differences, a necessary step toward helping the group reach the stage of conflict resolution in their development.

There is evidence in this excerpt of problem swapping, as described by Shulman (1984, 200–204). Sharing by group members points up the commonalities of their experiences and increases mutual-aid possibilities. The group members don't feel as different or alone as when they first entered the group. The norm of not judging others is introduced by a group member, which will make it more likely that group members will feel freer to risk using behaviors that seem uncomfortable at first.

Involuntary Group Members

All that has been said presupposes that group members are willing to attend and interested in what the group can do for them. They can also be expected to present their reasons for participation in a coherent way and to work with the group toward a clarification of purposes and roles. It does not always happen this way. Many group members are involuntary participants, who may be indifferent, angry, and withholding. Nevertheless, it is possible to induce this kind of member to cooperate.

To achieve collaboration, the worker will concentrate on developing trust by exploring personal or environmental issues that persons bring to the group. For instance, in a group of alcohol or drug abusers who are mandated by the court to participate in an educational and counseling program, there is denial, anger, projection, and guilt, as well as some genuine desire to reduce or eliminate substance abuse. The worker will want to listen to their stories, even though there are defensive distortions and projections, and then allow other members of the group to challenge this maladaptive behavior. If no member is willing to take on this responsibility, the worker will do so, exploring the problem, asking questions, and confronting the involuntary members with their behavior. In order for them to abandon defensive maneuvers and dysfunctional patterns of behaving, they will need to get something in return. That "something" is the belief that someone really cares about them, is willing to listen, and can provide some constructive help, perhaps even concrete services when needed.

Setting expectations for the initial structure of the session and maximizing choices, as suggested by Harris and Watkins (1987, 60–61), can reduce some of the resistance to counseling. Behroozi (forthcoming) also emphasizes giving group members choices, contributing to empowerment, and promoting competence for the involuntary group member. It is likely that involuntary group members are experiencing a loss of control and power and a lessening of self-esteem. Involving them in developing a contract for services, within the boundary of expectations set by the agency, can increase their willingness to invest in a helping process.

The way the contract is developed will vary, depending on the group. With a group of emotionally disturbed children, for instance, the worker will need to start with one or more activities that will permit some distance and gradually encourage closeness. In this case, the discussion of a working agreement about purpose and roles may be done retrospectively on the basis of an evaluation of their experiences of structured activities that were planned by the worker.

For a group in which there is focus on personal problem solving, it is helpful to contract around the use of constructive behaviors by the group members. This will enable them to deal more successfully with their perceived needs and presenting problems. Even with a "resistant" group, there will be some persons who are more willing and able than others to face the reality of their situation. Their participation encourages others to become involved in sharing views on individual and group purposes. However, Seabury (1976, 18–19) points out that the contract may not be feasible or realistic with some involuntary clients or those who are severely disoriented.

6. Recognize and Deal with Resistance in the Group.

WORKER ACTIVITY: *Assess the possible meaning of the resistance. Is it related to feelings that are generated from within or outside the group? Attempt to locate the source(s) of the resistance, perhaps by asking persons what they are thinking and feeling in the here-and-now of the group. You may want to share your sense of the obstacles that are getting in the way of their accomplishing their objectives. Reflect upon the concerns that are expressed and validate them. Depending upon the nature of the group and its stage of group development, you may want to allow them more distance and not confront the resistance directly. It may be serving a useful purpose for them. If it continues to prevent individual and group growth, it should be raised as an issue for resolution. Give them an opportunity for choices, eliciting their ideas for alternative solutions to whatever the problem seems to be.*

Resistance is a natural part of change. When a person gives up established patterns of thinking or doing, there is discomfort. For instance, when the young child goes to school and learns about ideas that are different from his or her parents', it will be difficult to accept these changes. The child's security is shaken, since the original beliefs are part of the child's self-concept. The early stage of group development means exposure to ideas, values, and actions that are often unusual for those in the group. In some cases persons who may seem to be resistant are simply adhering to their cultural norms. For these group members, it is perfectly natural to behave the way they do.

One reaction to change is to deny or avoid facing differences. Stability, in the sense of knowing what to expect, is a valued part of people's lives. Each new learning includes the pleasure of growth and the excitement of expanding one's horizons, but with it comes uncertainty about what the newness will mean. If the person has experienced prior successes, the comfort of such achievements will make him or her more ready and willing to change.

Being able to talk about one's resistance with others makes it easier to resolve. In a group whose members possess different degrees of readiness to change, those who are more positive can influence the more reluctant. The worker should not gloss over the differences or minimize them in order to inject a positive tone to the group. The worker needs to encourage members to note differences, recognize their existence, and help persons find similarities in their differing views. Resistance may be a healthy way for some people to protect themselves, and when this occurs, it should be respected (Corey and Corey, 1987, 141).

One form of resistance, especially with involuntary groups, is members' fear of not being in control of their situation. Group members should be encouraged to assume as much responsibility as possible and to participate in joint planning and decision making, and this in turn should increase motivation for participation. In working with hard-to-reach adolescents, Casey and Cantor (1983) urge group members to choose which activities to engage in, as a means of increasing their control of the group environment.

The group worker needs to assess members carefully enough that he or she knows how much resistance to accept and how much distance may be necessary in the development of trust, and when to be firm and challenge these obstacles to growth. Hurley (1984, 78) believes that the group worker should take the stance that he or she is not asking group members to change, but does expect the group to change. It is true that a group worker cannot change anyone. The person has to be willing to open himself or herself to new learning or the discontinuance of negative behavior. But the professional helper can create the conditions under which persons are willing to do the problem solving that may result in change.

☐ *Example of the Task.* In the teen girls group that meets at the Family Service Agency, the worker attempts to get the girls to talk about why they are coming to the group. She continually probes for more explicit reasons for what they expect from the group and seeks to have them elaborate on these reasons. The worker meets their resistance with challenges for dealing with the topic at hand.

WORKER: I wonder if we can talk more about that—why we're here, why you're all here. What ideas do you have? I think it's important to know why you're coming, because you come. But why?

(*Jan, in a low and almost inaudible voice, tells about being abused, and that's the reason she is coming to the group.*)

WORKER: Did you hear her, Barbara?

BARBARA: She said she feels she is being abused or may be abused.

JAN: You have to know how not to be.

WORKER: Is this why you're here?

JAN: Yes.

WORKER: That's why you're here.

JAN: Not be taken advantage of.

WORKER: Not to be taken advantage of. OK.

BARBARA: In what way?

JAN: I can think of lots of different ways.

WORKER: OK. What were you thinking of?

JAN: I don't know.

WORKER: Friends, school, boys, what were you thinking of?

(*Some of the girls discuss how much better it is to discuss their problems with their friends since they see them all the time and know them very well.*)

CATHY: So it's difficult [to discuss problems in the group] because once a week is actually not that much when you see them [friends] every day, call them on the phone at night, talk forever and stuff like that.

WORKER: Then why are you coming?

CATHY: My mother wants me to.

WORKER: All right, your mother wants you to. But why? (*Pause*) What's going on? The same with you, Joan, why are you coming?

☐ When the subject of their own problems becomes more threatening, the girls show more resistance and withdraw from the topic. As the social worker pushes them to discuss why they are coming to the group and, as it turns out, why they don't want to come, she attempts to help them involve other girls in the group. She is also continually dealing with their feelings about coming to the Family Service Agency.

WORKER: Girls, why are you getting away from discussing the group.

JAN: Because we don't want to talk about it.

WORKER: Yeah, why? Why don't you want to talk?

BARBARA: I think we've sort of all made a decision I'm not going to come anymore. We can't explain it to ourselves. Maybe it's rationalization. And we're afraid to talk about it because you'll convince us otherwise.

WORKER: OK. Does part of you want me to convince you?

BARBARA: Yeah, but the other part doesn't.

(*The girl goes on to tell how difficult it will be for her with transportation if she comes to the group.*)

WORKER: All right, so what is it about coming here and talking about yourselves? You don't involve Peggy. Peggy sits there and you permit it.

JAN: Do you know how many times you asked that question? And you got no response yet.

WORKER: Yeah, I'm pushing you today.

JAN: You are.

WORKER: Because I don't know what you're doing.

JAN: If we don't answer the question, you dump it.

WORKER: But you're not answering me. You're beating around the bush. And why are you here? . . . Today I'm really pushing you. I'm not sure you really know why you're coming.

In this situation, the worker thought that the group members could handle the confrontation about why they were coming to the group. But there is always the danger that some may flee from the demands imposed by the worker. Still others, when the worker maintains the focus on their reasons for coming to the group, interpret this insistence as strength. By challenging them, the worker is also implicitly recognizing a strength in them, an ability to express their ideas and feelings. she is also using the technique of involving them in the discussion and exploring the meaning of their experience in the group. Another important technique is to ask them to define the issue or problem. They will not be able to engage in problem solving unless this step is accomplished.

7. Introduce Structure in the Group.

WORKER ACTIVITY: *Offer specific procedures and guidelines of behavior to enhance organization of the group and define clear boundaries (confidentiality, etc.). Some of the development of this structure may be done jointly with group members, depending on their ability to participate collaboratively, or with their input. The use of structured activities could be another means of facilitating group interaction, developing relationships, and building cohesion in the group. The prescribed roles of the activity enable group members to try out certain behaviors that they may ordinarily be hesitant to use. The structure provides safety. The forms of organization (procedures, rules, activities, etc.) should be relevant to help the group accomplish its purposes. Groups with members who have many inadequacies will need more structure.*

Structure means organization. It is how roles, relationships, expectations, and responsibilities are arranged in certain situations. There is a formal structure, which includes the purpose, rules, office holders, and prescribed ways of interacting among people in a particular group or organization. This configuration includes operational procedures. People know the who, what, why, when, and how of group life. There is less chance of making a mistake in an interpersonal encounter if the social and behavioral rules are spelled out. That's the formal structure of an organization. The informal structure consists of the way persons relate to one another according to the norms that develop in the group. This pattern of relationships includes indigenous leadership, subgroups, isolates, and forms of communication and decision making.

People need and want structure. It provides order and stability. But if the formal structure is overly rigid, so that persons have little opportunity for making decisions, it can inhibit the development of creativity. Being creative is more likely to come as a response to an ambiguous situation. It is also true that lack of structure can lead to tension and conflict. When conflict is valued as an opportunity for resolving personal and group issues, it may be encouraged. In such cases, as in traditional T (training) groups or certain types of therapy groups, the structure is ambiguous for this very purpose.

For groups it is useful to provide structure initially, so they have the comfort and security of knowing what to expect. However, the group worker seeks to *involve the group* as much as possible in developing their structure. In this way, as group members have opportunities for decision making and self-determination, they can take more control of their transactions and demonstrate the assertiveness they will need for personal and group growth. For groups with more deficits, the worker must introduce more structure. For instance, younger children will often need more structure than older children. Persons who are developmentally disabled or have emotional problems will require many guidelines of behavior and consistency of expectations. The use of games, with its accompanying rules, is popular with children, because it gives them the chance to master certain activities. Role play can enable the players to try out previously untested behaviors. The structure of the role play allows for safety in using these new ways of expressing oneself.

☐ *Example of the Task.* First- and second-year high school students met as a group after school. It was formed by social workers from a community mental health center and Police Department, who co-led the group. The adolescents were at risk of school failure and some were on probation from juvenile court. The guidance counselors at the high school referred the students to the group and continued to meet with the social workers in a team effort.

The purposes of the group were to help group members feel better about themselves, have fun, and make good choices by learning problem-solving skills. The social workers were white, the group members black. The color difference became less of a barrier to working together as mutual respect and trust developed among the professionals and group members.

One of the boys in the group, David, was on probation and had a marginal academic record. He was extremely quiet, and teachers reported little interest in school. He said very little in the group. During one meeting the group did a role play where David volunteered to play a teenager who was drinking beer and became involved in a stealing incident at a shopping center. The workers played the parents. Other group members were David's older sister, store owners, and two police officers. The scene was the family having supper when the police officers came to the house to tell the parents about a drinking and stealing incident involving David. The ensuing discussion involved David being reprimanded by his parents and defending himself. After the role play the workers asked the group members for their reactions about how it felt to play the roles.

DAVID: I wish I would talk to my parents that way.
WORKER: What way, David?
DAVID: Just to let them know what's on my mind.
WORKER: You'd like to be more outspoken.
DAVID: Yes!
WORKER: That's not easy to do, is it?
DAVID: No!

☐ At that point, the worker asks the group whether they are able to bring out their feelings to parents. The reactions vary—some are able to do it more successfully than others. The worker asks how they can use the group to get better at it with their parents and other adults. David is given praise for being able to share his feelings with the group. He smiles and appears to feel better about himself.

David had more freedom in the structure of the role play to behave in a way that would ordinarily be unacceptable. But it was a play, and he could be somebody else, try something new. There were really three parts to this structured role play: first, the development of the story and characters with the help of the group members; second, the actual enactment; and third, the analysis of what happened and relating their experiences to the here-and-now of the group and everyday life. The role play had prescribed roles, rules, and a boundary that was clearly defined. The analysis of what happened during their portrayal of the characters gave new meaning to their behavior. Most importantly, they were able to experience what it was like to express the feelings. This was a small step for David in taking a risk. There is also a potential danger for David. If he were to replicate his actions from the role play to an actual outburst and confrontation with his parents at home, he could be severely reprimanded and lose ground in his relationship within the family. Therefore, the discussion of the role play needs to show how to express feelings appropriately—being assertive but not hostile.

8. Plan with the Group to Accomplish Its Purposes.

WORKER ACTIVITY: *Planning is always going on in the group. The involvement of group members in making decisions is an essential part of group work. The steps that are outlined below are the phases of this planning process—the subtasks to accomplish problem solving.*

> a. *Sharing of perceptions, values, feelings, and ideas about an issue, need, or problem*
> b. *Identifying common themes and defining the issue, need, or problem from the collective thinking of the group*
> c. *Seeking further information to clarify the nature of the problem, if necessary*

d. Reaching agreement on what the group will work on together
e. Partializing the issue or problem for accessible and manageable tasks
f. Considering alternatives for action and problem solving
g. Making decisions and determining responsibility for action

The social work values of self-determination, empowerment, mutual aid, shared responsibility, and use of indigenous leadership leads to collaborative planning within the group. The planning process resembles the problem-solving model that Somers (1976) describes in social group work. As the practice of social work is becoming more integrative, the elements of problem-solving are the common core of what social workers do. Although identified as a single task, planning within the group occurs throughout the life of the group. Planning and problem solving take place during a beginning contracting phase, then as part of a middle or work phase to accomplish the purposes of the group, and finally in regard to termination and the future.

☐ *Example of the Task.* Nurses and social workers from the oncology floor of a hospital formed a group to deal more successfully with job stress. The group was facilitated by two of the nurses as peer leaders. The leaders were trained in group leadership skills and offered ongoing consultation by a social worker with expertise in group skills. The group had been meeting weekly for a month at the time of this session.

NURSE A (*bringing out the problem of staff shortages*): We have to start recognizing the problems that we face. That's reality. A lot of people say we don't have short staff. Being short-staffed on the floor where the patients can walk and eat and talk and take showers for themselves is a lot different than being in a facility where these patients can't do much for themselves. . . .

NURSE B: We have to come up with some sort of solution. I think we really have to put our heads together and find the answers. We may not get them right away.

NURSE C: Our proposal for drawing up a letter is very good, and we can put down our recommendations and solution to problems.

WORKER: What would happen if you gave them a few case histories, real case histories, and said what could be done . . .

NURSE A: Possibly, but then just by the mere fact of the dates of these things, when they might occur. They don't happen every day, every week, or every month. But there are just some things that can't be avoided. We've had patients that have needed constant—and I mean constant—attention for that eight-hour shift. What happens to the other five or six patients you are responsible for? . . .

WORKER: But what kind of help could you get on such sudden notice? It wouldn't be someone trained for this unit.

NURSE A: We have floats all the time that come to our floor and still make us short, but at least we are going to get out at a reasonable hour. The patients are going to get a decent amount of care. There's no reason why, if another floor is less critical, they can't give up that fifth or sixth nurse there.

WORKER: So if the supervisor could make that judgment it would be up . . .

NURSE A: It would be up to the supervisor to send someone.

WORKER: Then the administration should trust that supervisor's judgment. If she says it has to be that way, it does.

In this meeting the group recognizes a large and pervasive problem. They perceive the cause of the problem as existing outside the group. The expectation is that some level of the administration will need to resolve it. However, the administration may identify the problem from a different frame of reference and not accept the way it was defined by the group—a need for additional staff to help them with patient care.

This is what happened. The group became more angry and upset, because they felt that the administration didn't hear them. In response to their lack of success, the group redefined the problem as lack of time to carry out all their responsibilities. They focused on what they could do *that was within their control* to increase the time with patients. Once they had that frame of mind, they recognized that some alternatives were available to them. They changed their recording system so it took less time and were able to plan how they could help each other when there were emergencies. They recognized that the stress might not go away, but they could take more control of what was happening to them.

The development of a more positive attitude—such as "What can I do to deal with the troublesome situation?"—was crucial in helping them approach the problem more successfully. Being able to continue their meetings as a problem-solving and support group provided needed nurturance and personal energy to gain satisfaction from the job. The use of peer leaders—two nurses chosen by the members themselves—identifies this group as a mutual-aid self-help group. The professional social group worker was a resource and consultant to the leaders but was not present at the meetings.

Tasks: The Environment

9. Arrange Physical Structure.

WORKER ACTIVITY: *Locate a room that is large and comfortable enough to accommodate the group, especially if activities are planned, that may require extra space. The seating should allow persons to have eye contact with one another. Refreshments might be used to create a more informal atmosphere.*

It may seem like a small matter compared to all the skills of helping, but the physical atmosphere in which a group meets is important. If the worker sits in a circle with the group members, it suggests that he or she is willing to foster a collaborative process and that power is shared. If persons in the group are expected to work together, they need to have eye contact with one another and read the nonverbal signs of communication. When there are co-workers, they should be sitting across from one another rather than next to each other, in this way co-workers are able to notice the body language of the other person as well as the eye contact.

For some groups the use of refreshments can contribute to the informality of the ambience and help people feel more comfortable, especially for a beginning meeting. However, if serving refreshments becomes a habit, it is advisable to ask group members to share the responsibility of providing them. When the worker takes on the role of provider on a continuing basis, it may be difficult to some group members to bring out differences or express anger, since the giving of food is often symbolized as providing love.

The quality of the room also has meaning for group members. If the room is comfortable, cheerful, and well furnished, it sends a message to the group members that the agency considers them important people. It can set a tone of acceptance, which may also contribute to greater trust in the group.

Finally, a word about audiovisual materials or activities, if they are to be used in the group. It is essential to try out all equipment before the group arrives. Many a group meeting has started off badly because some needed equipment was forgotten or did not work.

☐ *Example of the Task.* At the first meeting of a Public Assistance Client Group, the group worker describes the room (*Trainee's Handbook,* 1968, 19):

> ☐ The room in which the group meetings are held is a conference room in the Department of Social Welfare County Offices building. It has a window with a venetian blind and on the walls there are occasional pictures showing life situations: children playing, grown-ups in group activities, mothers with children, and single portraits of men and women. Near the door there is a bookshelf on which is placed a coffee urn, cream and sugar dishes, cups, napkins, and plates of cookies. There is a colorful cover on the bookshelf and the dishes are also colorful. In other words, the agency has done the very best to make the room pleasant and comfortable. A conference table is in the center of the room with chairs around it.

In this case the room was comfortable enough for group members to see and hear one another without any difficulty. They were seated around tables that were arranged together in a square. In this way the group worker and members were about equidistant from each other. When persons are seated at a rectangular table, so that eye contact is minimized and some group members are at one end, away from the centrality of the action, there is the tendency for the persons who are furthest removed (at the end of the table) to speak less often.

10. Act as a Broker for Needed Services/Resources.

WORKER ACTIVITY: *There are times when you might work with persons outside the group to secure services or resources that would benefit the group.*

Whenever possible, the group members should be involved in decisions about what kinds of services or resources are necessary. They might also be encouraged to seek these services or resources on their own or with others of their choice.

Since persons who enter groups may have a variety of needs, interests, or problems beyond what can be offered in the group, there are times when the worker arranges for some of these additional services. In order to avoid creating undue dependency, the worker can encourage the group member to seek out these other services on his or her own. In this case, the worker becomes a resource who imparts information to the group member. If group members are not able to take on this kind of responsibility, either because of age, illness, or lack of appropriate knowledge and skill, the group worker becomes more active in making the contacts for these services.

If group members are receiving other services as a result of the worker's efforts, it is desirable that contact be maintained with persons from another agency. In this way, there is the possibility of an interagency team approach on behalf of the group member. When this happens, it should be clear which agency person will be maintaining a coordinator role.

11. Identify and Involve Potentially Supportive Persons.

WORKER ACTIVITY: *Recognizing the importance of a healthy and supportive environment, the worker and the group and/or members might locate persons who could encourage growth and change. Seek to involve these other persons as additional sources of support. This will create an expanding helping network.*

Since the person, group, and environment are bound together as an interrelated whole, the people in the environment who can contribute to the well-being of the group members should be involved very early as part of a helping network. An ecological approach, emphasizing the relationship of persons and their environment, is a useful way to think about human behavior, since it takes into account all the factors that have meaning for the individual. Balgopal and Vassil (1983) discuss behavior as a reflection of this person-environment interaction. It is called *holism* (p. 29). Garbarino (1983) assesses the complicated equation of person and situation, stating that

> The individual brings both his personal and his species' biology ("nature") to each situation. The environment shapes the individual through reinforcement and modeling ("nurture"). Nature and nurture can work together or in opposition, and the level of risk or opportunity experienced by an individual depends on the interplay of these two forces. In extreme cases, facts of nature can all but overwhelm environmental differences. Likewise, environmental conditions can be so extreme (either in a positive or negative way) as to override all but the most powerful conditions of biology. This is human nature, to be whatever conditions encourage. (p. 7)

If the person's environment is healthy, he or she will have that much more opportunity to use existing strengths to the fullest and be successful. Evidence now exists on the follow-up of children who participated in the Head Start programs in the 1960s as part of the War on Poverty. Preschoolers from Head Start, when compared with children of a similar background who did not take part in the program, did better when they first entered school. However, when these children were compared with the general population years later, they lost ground academically. Since the gains of these early years had not been reinforced, they seemed to be lost or minimized in the years ahead. The need to continue an enrichment of children's social and academic environment into their school years became evident (Maeroff, 1985, C1).

SUMMARY

The tripartite focus of person, group, and environment represents the holistic nature of social work with groups. The emphasis in each of these areas may change at different times, depending on the variables of group purpose, composition, setting, and stage of group development. Some of the initial thinking of the preforming period may change as interaction among the group members and with the worker becomes a reality. Intervention is directed as much as possible at personal and group strengths, utilizing the abilities of group members to become involved in decisions that affect them. Terms such as self-determination, mutual aid, empowerment, respect for individual dignity, and appreciation of cultural differences represent the beginnings of group work that continue throughout the life of the group.

The group worker recognizes that starting in a new group can be difficult, especially if the group member is uncertain about acceptance because of the issues or problems that bring him or her to the group. The ability to be empathic with each person's condition and express a genuineness of feeling will create the conditions that are necessary for a working, helping relationship.

Whether it be a treatment, socioeducation, social action, or administrative group, there is attention to the socioemotional and task dimensions of group life. For groups that are more therapeutically or educationally focused, the socioemotional aspects will be more evident. With groups whose purpose is environmental or organizational change, the task will seem uppermost. However, to neglect either aspect completely will retard group growth and accomplishment.

REFERENCES

Alissi, A. S., & Casper, M. (1985). Time as a factor in social groupwork. *Social Work with Groups, 8* (2), 3–16.
Balgopal, P. R., and Vassil, T. V. (1983). *Groups in social work: An ecological perspective.* New York: Macmillan.

Behroozi, C. S. (forthcoming). A model for social work with involuntary applicants in groups. In J. A. Garland (Ed.), *Group work reaching out: People, places, and power*. New York: Haworth Press.

Brown, L. (1971). Social workers' verbal acts and the development of mutual expectations with beginning client groups (Doctoral dissertation, Columbia University, 1970). *Dissertation Abstracts International, 32* (3), 1627A.

Casey, R. D., & Cantor, L. (1983). Group work with hard-to-reach adolescents: The use of member initiated program selection. *Social Work with Groups, 6* (1), 9–22.

Chin, R. (1961). The utility of system models and developmental models for practitioners. In W. G. Bennis, K. D. Benne, & R. Chin (Eds.), *The planning of change* (pp. 201–214). New York: Holt, Rinehart & Winston.

Corey, M. S., & Corey, G. (1987). *Groups: Process and practice*. Monterey, CA: Brooks/Cole.

Garbarino, J. (1983). Social support networks: Rx for the helping professions. In J. K. Whittaker & J. Garbarino (Eds.), *Social support networks: Informal helping in the human services*. New York: Aldine.

Garland, J. A., Jones, H. E., & Kolodny, R. L. (1973). A model for stages of development in social work groups. In S. Bernstein (Ed.), *Explorations in group work* (pp. 17–71). Boston: Milford House.

Harris, G. A., & Walkins, D. (1987). *Counseling the involuntary and resistant client*. College Park, MD: American Correctional Association.

Hurley, D. J. (1984). Resistance and work in adolescent groups. *Social Work with Groups, 7* (4), 71–81.

Janis, I. L. (1982). *Groupthink*. Boston: Houghton Mifflin.

Maeroff, G. I. (1985, June 11). Despite Head Start: Achievement Gap Persists for Poor. *The New York Times*, p. C1.

Maluccio, A. N., & Marlow, W. D. (1974). The case for the contract. *Social Work, 19* (1), 28–35.

Schutz, W. (1961). Interpersonal underworld. In W. G. Bennis, K. D. Benne, & R. Chin (Eds.), *The planning of change*. New York: Holt, Rinehart & Winston.

Seabury, B. A. (1976). The contract: Uses, abuses, and limitations. *Social Work, 21* (1), 16–21.

Shulman, L. (1984). *The skills of helping* (2nd ed.). Itasca, IL: F. E. Peacock.

Siporin, M. (1975). *Introduction to social work practice*. New York: Macmillan.

Somers, M. L. (1976). Problem-solving in small groups. In R. W. Roberts & H. Northen (Eds.), *Theories of social work with groups* (pp. 331–367). New York: Columbia University Press.

Studt, E. (1968). Social work theory and implications for the practice of methods. *Social Work Education Reporter, 16* (2), 22–46.

Trainee's handbook: A case history of a public assistance client group (1968). Manhattan Beach, CA: Mehring Productions and the California State Department of Social Welfare.

TEACHING AND LEARNING IDEAS

1. If you are working with a group, think of how many tasks you were able to undertake during a beginning stage. Briefly describe what you did for each of the tasks.

2. Observe a group during one of the first few meetings. Can you identify any of the tasks from the chapter? Meet with the group worker to discuss your observations.

3. What are the characteristics of small group theory that typify a beginning stage of the group? Describe how this theory offers a rationale for one or more tasks during this early phase of the group.

4. What tasks were most comfortable and least comfortable for you? How would you account for the differences?

CHAPTER 9

The Middle

If group members have an opportunity for self-determination and can collaborate with the group worker in making decisions about the direction of the group, it is more likely that they will progress to the intimacy and maturation stages of group development. In order for this to happen, the conflict, or the expression of differences of the beginning phase needs to be resolved, so that the group can discover a commonality of interest and a need to work together. They also need to respect each other's differences. The increased interaction in their joint problem solving will lead to the greater intimacy and closeness that typifies this middle phase.

By this time norms of behavior have been developed through the expressed values of the worker and members. These norms should be accompanied by role behavior that will support the objectives of the group. The worker builds a social climate in the group in which group members can risk behavior that increases feelings of self-esteem and competence. As group members are able to feel better about themselves and more cohesiveness develops in the group, they become more willing and able to take responsibility for decisions that affect them and the group. Groups that function on a high level will be able to risk the controversy of differences, since there is more assurance of their differing views being accepted. In the diversity of ideas and feelings available to the group, there will be increased ability for problem solving.

The tasks of the worker during this middle phase (see Figure 8.1) continue with the person/group/environment configuration. The emphasis on person or group or environment will vary, even at the single meeting. The group takes on a more central focus during the middle phase, increased cohesion occurs, and there is more willingness for the group to work together. Group members feel freer to communicate and feel more empowered in their collective strength.

TASKS OF THE GROUP WORKER

Tasks: The Person

The focus toward the person in the group deals with those areas that strengthen group members and increase their competence. The uniqueness of the person is not lost as the group matures. In fact, the possibilities for personal growth and individuality can increase, since there are more opportunities for learning and experiencing adaptive behavior. One of the skills of the group worker is to go back and forth between the person and the group—seeking relationships, searching for similarities and differences, fostering mutual aid, and yet helping group members to understand the differences that may exist.

The tasks with some emphasis toward the person include enhancing self-esteem, encouraging self-understanding, relating individual issues to the group as a whole, and encouraging responsibility for action.

12. Enhance Self-Esteem of Group Members.

WORKER ACTIVITY: *Explore with group members how they assess their abilities and help them to recognize and accept their positive qualities. Reinforce the use of their strengths. Arrange for activities that will enable group members to exercise those characteristics that contribute to a positive self-image. Encourage persons in the group to offer feedback to one another that will enhance mutual aid.*

The encouragement to use personal strengths dates back to the early days of group work. It is a key ingredient in planning activities and contributing to feelings of self-worth. Encouraging members to use constructive qualities to contribute to the group as a whole remains a basic tenet of present-day group work. As persons are able to think and act positively toward themselves and others, it is assumed that they will be able to lead more enriched lives. The concept of mutual aid in social work groups, first proposed by William Schwartz (1961) and elaborated upon more fully by Gitterman and Shulman (1986), emphasizes the collaborative power of the group for socialization, problem solving, and community action. In a mutual-aid model, the group members are encouraged to take responsibility for helping one another. The worker takes every opportunity to support and reinforce group members' existing strengths and to enable them to increase their capacities for problem solving and shared helping.

Although clients of social agencies want to feel good about themselves, vestiges of past defeats remain: unfulfilled love, guilt, lack of accomplishments that lessen feelings of self-worth. To be Somebody, to be appreciated as a person even with faults, is a basic striving. If legitimate avenues for success, recognition, and power are not available, some persons will use negative behavior, even self-destructive behavior, to gain attention. Many of these persons may feel emotionally vulnerable, especially when they overemphasize their negative attributes and minimize their positive qualities. Potentially creative and constructive energies are used instead to maintain defenses and ward off further psychic damage. How people are treated by others, especially the family and authority figures from an early age to the present, shape the self-concept. The development of self-esteem is related to the feelings of competence from these early experiences, as discussed by Erikson (1963, 247–274) in the completion of life stages.

Empowerment of group members, another aspect of developing self-esteem, is embodied in the tradition of social group work and should result from the "enabler" role of the group worker (Pernell, 1986, 108). Hurayma and Hurayma (1986) discuss empowerment as both a goal and a process; the role of the group worker is seen as that of helping members get in touch with resources, develop self-knowledge, and learn necessary skills for increased achievement.

☐ *Example of the Task*. At a residential treatment center for children with emotional problems, the group worker organized a Middle Eastern Dance Group for young adolescent girls. The worker had previous experience as a teacher of dance and started the group in response to interest in dance by the girls. The worker dressed in Middle Eastern costume and had other costumes and materials available for the group members to wear. The weekly meeting included a "rap session" at the end of the dancing.

At the second meeting Susan arrived twenty minutes late after seeing a therapist for an individual session. The group had already worked on several steps and demonstrated beginning proficiency in these movements. Susan appeared intimidated upon entering the group. The worker welcomed her and asked for volunteers to "catch Susan up" with the others. Grace helped her with "costuming" (Grace had asked for and received worker's help with her own costume at the beginning of the session). Sarita demonstrated arm and slow movements. The girls had teased Sarita earlier about her clumsiness, but the worker had positively reinforced those steps in which she had done well. Betty efficiently "broke down" and taught Susan the faster body movements. Interestingly, these girls were in conflict at the prior contracting session. Susan quickly caught on, and the session continued. The increase in group cohesion was evident.

In this situation the worker had modeled helping behaviors, and the group members, given the opportunity, responded by helping Susan. As these girls were able to assist Susan, they also became strengthened. They felt better about themselves and received praise from the worker, which reinforced these positive qualities. The norm of mutual aid was introduced, and since it was successful, it is more likely to continue for the benefit of the group members and group itself.

13. Encourage Self-understanding by Group Members.

WORKER ACTIVITY: *Explore with persons in the group the meaning of their behavior. Help them to elaborate on thoughts, feelings, and bodily reactions that will increase the awareness of themselves. Encourage feedback within the group so that the group can become a means of reality testing. Enable the group to recognize inconsistencies between thinking and behavior. Clarify or interpret patterns of behavior or how past events contribute to present functioning. Confront the individuals in the group to examine the consequences of negative or maladaptive behavior.*

For treatment groups, in particular, personal development through self-understanding is a key ingredient of the helping process. Persons who are able to recognize the reasons for their behavior are more able to control what they do. The self-aware person can act more purposefully given an array of choices. Group members bring to the group unresolved conflicts and many personal needs, many of which are in various degrees of fulfillment. Perhaps unwittingly, he or she may use the group to satisfy these needs and in so doing will divert it from its purposes. This happens to some degree in all groups. For the treatment group, one purpose of the group is helping members become more understanding of how they act out their social and psychic needs.

Dealing with these hidden agendas is a task for all groups. It is a delicate situation for groups whose primary purpose is social action, system change, training, or administration. Since the purpose of these groups is task completion rather than personal change, should there be any attention to self-understanding? When personal issues and problems interfere with the group agenda, yes—they need to be addressed. However, in a social action or administrative group, the personal diversion is discussed in relation to helping the group return to the task—not as an issue in itself that requires further probing for greater personal awareness. For instance, in task groups all the support and involvement techniques are used, and group members should be able to express their feelings, but the focus is not on understanding the derivation of behavior. The focus is on completing the task. Feelings and ideas are expressed in order to enhance the problem solving in the group.

Since self-understanding is usually associated with treatment groups, the following illustration brings out worker techniques for enhancing awareness of behavior.

☐ *Example of the Task.* This is the eighth session of an adult treatment group at a community mental health center. The purpose is to enhance group members' ability to interact on an interpersonal level. The goals are to enable them to gain insight and understanding about the behaviors that are creating difficulties for them in daily living. They meet on a weekly basis for one and a half hours. [Parts of this meeting will be used as examples of this section, "Encourage Self-understanding of Group Members," and "Relate Individual Issues to the Group as Whole" (see Task 14).]

The group began with the group worker telling them that Bill, the co-leader, was still sick (he had missed two prior sessions because of illness). He would need time to recuperate but would definitely be joining the group in two weeks.

SHARON: Can I start? Well, I've been thinking a lot about getting older. My birthday is in two and a half weeks, and I'll be twenty-seven. I guess I'm afraid to get older because then people around me get older too, like my parents. I guess I'm afraid of when they're not around, you know, if they die. Does anyone else get fears like that?

BARBARA: Yeah, I know what you mean, I think. I'd just go crazy if my mother died now. We didn't use to be that close, but we have been getting closer in the past two years. She's the only one I can turn to now.

CAROL: I can't even think of what it would be like if my father died. It was too horrible to deal with when my mother died.

WORKER: How old were you then, Carol?

CAROL: I was nineteen. Wow, that was really something when someone dies really quickly without you knowing about it until it's all over. Boy, it's scary!

WORKER: I'm hearing it in different ways, but what people seem to be talking about is fear of losing someone close to you. What do you imagine the fear to be about?

☐ Worker identifies a theme that several group members are feeling—the experiences of loss and abandonment. The technique of exploration is used to help them elaborate and think more about the possible meaning of these feelings.

SHARON: Well, if I had Sid around, it wouldn't make me so afraid. Here I am almost twenty-seven, and I'm not married. What I'd really like for my birthday is a ring, but Sid still doesn't want to get that involved. But I know that if he were around, it wouldn't be scary for me. Don't get me wrong, I love my parents, and it would be terrible if they died, but if there was someone else there, it wouldn't be so hard to cope with. Especially if it was Sid.

WORKER: Sharon, what would having that other person there do for you?

SHARON: I guess I wouldn't feel so lonely like I was abandoned. I don't like being alone. I can if I have to, but I try not to be.

WORKER: So Sharon, let me see if I understand what you've been saying, that part of your fear of losing someone close to you is the feeling of being abandoned or left feeling empty and to have someone around would fill up the empty feeling.

☐ The worker is using the technique of reflection to demonstrate understanding of what the group member is saying.

SHARON: Yeah, I don't know if I would call it empty though, but I guess it would feel like something was missing.

WORKER: I wonder how other people in the group are experiencing what's being discussed?

☐ The worker had a choice—to continue further exploration with Sharon or to involve other group members. She chose the technique of involvement.

BARBARA: I guess when you talk about losing someone, it doesn't have to mean dying, because when I had my kids taken away, I felt like I had nothing left inside of me. Nothing made sense anymore. I didn't even care if I lived or died then. Now that my daughter's with me, I feel things again, but I know it won't feel right until I get my son back.

WORKER: How do you understand having feelings at one point and then not having them at another?

☐ The technique of exploration continues to help Barbara sort out her feelings and look more deeply at the source of her changed reactions.

BARBARA: That's easy, who wants to feel all that pain? I made myself an expert at that since I was a kid.

WORKER: How were you able to find such a foolproof way of protecting yourself?

BARBARA: Well, you had to. My mom never really had too much time for any of us. So we pretty much did our own babysitting with each other. She'd have different guys over all the time. I used to laugh when my little brother would ask one of them if they were our father. By then I didn't care. I just went out and hung out with my friends. I didn't care what she did, and she didn't care what I did. She screwed around with all of these guys and so did I.

The worker guided the group gently into exploring their feelings, using *reflection* to demonstrate listening and seeking *involvement* from the group in regard to their common theme of loss, abandonment, and the resulting pain from such separation. Their fear of closeness and intimacy is obviously affecting relationships with other people. Being able to recognize pain and knowing that other group members have also experienced it may make it less fearsome. The group should feel freer to risk closeness, since they have been able to ventilate their concerns and receive support from the group worker and members.

Self-understanding is occurring as group members become more aware of the meaning of their feelings and how these feelings impact on their behavior.

14. Relate Individual Issues to the Group as a Whole.

WORKER ACTIVITY: *In order to enhance mutual-aid possibilities, seek linkages wherever possible between what individuals are discussing and related interests or concerns within the group. The relationship between the individual and the group is strengthened as you can make these connections. In some cases, a person's issues may represent what others are thinking or feeling, and you might ask if others share what is being said. At other times, persons may inaccurately attempt to speak for the group. When this occurs, it should be recognized and pointed up. At all times group members should be encouraged to speak for themselves.*

The skillful weaving back and forth between group member and group issues strengthens the relationship between the person and group. The commonality of needs, interests, and problems is what brings group members together. The recognition of their common needs and the use of the group for problem solving are primary rationales for group work. A delicate balance is necessary— not to rush so quickly from an individual concern to the group that the group member feels neglected and yet, on the other hand, not to dwell exclusviely on the individual, so that the group becomes a mere audience. During the beginning group meetings, the balance is slightly more toward the individual, since it is important that personal issues become known and appreciated at the outset. As the group continues and develops cohesiveness, members are drawn in more fully.

Each person's actions have meaning for the group. As the interaction unfolds, group members compare, contrast, rank, and evaluate the behavior of others. The linking of individual to group issues brings to the surface what may be the underlying dynamics of how people are relating to each other. It helps the group to mobilize its problem-solving potential. When personal change is a goal, as in treatment groups, the collective strength of the group has healing effects, as group members provide needed resources, offer support, and explore the meaning of behavior with one another.

☐ *Example of the Task.* This is a continuation of the meeting of the adult treatment group that illustrated encouraging self-understanding. Although understanding of behavior is still highlighted, the dimension of relating individual issues to the group as a whole becomes clear as well.

The reader will remember that the worker mentioned to the group when the meeting started that her co-leader, Bill, would be absent for another two weeks because of illness. It just so happens that the theme of discussion is on loss and abandonment. At this point in the meeting, she explores with the group the possible connection of their feelings of loss and Bill's absence.

WORKER: What keeps coming up in my mind about what people are talking about is the fear of feeling close to or trusting and caring for someone and then feeling you're at risk of possibly losing them or that they'd leave you and the feelings that you'd experience then. The emptiness or aloneness. What it reminds me of is what happened here in the group. Where people have been used to Bill and me running the group. He's someone that I think everyone has some type of feelings about, and he hasn't been here for three weeks. Which is a form of loss, even though it's temporary. Can anyone relate the two topics that were being discussed and the issue involving Bill being sick?

☐ Worker reflects what group members are feeling about loss. She explores the meaning of what they are saying and Bill's absence. Worker attempts to bring in the group as a whole.

SHARON: Well, you said he is returning, right? I guess there's a similarity. I was kind of used to having him around, and now it feels kind of different without him being here. I miss him. I like having a male therapist's opinion. Don't get me wrong, what you say is important too. But I really respect a man. Like my father has always given me good advice, so a man's opinion means a lot to me.

WORKER: Sharon, I wonder if there is a similarity between the feelings you experience when your father leaves on business trips and that of Bill not being here?

☐ Worker now focuses on Sharon's concern about her father and Bill's absence—an individual issue.

SHARON: Not close similarities, my father is my father but, yeah, I miss him. But I feel like that when anyone isn't here. Like when John didn't come for two weeks (*turning to John*). You know you had made a promise to come for the first ten sessions. I was disappointed that you didn't show up and keep your promise. That's your business, I guess, but sometimes you have some good things to say.

JOHN: I explained to all of you that I couldn't get a ride in.

SHARON: If you wanted to give me a call, I could have picked you up.

JOHN: Well, it's too late now.

WORKER: John, how are you feeling about what Sharon is bringing up?

JOHN: Kind of backed against the wall. It wasn't intentional for me not showing up. No big deal.

RUTH (*Quietly at first*): Sure it is. There's times I don't want to come, but I still do because I hope I'll get something out of it.

WORKER: Ruth, how do you see why some people might not show up for group?

RUTH: I think they're afraid that maybe people will know too much about them and might end up not liking them.

WORKER: What are some of your reservations about coming to the group?

RUTH: I guess that's it. The more people know about you, you can get hurt. They could decide they don't want you anymore, or you're no good for them.

CAROL: You know that reminds me of my first outpatient appointment. I met this psychologist, and the next day or so he had a heart attack. That's terrible.

WORKER: Are you making any connections for yourself?

CAROL: No, why?

WORKER: I wonder if you had any thoughts that you had something to do with it?

CAROL: (*Laughs.*) Well, I did think it was right after I left. Maybe I just overwhelmed him with my problems, and he just keeled over. Who knows?

WORKER: That's a lot of power to bring on a heart attack in someone, especially if you don't know if he's had a history of them before or anything about his health.

CAROL: I guess I should check that out before I start working in therapy with someone. Do you have a history of heart attacks, or health problems? (*Group laughs.*)

WORKER: I wonder if there's the thought that you might have something to do with Bill's illness?

CAROL: Well, I can't say the thought didn't cross my mind.

The themes of closeness and affection toward others in the group are part of the discussion. These feelings are typical of a middle stage of group development. The fact that some members were able to associate closeness toward others with being hurt emotionally was significant. Being able to discuss the relationship of intimacy and emotional pain means that there is a high trust level in the group—also a characteristic of a more advanced stage of groupness.

The group worker was astute in considering the possible link between loss as expressed by the members and Bill's unavailability. The feelings of guilt are also expressed. Since a group member was able to discuss her perception of how she may have caused Bill's illness, it is likely that others have the same beliefs. The worker's next step would be to see if more members share similar feelings. If the members can recognize their discrepancy in thinking (I like Bill—Bill is sick—I caused his sickness—I am bad—I feel guilty), it may relieve some of the guilt. The net result of their discussion, which includes ventilation of feelings and cognitive understanding, will be their willingness to risk engagement in building relationships.

15. Encourage Responsibility for Action.

WORKER ACTIVITY: *On the basis of an assessment of individual and group maturity, encourage persons to assume as much responsibility as they can handle. Support self-determination. Offer choices or involve group members in the consideration of alternatives for decisions. Ask how group members plan to take responsibility, either for activities within the group or in relation to outside events.*

Taking responsibility is a risk, since there may be failure as well as success. However, each time individuals demonstrate responsible behavior that leads to action, the possibilities for growth and change increase. Group work is action-oriented. The values of taking responsibilities for personal and group development, as well as the betterment of society, remain at the core of social group work practice.

Even with persons who have many limitations for taking responsibility, either because of age, infirmity, or organizational constraints, the worker will offer choices for decision making. These choices can contribute to more personal autonomy and empowerment within the group. In the incremental steps toward increased responsibility, small gains lead to further risk taking. People are able to take responsibility because the group is a supportive environment for change.

☐ *Example of the Task.* The group was meeting on an outpatient basis at a community hospital. All were being treated for breast cancer.

It was clear that Jane was going to die within a few days. Group members were skirting this, and I asked them what they thought was going to happen next. They began to discuss Jane's pending death with a lot of anger over Jane's estranged husband. It appeared too painful to see the part of their anger that was directed just at the situation—after all, in addition to their close relationship with Jane, what was happening was very close to each of them, as they all had been diagnosed with their breast cancers around the same time as Jane. Lots of venting of rage . . . plans to boycott the viewing and the funeral. Asked them what they would need to do for themselves then . . . since they all agreed that staying away from the funeral was for Jane. Lots of discussion followed, with some crying, some physical reaching out to each other. And then a plan—to have the hospital chaplain provide a private memorial service with each of us saying what we wished.

Some raw feelings were exposed by the women in the group. It was the group's trust that allowed for that expression. The "reaching for feelings" and encouraging responsibility for action by the group worker would have met with far different results had the group not moved to this high state of cohesion.

It was obviously important for the women to ventilate their feelings. However, if it stopped at that, the only result would be frustration and further anger without a constructive resolution. When group members bring up problems and feelings associated with them, the group worker gives members an opportunity for a full expression of those emotions. But once the problem and feelings are identified, it is then necessary to look at the choices of what they can do about it. Even small decisions can help.

There are some cautions, however, about encouraging expression of feelings. If it is done too early in the group, before sufficient trust and groupness have taken place, some people may become overwhelmed by anxiety from the intensity of the feelings, and then withdraw from the group. Facilitating exposure of feelings needs to be moderated according to the stage of group development. As in the example above about the women with breast cancer, the group members could tolerate the emotional release because the level of group cohesion and trust was high.

Tasks: The Group

When the group enters into the middle stage, its members are still searching for appropriate roles for themselves and determining their status in relation to others in the group. Internal leadership within the group may still be in a state of flux. As the trust level builds in the group, with increased acceptance of one another's shared values and greater acceptance of differences, communication is freer, and there is a need for conflict negotiation. Purposes may become redefined as previously unavowed goals are expressed. Group members feel freer to accept challenges for increasing their self-awareness or using creativity in accomplishing tasks. Group members feel more a part of the group as their beliefs and behavior practices are incorporated into the norms of the group. The tasks that emphasize groupness are meant to deepen the group's abilities to solve problems, by enhancing their relationship to one another.

16. Recognize and Negotiate Conflict.

WORKER ACTIVITY: *When conflict occurs, attempt to involve group members in identifying its source. If the conflict is related to an issue within the group, treat it as an opportunity for a broader discussion of alternatives in problem solving. Validate the differences being raised in a conflict situation. Encourage communication to represent the points of view. Seek possible areas of agreement. If the conflict seems related to a displaced emotion from outside the group, attempt to help the group member or group recognize it as coming from an outside source. Attempt to relate it to an issue within the group or to a generalized concern that may involve more persons in the group. In some cases, it is helpful to seek a goal or project where people need to work together to accomplish the goal (superordinate goal), creating more positive feelings for one another.*

Conflict can be destructive or a stimulator of growth. It is usually perceived as negative when there is an attack on a person or the group. It may be a displacement of anger that stems from outside the group. When these hidden agendas surface, it is difficult to understand them, since their source is not known.

The conflict may be the result of transference—an emotional reaction toward someone in the group that has its source in some significant person in the member's private life. Yalom (1975, 41) refers to transference as "a specific form of interpersonal perceptual distortion." For instance, it is not uncommon for group members to have feelings for the group leader, positive or negative, that are related to unresolved attachments to other authority figures, such as a parent or teacher. In group therapy, issues of transference become the central focus of treating personal problems. Unless group workers are trained to practice group therapy and deal with the unconscious feelings that may underlie these transferences, it is best not to probe for the deeper meaning behind them.

When conflict occurs that seems to have its roots outside the group, the worker needs to find out more about how persons are perceiving the problem. In this way the worker is in a better position to understand the meaning of the situation in order to intervene appropriately. Whenever possible, person-directed conflict that is a form of "tension release" (Bernstein, 1973, 77) should be related to a topical issue facing the group. When the conflict is in the form of a realistic issue, it can be more rationally understood and resolved.

Controversy, a milder version of conflict, often means the expression of opposing views and can be a natural occurrence during problem solving as a means of sorting out ideas and feelings. The worker may introduce a norm that differences are acceptable, for the group can benefit from the richness of alternative approaches. Conflict or controversy is an expected part of the beginning phase of group life. The worker encourages clear communication and the use of feedback as a means of clarification. Selective listening, double messages (one communication having two and often opposing meanings), and emotionally charged words contribute to distorted communication.

As members present a range of values and behaviors from other reference groups, the group needs to deal with these differences within the context of group purposes. Some may be accommodated, others rejected or modified. The process of resolution can be controversial. Conflict is also part of the phase of intimacy and maturation within the middle phase of the group. By this time it represents a level of group member achievement in the continuing pursuit of individuality within the group.

☐ *Example of the Task.* In the group of mildly retarded young men described in Chapter 6, there were a series of conflict situations involving John and the other group members. John demonstrated resistance to participating in the group, possibly because of his fears of rejection. By the fifth meeting, the group developed more cohesion and a willingness to risk new social experiences. They want to go to a restaurant in the community for dinner. John resists, and hostility is expressed toward him about being a deviant in the group.

WORKER: Is it agreed with everybody that we want to eat out?

☐ INVOLVEMENT: Seeks consensus or indications of resistance as a basis for further planning.

TED: It's agreed with me.

WORKER: Outside next week.

☐ SEEKING INFORMATION: Continues focus on participation in planning.

BOB: If it's agreed with you, raise your hand.

MOST OF THE BOYS: I.

BOB: Do you agree with all of us (*focusing on John*), do you agree?

(*John does not want to eat out.*)

JACK: Why not?

BOB: Even if he didn't agree, we'd still win because—how many, one-two-three-four-five.

JACK: How about you, Mr. Rogers?

BOB: What do you agree, Mr. Rogers? It's actually your idea. It's up to you.

WORKER: It's up to you fellows.

☐ ACCEPTANCE: Demonstrate belief in their self-determination.

BOB: It's OK then.

WORKER: Would you like to eat out (*referring to John*), what do you think?

☐ SEEKING INFORMATION: Wants to know John's thinking so he could discuss his feelings of resistance within group.

JOHN: I'm used to eating here.

JACK: Oh, man.

BOB: Wait a minute. One can't mess up the whole bunch. You forget it takes one apple to spoil everything so we can't actually let . . .

WORKER: Don't you think we might want to let John tell us . . .

☐ ENCOURAGING IDEAS AND FEELINGS: Gives John an opportunity to respond so issue of resistance could be discussed in group.

BOB: Wait a minute. Let John explain why he don't want to eat out.

JOHN: I'll tell you why. Because I'm used to the prices here, and I like coming right from work right to here.

WORKER: I guess you're used to the Y, you know people here and you know what to expect. If you go to a different place, everything is going to be new to you.

☐ ACCEPTANCE: Expresses empathy for what John may be feeling—joins with resistance.

TED: It's going to be new to us, too.

BOB: It's going to be new to us, too, Mr. Rogers, but that's the only way you can make friends. How do you expect to make friends?

WORKER: You figure this is the way of learning.

☐ REFRAMING: Puts desire for new experiences in positive context of learning.

The worker's assessment is that John is feeling insecure about facing a new and challenging social situation. His past history at the residential school and in the group reflects these fears and his resistance to meeting new people. John needs support as a person who is valued. It would be helpful for these concerns to be expressed by John, so that the problem could be identified and discussed for problem solving. If it seems that John is unaware of his pattern of defense or reluctant to deal with it, the worker may raise the issue with the group about the possibility of group-member ambivalence regarding eating at a restaurant. If some of the group members could bring out their reservations, it might enable John to do the same. If this did happen, the group members would be exercising leverage on John to be more open about his feelings.

On the basis of this assessment, the worker works on two levels—helping John to identify the problem and encouraging group-member decision making about eating out. With encouragement from the worker, Bob says, "Let John explain why he don't want to eat out." This opens up the possibility of discussion by John and others in the group about what it will mean to have supper at a restaurant in the community. With considerable pressure on John from the group, the worker offers support by joining with John's resistance. The intent of this worker technique was to lessen the threat to John and, possibly, to increase his receptivity to a discussion of his feelings about not wanting to eat out.

17. Redefine Group Purposes.

WORKER ACTIVITY: *If the original contract seems to be changing or is becoming more ambiguous, ask whether persons are still clear about the group purposes or whether there needs to be more time to clarify the original intent. When additional purposes are identified, consider with the group whether these should be included and what their meaning is for the group.*

There could be many reasons why people join groups. Initially, some of these reasons seem primary and are the basis for developing a contract on what they will do with other group members. For instance, a mother participates in a Parent Group to learn how she can be more helpful to her young son, who is having problems in school. She is also having marital conflict but is not in the group to examine personal behavior in relation to her marriage. However, it becomes more apparent, as parents discuss relationships with their children, that the marital situation has a bearing on the child's behavior and performance in school. As the parents recognize that link of family environment and reactions of children, they may want to shift or broaden the group purpose to include personal issues of the parents themselves. If and when this occurs, the original contract needs to be renegotiated to include this broader focus.

The contract should always be clear and acceptable to the group worker and members. The clarity of the contract allows the group worker to focus the activity on those areas that will enable the group members to fulfill their purposes. The contract may change several times in the life of the group, depending upon the needs or interests of the group members, the stage of group development, and environmental circumstances. Each time this happens, the group should be aware of its changing boundary.

☐ *Example of the Task.* This group is for parents of handicapped children, meeting at a community mental health agency. They utilize a mutual-aid and problem-solving approach, focusing on issues of individual, family, school, and community interaction to meet the special needs of the handicapped child. The group is open to new members and for recontracting with existing parents after each eight-week segment.

The meeting being described is the last one of the eight-week period. Most members are planning to continue. There has been some discontent expressed about the direction of the group and a desire for a change. Specifically, there was a split between those who wanted to use the group for the expression of feelings and others who wished to spend more time in exchanging resources.

The group worker asked members how they would like to see the group's focus change to better meet their needs. Some members said they would like more concrete problem solving and resource sharing. The worker asked if others saw this as a priority and something to develop further. Betty stated her desire that the group not become too task-oriented. She stated that she sometimes felt like the only one expressing feelings. The worker offered support for her risk taking and asked if others shared her concerns. Gloria stated that she had come to count on Betty to express what "we all sometimes feel." The worker asked Betty what she would like from the group when she's feeling like the only one bringing out feelings. Betty said she hoped others would express their feelings—she can't assume the responsibility of being the only one. The worker reflected on what was happening in the group, sharing the observation that some group members wanted to be more task-oriented and others more open about their feelings. Charles stated that he wished other group members would share the responsibility for providing the group with more resource information. The worker encouraged others to help in this way.

The worker asked the group to consider how the meetings might be structured to meet both the expressive and task needs of the group.

In the parents' group, the group purpose seemed to incorporate the range of needs, from personal to community action. The group worker reflected their concerns and helped them explore ways to incorporate their interests into the ongoing operation of the group.

Every group should attend to the socioemotional aspects of group life and the need to do something, such as accomplish a task or solve a problem. Depending on the purpose and type of group, the socioemotional or task elements will often predominate. If the group becomes too heavily invested in one direction or the other, there may be group member dissatisfaction or more reduced accomplishment than the group could expect. For instance, if a treatment group spends all of its time on the ventilation of feelings, without considering what group members will do with these feelings to solve a problem, the group could experience excessive anxiety and frustration in having feelings exposed without any further resolution. On the other end of the continuum, if an administrative group is so task-oriented that it does not offer support, recognize feelings, or involve group members in the decision-making process, there can be dissatisfaction with the group and actually less productivity in the long run. There is a need for some balance of both the expressive and task dimensions, although one or the other may be weighted more heavily according to the purpose of the group.

18. Build Relationships and Group Cohesion.

WORKER ACTIVITY: *Relationship building involves the demonstration of acceptance, caring, empathy, and being genuine as a person. You are able to "start where people are" and continue to be responsive to group member needs and the group as a whole. You are an active listener, giving indication that you either understand what the person is saying or are willing to ask questions for further clarification. Your use of language is clear, voice tone consistent with the presenting situation, body posture responsive, facial appearance expressive with appropriate affect. Building group cohesion means involving the group in decision making, contributing to a healthful climate in the group and permitting the group to exercise its autonomy when it is ready.*

The relationship of group worker and members of the group is the foundation for helping. While the technical skills of the professional are important in the problem-solving process, the basic determinant of success in the group will be whether the worker has been able to convey nonpossessive warmth, empathy, and genuineness in relationships with group members. In writing about effective casework practice, Fischer (1978, 191) cites these characteristics of the helper as being the only ones identified with successful outcome in treatment. Basically, group members want to be respected as having personal worth. Persons in the group can understand that others may not accept their beliefs or actions, but they still want and need the affection that comes from caring and concern for their well-being.

The helping relationship should be established during pregroup forming and at the very beginning of the group. It obviously will continue throughout the various phases of the group, using affectional ties to build trust and cohesiveness. The group worker serves as a role model for group members in building relationships with one another. The middle phase, especially the stage of intimacy, exhibits more open communication and a willingness to have closer ties. By this time group members are becoming more cohesive through their involvement in decision making and collaboration regarding future directions. The group worker is mindful of ways to continue the give-and-take of relationships.

☐ *Example of the Task.* Use of activity is a way to enhance interaction with this children's group, ages eight to ten. They are meeting through the mental health service of an army community hospital. The five youngsters have all been traumatized (abuse, molestation, abandonment) and meet weekly to enable them to trust others, appropriately share feelings, modify acting-out behaviors to appropriate social behavior, and encourage peer interaction.

The activity this day was a game in which masking tape with the name of a famous person or character is put on the child's forehead. The object is to guess the name that has been taped to one's forehead, and other members give hints as to the identity. This activity was used to promote group interaction and cooperation. Some members wanted the group worker to play. She set the guideline that all the members would discuss the character, agree on the choice, and then she would play. Once the character was agreed upon, she accepted the group's decision and played with the rest of them. This part of the activity was the first opportunity the group had to work together and cooperate. Afterward, there was reinforcement (verbal) for the cooperation and creativity.

This little gain in cooperative behavior could be viewed as a step toward larger achievements. The reinforcement of their working together added a measure of self-esteem and increased the possibility of more socially desirable behavior. For the group members to take some control of their environment is important for their developing autonomy. The development of cohesiveness or a "we" feeling takes place as group members can experience what happens in a group. It is a shared engagement and mutual responsibility between group worker and members.

19. Clarify Norms and Roles.

WORKER ACTIVITY: *Norms are established modes of acting or standards that are typical for a particular group, such as starting and ending meetings on time or shared participation. Roles are specific behaviors that are used in certain situations, such as being an initiator of group activity or the critical evaluator in a group. Norms that support the accomplishment of group objectives need to be introduced, defined, and reinforced. The use of constructive roles should also be clarified and reinforced. Helping roles of the worker will serve as a model for group members to use some of these behaviors.*

All groups need rules and regulations so group members know what they can and cannot do. These rules are often imposed by the organization, because they make sense in the best judgment of the administration. Once the group begins to meet and persons act in accordance with their own values, they may or may not accept the expected behavior of the agency or group worker. When practices within the group are accepted by the group members, they become the norms.

The development of norms can be part of the testing of the power of the group worker during the beginning phase of the group. The group members may deviate from stated expectations in order to see if the worker will adhere to these standards in the face of their nonconformity. For instance, the meeting is supposed to start at 3:00 P.M., but the group worker waits until 3:15 P.M. to begin in order to accommodate latecomers. If this practice continues for the second meeting, it is likely that even those group members who hitherto have arrived on time will now come a little later. If the group worker continues to delay the scheduled starting, a norm has developed that meetings don't start on time.

Group members with more status and power will have greater ability to influence norm development. Since group members need acceptance by the group, they may be swayed toward norms that are favored by these indigenous leaders. The group worker needs to know which norms to be firm about and which ones he or she is willing to compromise on. For instance, the norm of lateness may lead to a negotiation about a different time to meet, whereas a norm of several persons talking at the same time is one the worker may decide to change. At any rate, norms can be an important source of behavior enforcement, especially when they develop from the combined value systems of persons in the group.

Roles may be formal and informal. Depending upon the needs within the group, persons will usually adopt informal roles to help accomplish group purposes. The two most common distinctions of roles are those that address socioemotional needs and others that are essentially task-oriented. A combination and balance of both kinds of roles are helpful to the group. Roles can be prescribed in order to influence changes in behavior. For instance, a quiet member might participate in role play where there is an expectation of more assertive, active behavior. If the person gets positive reinforcement for this kind of behavior, he or she may be willing to move somewhat in that direction in the normal course of interaction.

☐ *Example of the Task.*   This is the ninth meeting of a group of inner city black adults who are experiencing poverty and alcoholism. It is part of an alcoholism rehabilitation program of a community action agency.

The group worker is attempting to challenge a norm that has developed in the group of sharing past experiences or storytelling. It may be a way for them to defend against an examination of their current behavior.

Bob often talked about being arrested and sent to prison. He talked about stealing a police car. The worker asks if he is trying to figure out why he did it. A little later Bob shares with the group what it was like in prison. The worker asks if the experiences of being confined have something to do about how he was feeling right now in the group.

A practice question is how much to confront this norm and seek to have them change it. Is it best to accept this behavior as a protection which they need at this time in their lives? Since they were showing signs of closeness in talking about wanting to help one another, it seemed appropriate for gentle exploration of the meaning of their behavior. Being in an intimacy phase of group development suggested that there was some trust in being able to discuss their relationships with one another in the group.

It may be difficult to change these or other norms that offer a defense against introspection. Although self-awareness was one of the purposes of the group, it was also recognized that group members were facing poverty, discrimination, lack of formal education, and unemployment—a host of environmental factors that contributed to life stress and feelings of being defeated. They needed to be able to use the group to learn about community resources, become motivated to participate in training programs, learn social skills, and receive support for their strengths.

Norms need to be developed, if possible together with the group members, in order to foster the accomplishment of these group purposes. If members are not able to demonstrate certain roles that move the group toward these objectives, the group worker must become more active in fulfilling whatever helping roles are necessary. The group worker's example will enable group members to exercise leadership when they are ready and able to do so.

20. Continue Problem-Solving to Complete Personal and Group Objectives.

WORKER ACTIVITY: *Problem solving is an ongoing activity of the group. It is a continuation of the process of planning (see no. 8) that was started in the* *beginning stage. During the middle stage, you should be able to expect the group to take increasing responsibility for defining the issue or problem and work toward constructive solutions.*

Each time a problem is introduced into the group, the worker and group members will need to consider its meaning and eventual resolution. In the beginning phase, there may be a sharing of many problems and the ventilation of feelings that accompanies the disclosure. While this continues to some extent in the middle phase, there is usually more togetherness and direction by this time, to focus on areas that have more personal risk in their self-disclosure. The redefining of problems may bring out issues that were too sensitive for discussion at first. Group members feel greater emotional safety, and the boundaries of confidentiality are more secure, so that communication is open and reciprocal. The informal leadership structure has developed to the point where group members are able to exercise greater responsibility for planning and action. The group worker accepts this shift and supports group member initiative and assertiveness.

□ *Example of the Task.* A student-assistance counselor in a high school meets weekly with adolescents who are at risk of using drugs. The group provides a place where these students can discuss topics of interest to them, some of which are related to substance abuse. Students are referred by an interdisciplinary team.

A girl, Wendy, who previously did not seek help from the group or disclose personal information said that she would like to tell the group something and asked if they could keep it secret. The group members nodded. Wendy told them that, while she was in another state at a fraternity house party, a girl came up to her and made a pass. She wondered what the group thought of this. The worker looked to the group to respond. They reacted with "EUU!" They discussed homosexuality generally in a negative light. The worker sensed that it was too threatening to discuss this subject, and they seemed unwilling to pursue what may have been Wendy's potential lesbianism. The tone of the group was "us against them" (heterosexuals versus homosexuals). The worker intervened to say that homosexuality was common, and that group members were going through a period in which they were choosing a sexual orientation. The worker also pointed out that people sometimes changed orientation after high school. Wendy brought up the fact that sexual preference is often seen as a continuum from homosexuality to heterosexuality, and that people may find themselves anywhere on the continuum.

The group discussed something else. Wendy turned to me and said she hoped the group would keep what she said confidential. The worker told her to say that to the group. She did, and they reassured her.

This was the beginning of Wendy's use of the group to discuss her concerns. The topic of sexuality is one of great interest to teenagers, but they feel awkward in discussing this topic and in exploring their own sexual identity. Wendy may have been exploring the group's reaction to see if she could go one step further and discuss her own feelings about homosexuality. The worker might have asked Wendy what it felt like to have someone approach her sexually when she was not interested in her. However, this was not what Wendy was asking, and it may have been premature to have her self-disclose more than she was ready.

There is another factor which limited the worker's use of the exploration technique. The group only meets for forty minutes—the time for a regular class period. The shortness of the time presents a constraint on the depth to which the group can discuss a problem. Because of this restriction and the fact that the group only meets for eight weeks (they can recontract for another eight weeks), means that the group should take on more of a socioeducational rather than a treatment focus. If group members really want to resolve social or emotional problems, they could be referred to a community agency where there are fewer limits on what they can discuss. The problem-solving aspect of this kind of group would be to learn how to clarify the meaning of a problem, use themselves and the worker to gain additional knowledge about it, and consider the choices they have for decision making. They would be learning the skills of problem solving and receiving support from the group in this process.

Tasks: The Environment

The roles of the group worker encompass many helping functions. The worker with a commitment to environmental modification, which will contribute to group member and group needs, works with the group to achieve system change, if this becomes necessary. With social action or administrative groups, system change is part of the group purpose, and it seems more obvious how the environment will impact on the group. However, even for treatment or socioeducation groups some aspects of the family, organization, or community will influence personal behavior. When environmental forces can be mobilized to support group member functioning, there is a greater possibility that persons will be able to reach their goals. It may not be a question of personal or environmental goals. The skill of the worker will be to engage the person/group/environment relationship in such a way that common needs and interests are identified, and there is reciprocal nurturing.

21. Mediate Differences Between Group and Environment.

WORKER ACTIVITY: *With mediation, an attempt is made to bring together those persons from the group and environment to discuss their* *perceptions of the issue or problem. If these persons can agree on the nature of the problem, it becomes a matter of problem solving to seek a solution. Every effort is made for persons to feel at ease. Sides are not taken. There is an attempt to help persons recognize how they are affecting one another and to support mutual feedback. Differences are identified and explained. Areas of commonality are located, especially where they serve the interests of both parties. With these commonalities in mind, creative solutions are sought which involve input from all those participating in the mediation effort.*

In introducing the mediating role of the social worker in the group, Schwartz (1961) makes the assumption that the individual and society reach out to each other for mutual fulfillment. In social system terms, the person, group, and environment are interrelated and linked within a boundary of common need and interest. Often obstacles interfere with these symbiotic relationships. When people communicate, different values and social backgrounds bring varied perceptions of meaning to their exchange. Feedback—the shared reactions to the impact of the message, from the receiver to the initiator—increases awareness of the meaning of communication. During mediation, clarification of the meaning of communication can bring about a commonality of views and interests amidst the diversity of thoughts and feelings. The recognition of this mutuality can create collective energy for those involved and lead toward integration as a means of problem solving. In integration as a form of conflict resolution, those involved in a dispute often develop a more creative and satisfying solution than either party had proposed (Follett, 1941). This usually happens when the problem is addressed in a new way, perhaps extending the original boundaries of thinking.

The group worker attempts to build the conditions for trust so that open communication is possible. Although commonality of interests is the bond, persons still need to have their specific interests and views validated. Personal thoughts and feelings are seen as a mark of individuality, which persons often want to maintain. If persons can feel that some of their diversity is acceptable, it is more likely that they will want to seek out the commonalities. The group worker will first want to have persons in the group agree on the nature of the problem. The mediation effort is essentially collaborative problem solving in action.

☐ *Example of the Task.* On a psychiatric ward of thirty men, the group worker organized a patient government program. Patient representatives were chosen in an interesting way. The dining room was arranged for the patients to sit at five separate tables, and six to a table. The group worker rearranged the tables so that indigenous leaders were distributed among all the tables. This was done by the use of a sociogram, which is a charting of chosen relationships in a group. Patients were asked to select three persons that they would like to have at their table. Natural subgroupings were identified from their selection. As much as possible, patients were able to sit with some of those that they had chosen. After the seating arrangement was completed, each table was asked to select a patient representative for their ward program. Usually the indigenous leaders were picked. This plan also served as a good means of enhancing communication about ward activities, since the leaders were the ones who were more likely to talk to those at the table.

A "management" problem arose one day. Some of the patients who were supposed to do the dishes in an alphabetical rotation system refused this assignment. Other patients who had to take their place became angry. To try to resolve this problem, the five patient representatives met with the head nurse and group worker as mediator. They decided that dishwashing would be the responsibility of each table on a rotating basis. Patients at the table would be given the responsibility of deciding who would do the dishes at their table. There was less resistance to this idea since patients had more control in decision making, and there was group support as well as peer pressure to handle this assignment.

In working toward solving the dishwashing situation, the problem was clearly identified. From an administrative point of view, the patients had to wash the dishes. Leaving it up to the group to decide how this would be carried out was more therapeutic, since it involved patients in making decisions and handling responsibility for their living arrangement. The head nurse could accept this plan, because it was consistent with the therapeutic purpose of care for the patients. It was regarded more positively by the patients since they had more power to control this aspect of their ward responsibility. It also was a task that contributed to greater cohesion in their table group.

This small group could also make decisions about other group living situations. It offered a structure that allowed for mediating differences of the group and its ward environment. The group worker met with the table representatives to consider wider ward activities as well as to resolve any problems that arose. It was also possible for the group worker to meet with a separate table group and act as a mediator for problems within the small group. He acted as a resource to the patient representatives in regard to their group leadership issues. This professional function is similar to what might take place in the community when a group worker might act as a consultant to a self-help group.

The solution to the dishwashing problem was an illustration of integration as a means of resolving conflict. Neither party to the dispute had to compromise its position. The way it was handled served the therapeutic purpose of the ward staff and patients. It also allowed for some trade-offs. Some patients who preferred washing dishes might arrange to do that chore rather than something else that needed to be done. A few of the patients who refused to wash the dishes might change their minds because decision making was left up to the small group. However, they could also trade off with other patients for jobs that were more to their liking. It offered a flexible and yet efficient system for ward management as well as therapeutic gain for the patients.

22. Advocate for Change or Additional Services.

WORKER ACTIVITY: *When some part of the environment is creating an obstacle to the group (e.g., a discriminatory practice by a housing authority), one might exercise influence on behalf of the group or for an individual in the group. Advocacy involves explaining the needs or problems of individuals or the group to those in the environment who are able to make the necessary changes. This kind of communication can increase understanding of the issue or problem and enhance the possibilities of a successful resolution. Advocacy also occurs when working with persons in the agency or community to gain access to resources or opportunities that will benefit group members.*

The group worker encourages group members to take responsibility for being assertive about their needs. This may take the form of members advocating for themselves when they face barriers in their life situations. The group could be a place where these assertiveness skills are learned, and if the group worker uses assertion in the group, his or her example will serve as a model for group members.

When it is not feasible for group members to act in their own behalf, either because of age, handicap, or circumstance, the worker will assume this responsibility. It is done with the conviction that the environment needs to be supportive for growth of the individual and group. Many positive changes could be taking place in the group. However, when group members leave the group, they may face pressures to maintain their previous patterns of behavior, some of which may be dysfunctional. This will often occur with families, where the changed behavior of a family member who has been in treatment will be perceived as a threat to the family balance. In other situations, the obstacles to positive growth may be within an organization or the community.

In an advocacy role, the worker uses his or her influential position and professional skills to exercise leverage for needed services on behalf of the group or group members. When it is possible to join with others in coalition to support these changes, it is more likely to succeed. Besides securing additional resources, there may also be advocacy to change policies and procedures to ones that are more favorable for clients. This is especially important when discriminatory practices limit opportunities for enrichment, treatment, or basic needs, such as housing.

When one or more persons outside the group are identified as barriers, the group worker will need to develop the necessary communication to explain the problem and enlist the support of these outsiders. Many times the obstacles are not presented maliciously. There may be a difference in perception—the group sees it one way, persons who seem to be barriers see it another way. Once the situation is explained, there may be more commonality than expected. This type of communication for purposes of clarification is similar to what might happen in a mediation effort. However, in mediation the worker enables two parties to reach a better understanding of their differences and work toward a solution. In advocacy the worker takes a position to influence a person, group, or organization on behalf of clients. The influence of the worker can obviously be important, since this person has or represents power that can be used for negotiation. The group members may have minimal power and therefore be discounted in trying to deal constructively with influential persons in the environment.

☐ *Example of the Task.* A group worker provided services to tenants of a low-income apartment house, including primarily blacks and Hispanics. In the initial assessment, the worker found that two extended families and their friends composed about half the resident population. These family groupings were in conflict with one another. It was also found that the leaders were the women of each family. In trying to decide on where to begin, the worker asked people in the building what they considered to be their major needs or problems. Since the worker wanted to create more of a mutual-helping climate in the building, so that the residents could work cooperatively, the need for conflict negotiation between the families seemed obvious. However, the tenants also complained about the lack of heat and hot water for three weeks. The repairs had been promised, but there were delays. The tenants became angrier.

The worker used the inadequate physical conditions of the building, such as the heating situation, to bring the families together. The worker acted as advocate to contact various persons who might be able to help. Before contacting the building agent who was responsible for repairs, the worker met with a Legal Aid lawyer to find out more about tenant rights. Other professionals, such as the social worker from the Department of Social Services, were also involved for additional advice and support. The tenant families planned a strategy with the group worker to involve the building agent in a direct confrontation. During this meeting, the families, with the help of the worker, presented the problem of the repeated delays of repairing the heating and other inadequacies in the building. Now that the families were joined in their demands, it was more difficult to avoid their concerns. The group worker was also forceful in bringing out the needs as he saw it.

Although the living conditions seemed like the more urgent need (partializing and prioritizing the problem), it was necessary that the residents should cooperate in the plan for solving their problems. The urgency of improving their living conditions became primary and served to bring the tenants together to communicate about their needs. This superordinate goal overshadowed their rivalries and lessened their conflict. The social worker used his knowledge of the community to locate persons who could be resources in providing more valuable information (tenant rights) or skills (bargaining) to assist the residents in influencing the building department. The group worker took a large part of the leadership in these initial encounters with persons in the community. However, as the two families and their friends were able to coalesce in regard to their common need (living conditions), their informal relationships were somewhat rearranged. The energy devoted to internal dissension was now redirected toward their common problem. The empowerment that resulted from their unity was channeled into assertive behavior in their session with the building agent.

23. Collaborate with Other Professionals.

WORKER ACTIVITY: *This is similar to the development of a support network (see no. 11). However, in this kind of function, a team approach with other professionals provides an array of services in behalf of the individuals and/or group.*

Social workers often join with other professionals to coordinate services, enlist additional resources, and collaborate in helping clients. A basic premise of social work is that the "whole person" must be considered in any intervention plan. This may require a team approach of persons within the agency or, in some cases, on an interdisciplinary basis. Treating the whole person may mean working with the family, arranging for job-training skills or referral to a leisure-time agency for recreation. When various professionals work together to assist in individual, group, or system change, they need to communicate with each other about their activities, so that there is consistency in their helping approach. Without the joint planning and exchange of ideas, professionals may be working at cross purposes with one another.

With the pressures of time and productivity in many agencies, there is sometimes resistance to collaboration. Professionals may not always agree with what other agency persons are doing with the clients they are both seeing. They may not be willing to risk the competition or confrontation that could result from sharing strategies or interventions. Confidentiality may also be a factor in reducing possibilities for collaboration. Clients should give their permission for information to be shared with other professionals. Some clients may be reluctant to reveal personal data outside the agency. In these cases, the client's right to confidentiality should be respected.

At times staff in the helping professions will collaborate to resolve social problems in the community. The responsibility for arranging such a meeting usually rests with whatever social agency or governmental body is willing to initiate such action.

☐ *Example of the Task.* Elected officials of a township committee became concerned about the increased drug use and crime among juveniles. They organized a Task Force on Youth and invited professionals who served the youth population to participate in planning and proposing programs to deal with these problems. Staff from the police, health department, family counseling, recreation, schools, and child protective agencies were called together as the initial planning group. The township manager chaired the meeting. After they explored and defined the problem, it was recognized that several agencies were working with youth without any knowledge of what others were doing. There was unnecessary overlap of services, which proved to be costly to the community and confusing for the youth and their families.

The sharing of information on the Task Force about what agencies were doing was helpful. Some staff agreed to cooperate on joint projects. The Task Force on Youth became an ongoing collaborative organization. A Family Service Agency was able to get some funding from the United Community Fund for a part-time staff person to develop a delinquency prevention program. This person arranged for a joint program with staff from the police department, high school, and recreation department to serve adolescents who were at risk of becoming juvenile offenders. Adolescent life-skills groups were started at the high school, at different times by staff from the community and school.

The Task Force on Youth expanded to include parent and student representatives from the high school. During the monthly meetings, there was continued communication about what agencies were doing and how they could work together. There were also community workshops on issues relevant to adolescents and their families, a Youth in Action program for adolescents to take responsibility for planning and implementing youth programs, a booklet on community resources for referral purposes, and a survey on problems of youth so that subcommittees of professionals, parents, and young people could collaborate in planning programs regarding the most pressing adolescent needs.

Collaboration does not have to take the elaborate form of the Task Force on Youth. It may mean that a school, wanting to develop a better system of using community resources, will invite in representatives of frequently used agencies to discuss a strategy of cooperation. Any agency person could initiate collaborative activity. Although the resistance that was mentioned earlier is real, there are also many benefits to joint sharing. With less duplication of services, staff will not be pulled in so many directions. The pooling of ideas may lead to more creativity in shaping intervention plans. Staff could also test out their thinking on one another and be a source of support.

The Task Force on Youth was innovative since it included parents and youth as well as agency representatives. Professionals sometimes make the mistake of planning programs for adolescents without sufficient input from youth. Young people want to be involved and take responsibility for their future. Being able to participate in some level of decision making with community persons is a step into adulthood for the teens.

Collaboration takes time. Many agency staff persons balk at extra meetings, which sometimes are nonproductive, so a useful design for cooperative sharing is to hold luncheon meetings on some kind of regular basis. Professionals are usually interested in expanding their resource network and can see the benefit of joint communication as making their jobs easier. When collaboration cannot take place in the form of a meeting among professionals, the telephone can be a help in acquiring information that can be helpful to clients.

The role of the group worker in regard to group/environment tasks can provide a bridge to community social work. The skills of mediation, advocacy, and collaboration should be part of every social worker's professional repertoire. They add a dimension of breadth to the array of intervention possibilities.

SUMMARY

The middle stage, encompassing intimacy and maturation, is when most of the work of the group takes place. During this time, person and group are separate but related. The group is meant to enhance individuality. There are varying degrees of emphasis toward the person, group, or environment and their interrelationship. The tasks that have been outlined address what the group worker can do to create a more favorable climate for individual growth, group development, and environmental responsiveness to the needs of those in the group and the group as an entity.

Not all these tasks are useful for every group. For groups oriented to personal change, there will be more of a balance toward the individual but always within the context of the group experience. With task groups, the group and environment become more prominent in the worker's activity, but never to the neglect of the individual. The variety of practice examples points up the applicability of these tasks to many types of groups and situations.

The ending stage in the following chapter will continue to highlight group work tasks during this crucial and often undervalued period in the life of the group. This is a phase of transition for the group. How termination is handled will often shape the direction of future relationships with other people.

REFERENCES

Bernstein, S. (1973). Conflict and group work. In S. Bernstein (Ed.), *Exploration in group work* (pp. 72–106). Boston: Milford House.

Erikson, E. H. (1963). *Childhood and society* (2nd ed.). New York: W. W. Norton.

Fischer, J. (1978). *Effective casework practice*. New York: McGraw-Hill.

Follett, M. P. (1941). In H. C. Metcalf & L. Urick (Eds.), *Dynamic administration: The collected papers of Mary Parker Follett*. New York: Harper & Row.

Gitterman, A., & Shulman, L. (1986). The life model, mutual aid, and the mediating function. In A. Gitterman & L. Shulman (Eds.), *Mutual aid groups and the life cycle* (pp. 3–22). Itasca, IL: F. E. Peacock.

Hirayama, H. & Hirayama, K. (1986). *Empowerment through group participation: Process and goal* (pp. 119–131). New York: Haworth Press.

Pernell, R. B. (1986). Empowerment and social group work. In M. Parnes (Ed.), *Innovations in social group work: Feedback from practice to theory* (pp. 107–117). New York: Haworth Press.

Schwartz, W. (1961). The social worker in the group. *New Perspectives on services to groups: Theory, organization, practice* (pp. 7–34). New York: National Association of Social Workers.

Yalom, I.D. (1975). *The theory and practice of group psychotherapy* (2nd ed.). New York: Basic Books.

TEACHING AND LEARNING IDEAS

1. Select three tasks from the middle stage and write a narrative account of how you carried out each task.

2. Do a content analysis of a process recording of a group by identifying every technique of the worker. Attempt to match the technique with a task. Locate clusters of worker techniques for each task.

3. In an analysis of a group recording, video, or audio tape, what are the relative frequencies of tasks that emphasize the person, group, or environment? Do you notice any trends from person to group or group to person? If so, can you account for this occurrence?

4. Construct a simple questionnaire that identifies all the tasks of the middle phase with a brief description of each task. Send this instrument out to social workers in the community who have groups in the middle phase. Notice similarities and differences in responses and make some assumptions about the differences. Does this suggest any research topics?

CHAPTER 10

The Ending

Endings in groups are often difficult. There is the need to separate from the closeness of relationships. The comfort and security of a known structure will be gone. There may be the anxiety of starting something new. In terms of time, it is relatively short, even though it is suggested that issues about termination should start several weeks before the actual ending date. Some writers consider it a neglected area (Mayadas and Glasser, 1985). Why the avoidance, if this is the case? Perhaps some of the reason for the lessening of attention to ending is the pain that is associated with this experience in people's lives. When there is a separation from those who offer caring and have the quality of empathy, feelings of loss and possibly abandonment can take place, unless there has been adequate preparation for the separation. There are times when separation is unplanned and sudden, such as a death of someone who is close or simply a departure without saying good-bye. The unexplained absence of persons who have special meaning may introduce more caution regarding intimacy or contribute to hesitation in facing other separations. Ambivalence is expected during this time—possibly happiness about ending because of satisfaction with what has been accomplished but also denial, avoidance, regression, or anger about losing the bonding that has taken place. These mixed emotions occur in groups that have achieved a high level of closeness. For groups that are more task-oriented and do not achieve as much intimacy, the emotional losses associated with separation are not as great.

If the group worker has not successfully faced the personal meaning of ending experiences, it is likely that separation will not be done with the sensitivity that is necessary. Since the ending phase can rekindle strong emotions about old losses, it may be covered hurriedly, if at all—"a sort of institutionalized repression" (Fox, Nelson, and Bolman, 1969, 63). The worker may feel vulnerable in recalling the inner turmoils of loss and in being subject to the expected anger from group members about leaving the group. Self-disclosure by the worker could be helpful in modeling the expression of feelings and presenting oneself as more genuine and open.

ENDING THE GROUP SESSION

A natural kind of ending that occurs all the time is the closure of a group session. Each time a group meets, there is a beginning, a middle, and an ending. The beginning may require an introduction about the agenda, if it is a task-oriented group, or some comments by the group worker to set the tone for a treatment group. It is a time to clear the air or prepare the group for what comes next. The middle is obviously when the problem solving is done. During this period, the work of the group should be consistent with the expectations set up in the beginning. The ending should include a summation of what happened and plans for another session.

In psychodrama there is a structure that includes all these elements. The group starts with the Warm-Up, followed by the Action, and ending with Closure. The closure experience encourages participants to offer supportive feedback to the protaganist (the central figure in the psychodrama) and share feelings about the enactment (Blatner, 1973, 11–13).

Besides clarifying any points in the discussion or making further preparations, it is suggested that the group worker allow some time at the end of each meeting for processing what took place in the group that day. Setting aside ten minutes or so for summing up each session should be discussed with the group during the early meetings, so that it is understood as part of the process of individual and group development. If group members can agree that this is a valuable use of time, which needs to be protected, it will make it easier for the worker to restrict new and potentially time-consuming topics from being introduced toward the end of a meeting. The expectations about how to use these last ten minutes should be made clear. The worker might make a statement asking group members to share their reactions about the meeting in a general way, or more direct questions could be asked: "Could you briefly summarize what this session has meant to you?" or "Was there anything unfinished for you today that you would like to continue in our next meeting?" (Corey, Corey, Callanan, and Russell, 1988, 144). In open groups where there is a constantly changing membership, it is especially necessary that the beginning be an introduction and orientation for new members and the closing be a time for sharing thoughts and feelings and saying good-bye. The open groups may serve as a transition to other experiences, such as an orientation group for incoming residents of an institution. Termination from this kind of group could set a tone of receptivity for increased involvement in other activities beyond the group.

PLANNED ENDING WITH THE GROUP

Work with socioeducation groups is becoming increasingly time limited and usually short-term, about eight to twelve sessions. Among treatment groups, there is a trend to meet for shorter periods of time. Many of these groups will meet for a specified number of weeks, in the expectation that they will assess their progress at the end of that time and then recontract for additional weeks if it seems desirable. With task groups, such as those that meet for social action or administrative purposes, the number of meetings is determined by how long it takes to accomplish the task. In most cases, groups know about the ending date from the beginning. This means that the group worker can prepare group members for termination well in advance.

Needs of Group Members

The ambivalent feelings at the end—satisfaction with personal or group progress and sadness from the ending of meaningful relationships—can be confusing for group members. The denial, anger, or flight that is characteristic of this stage may be due to the painful experiencing of loss, but is may also be a reaction to the confusion that results from mixed emotions. This period of preparation for separating from the group is extremely important, because it can help group members understand the varied feelings and the meaning of loss in their lives (Garvin, 1987, 212), consolidate the learning that has taken place (Corey, Corey, Callanan, and Russell, 1988, 143), and maintain and generalize the gains that they have made to other aspects of their lives (Toseland and Rivas, 1984, 333).

Reemphasis on the Individual

It is typical of an ending stage for group members to show signs of withdrawing from the group. There may be an increase of absences, less willingness to assume responsibility for decision making, and more dependence on the group worker. In many ways the group resembles a beginning phase when approach-avoidance (Garland, Jones, and Kolodny, 1973, 29–30) was a characteristic of behavior. It reflects a fluctuation between willingness and unwillingness to participate in the life of the group. The group worker needs to avoid being punitive during these instances of what seems to be irresponsible behavior. Seeing these signs that group members are distancing themselves from the group, the worker will use these occasions as opportunities to discuss their impending separation—what is happening within the group and how individuals are dealing with separation. He or she should recognize that group members need to leave the group with a clear sense of themselves and the special qualities that characterize their values, thoughts, and feelings—the indivualization process of self-identity (Fried, 1970, 450; Henry, 1981, 259–261). Henry (256–258) discusses the shift from an interdependent contract, which started in the beginning stage and evolved through the middle or work phase, and enabled group members to work together, to an independent contract during the ending period. The independent contract is a personal commitment about how the group member will use the gains made in the group.

Group cohesion, which is a consequence of the maturation stage, is no longer a high priority. Efforts may even be made to reduce group attraction (Toseland and Rivas, 1984, 340–341), including activities that are more individualistic in nature to help group members wind down and be more comfortable in the distancing of termination. Wayne and Avery (1979), working with parent abusers, shifted from a discussion approach to the use of crafts toward the end of the group. They felt that it lessened the intensity of the group experience toward the end, led to more independence, self-confidence, and sense of completion for the group members. However, during this time, the group still needs to complete any unfinished business, whether it is in relation to how group members are related to one another or to the group worker (Corey and Corey, 1987, 209). In task groups, this may be a particularly active time, as group members are busy with the final preparations for a project or are busy making decisions on how to conclude their planning agenda. The group needs to seek a balance between ending their work and allowing group members to find the separateness they need in order to make the transition to new relationships. For person-centered growth and treatment groups, the balance will be toward individuation. There is not as much need in task groups for group members to distance themselves as part of the ending stage, since their investment of energy has been related more to a project than to relationships.

TASKS OF THE GROUP WORKER

The group worker will continue many of the tasks of the beginning or middle stage. This is especially the case in regard to enhancing self-esteem, encouraging self-understanding, relating individual issues to the group as a whole, encouraging responsibility for action, recognizing and negotiating conflict, planning, and problem solving to complete personal and group objectives. This is also true for activities with an environmental focus, such as acting as broker, mediator, and advocate, and collaborating with other professionals. However, other tasks are specifically related to the ending stage and these will be discussed with practice illustrations.

Tasks: The Person

24. Review and Summarize Individual and Group Progress.

WORKER ACTIVITY: *A successful separation will involve a review and evaluation of individual and group progress. Ask that they review the experiences that had the most meaning for them—the positive and negative. Help them to recognize the gains that they made. Discuss the extent to which they believe that their objectives were met in the group. Summarize the sequencing of events that were brought up in the discussion.*

This is the time to look back and sort out the various experiences that had meaning for group members and the group worker. The spirit and practice of collaboration is carried into the final stage. The worker also reviews what was meaningful to him or her, partly to model openness and realness about the quality of caring and to underline the significance of events that occurred during the group, but also to bring closure to the investment of energy in relationship with group members. It is useful to discuss negative as well as positive perceptions of the group. The group worker may unwittingly give the message that he or she only wants to hear "the good things," perhaps to confirm the members' ability to demonstrate progress or satisfaction. Unless the negatives are also shared, it is likely that they will be brought into a new relationship in some disguised form.

During this review and evaluation, persons will have the opportunity to recognize what changes in thinking or behaving might mean for them. One advantage of the group is that group members can offer feedback to one another to insure more self-understanding. The greater awareness of gains made in the group compared to a first meeting will help in the integration that is necessary to stabilize growth and change.

☐ *Example of the Task:* It is the thirteenth session of a group work class, and two more are still upcoming. The design of the course was to analyze student practice material according to knowledge, values, and techniques of social work with groups. The class functioned as a small group and also profited from experiential learning in the examination of their own process as a group and from the modeling by the teacher. They set aside time to begin an evaluation of their group experience.

During the early part of the class, they discuss the extent to which students were able to experience their own stages of group development. They bring out the importance of trust, the inclusion/exclusion issue and the differences and similarities of being a class and a group. They discuss what made them feel like a group, including the sharing of their experiences and their commonalities in being students. They talk about the delicate balance between bringing out personal feelings and staying with the practice issues from student presentations and the readings.

BILL: I felt essentially good about what we've gone through and the way the class is set up. . . . I don't know why we've done that though. I don't know how to apply that—the fact that I feel comfortable about that or I'm feeling pretty good about what I'm doing. In focusing on other people's work, you know, I felt afterwards, really, "whew," "wow," I presented my work. You know, I presented part of me or something. It wasn't that bad. It really made me feel like a graduate student. Here I'm presenting. Today I'll be video-taped. It made me feel like I thought it would be when I first came here. I just don't know how I can take that and apply it to the task group that I'm going to be working with.

WORKER: What you're saying is how can we extract out some of the experiences that we've had, perhaps some principles, that we could use to identify and then think about how we can apply some of these same kinds of principles to other groups, task groups that we are working with.

BILL: I've been in task groups before, but we've never stopped and said what have we gone through. So this is one of the reasons I wanted us to evaluate ourselves. We will be running task groups, and now we will be feeling what it's like to be a member of a task group. And before when I was a member, I just never set aside time to be aware of what I was feeling and doing and what the group was going through. I didn't have enough foresight to think of group dynamic theories. Now is the chance. It will be nice.

WORKER: Setting aside some think time.

BILL: Yeah.

Bill welcomes the opportunity to review and evaluate what the class has done together. He is searching for meaning—for what happened in the class group and for himself. The worker uses reflection to bring out what Bill seems to be saying. This enables Bill to go on with a further explanation of what he hopes to gain from their evaluation time. Being able to identify group work principles from their experience of being a group has a great deal more meaning than simply reading or discussing it in a more abstract way. The students can see more clearly how to apply these concepts to their agency groups. This type of evaluation combines the cognitive, emotional, and sensory dimensions of learning. It is a more total educational experience, similar to what Kolb and Fry (1975) describe as "an integrated cognitive and socio-emotional process" (p.34) in their discussion of an applied theory of experiential learning. The review of individual and group progress with social work type groups offers the same possibilities—inductively taking from the group experience what has meaning, seeking to integrate it with aspects of the self, and, finally, discovering new meaning and new behaviors to meet present and future challenges.

Tasks: The Group

25. Deal with Feelings and Attitudes about Separating from the Group.

WORKER ACTIVITY: *A range of emotions is usually present during a separation phase. Group members may feel pleased to be ending the group,* *especially if there are feelings of accomplishment. If affectational ties were strong, there may be denial, withdrawal, regression, and anger since they are experiencing loss in their relationships with one another. Encourage group members to express their feelings. You should bring out your own feelings in order to model self-expression and also to bring out your affection for the group members. If persons do care for one another, help them to express it (if it seems appropriate). Invite any anger or disappointment that may exist (if it seems appropriate). Invite any anger or disappointment toward you for leaving them and normalize these feelings.*

It was mentioned earlier in the chapter that ambivalence is a typical reaction when the group is about to end. There are many feelings—good, bad, and difficult-to-categorize. This is a time of sharing for those who are able to do so.

For some persons it is more difficult to discuss affection and caring than anger and hostility. When it is too much of a risk to express loving thoughts and feelings, these emotions may come out negatively. Anger may seem safer. To express affection toward another person makes one vulnerable, since the good feelings may not be reciprocated. The anger that is sometimes expressed toward the group worker during the final sessions may actually be admiration or fondness in disguise. It may also be anger at the worker for ending the group and contributing to their feelings of loss. When this happens, the worker should not be punitive or defensive. The feelings should be accepted for what they are—a part of termination. The anger should be recognized and validated, even encouraged. The worker uses these techniques—encouraging the expression of feelings, reflection on what is happening in the group, and exploration with the group of the meaning of their anger—to help group members reach greater understanding of these feelings.

Self-disclosure by the group worker is particularly important in the exchange of thoughts and feelings. When the worker models the sharing of feelings, group members are encouraged to express themselves. It is an opportunity to strengthen the bond between worker and members and thus enrich the meaning of the group experience.

Using a structured activity can help facilitate the evaluation of the group and the display of affect. This might take the form of dividing the group into twosomes or threesomes, who meet briefly to discuss their personal review of the group. This is a particularly good way to get at negatives, since persons are more likely to bring out strong feelings within the protection of a subgroup. They may or may not want to share their discussions with the larger group, although, once negative emotions are verbalized, it may be easier to discuss them freely. Another possibility is to use a silent activity like "sculpting," where group members and the group worker demonstrate a feeling by taking a particular body position, like a statue in a pose. They are then asked to explain the meaning of their pose to the group, which can lead into a discussion about the range of emotions. However, it is necessary to help group members bring out their thinking as well as their feelings. Some persons may find it easier to disclose thoughts than feelings, and this should not be discouraged, even though there is the danger of intellectualizing—persons becoming too conceptual and avoiding the feeling dimension completely.

If the group has not been accustomed to discussing feelings, it will be difficult for such disclosure to take place at this time. Indeed it is questionable whether it would be beneficial to unload a lot of feelings during final meetings. Unless group members have sufficient time to deal with "heavy" feelings, so that their meaning and impact on the group members can be resolved, it is better to limit this kind of expression. Since it is not possible to foretell what will happen when persons are invited to express their attitudes and feelings, deep emotions may be brought out. If group members take this risk of self-exposure, and there is no time to help them come to terms with their feelings, they will feel angry, confused, and guilty for displaying such affections. Some group members will see termination as the last chance to discuss previously undisclosed thoughts or feelings. It is for this reason that it is suggested the group worker start the review and evaluation process early enough to work through some of these bits of unfinished business. The longer the time that the group has been meeting, the earlier the group should start dealing with the ending (allow at least three weeks).

☐ *Example of the Task.*   A county welfare office has organized a group of women who are interested in getting their Graduate Equivalency Diploma (GED)—a high school diploma for those who dropped out of a regular high school. There are ten women, all black, mostly young mothers who participate in a formal educational program prior to the group meeting. The purpose of the group is to help the women offer each other mutual aid, learn problem-solving skills, improve social relationships, and offer support for them to stay in the classes in order to get their GED.

WORKER: How do you feel about leaving the group?

ANN: It's kind of scary. I'm wondering if we're going to mess it up.

☐ Other group members tell how nice it will be to get the GED.

WORKER: You sound like you have mixed feelings—happy and yet thinking about whether you have the right stuff to make it.

BETTY: I'm going to miss the moral support.

WORKER: We've shared so much. I've seen so many changes. What were some things that were really good—some things that you didn't think you could do and found that you could?

JEAN: I remember when Barbara called me up and said, "Jean, you're going to school today." I didn't feel like going, but I went after she called.

WORKER: What will it be like for you after you leave?

BETTY: You'll meet other people who are interested in what you're interested in. Even if you did keep some bad company or were with people who didn't have any get up and go, now you'll be around people who have some determination. It's like life in a bucket of crabs. You hang out with those crabs that don't have anything, they'll keep you right there with them. You manage to flip over the side of the basket, the world is there, and it's wide open. There's always somebody there to help you along—someone to give you push.

The group worker encourages communication about ending. They review, say what's on their minds, give and receive reassurance, and search for the meaning of their experiences together. The mutual aid is evident as Jean discusses the encouragement she received from Barbara to attend classes. Betty recognizes that completing the GED will mean increased opportunities and new friends, and that more will be expected of her. The group members wonder if they will be able to meet these additional expectations. Sometimes the uncertainty and fear of failure in a new situation will prevent the person from breaking out of a familiar mold. Support and encouragement along the way may be enough for persons to take the risks that are necessary for growth. The group has helped to reinforce feelings of competence and self-worth—the desire for new challenges.

Tasks: The Environment

26. Plan for the future.

WORKER ACTIVITY: *Involve group members in a discussion about their plans after leaving the group. Ask how they might be able to make use of experiences in the group with persons outside the group. Suggest that they anticipate future events and consider how they will deal with these new encounters.*

The ending should provide links to new beginnings. The prior example of the GED group pointed out how the completion of the GED was a step to new opportunities—jobs, school, and social relationships. The worker can help the members think about how they will use the gains they have made in the group. The weeks before the group ends should be treated as a period of transition. Group members must integrate what they have learned but also anticipate how it will be used—to try it on for size. The excitement and fears about newness are tried out in the group, and thus the group becomes a place for reality testing—looking at feasibility, resources, skills, attitudes, and whatever else is necessary for a successful transition.

☐ *Example of the Task.*   The excerpt that follows is a transcription from a Public Assistance Client Group (*Trainee's Handbook: A Case History of a*

Public Assistance Client Group, 1968). It is the twelfth and last session. All the group members are women who were having difficulties in their regular agency contacts (excessive distrust, reluctance to ask for help, strained communications, etc.). The composition was ethnically mixed.

WORKER: Well—we've talked about a lot of things these past twelve weeks. Is there anything you'd like to pull together from all these sessions?

HELEN (*To worker and group, laughing*): Yeah—I'm not scared anymore about talking back—because I've seen a program on TV of—ah—bravery and cowardness and I don't want to be a scrawny little ol' coward. (*Giggles.*)

SARA (*To group, laughs*): You know—I was telling you I talked back to my father—you know—I act real brave and everything. And inside I'm scared like hell. (*Group laughter*) I'm scared. (*She laughs.*) And if my father knew that, he'd come in here and knock the hell out of me. (*Group laughter.*)

PEGGY (*To worker and group*): Well—I decided I'm not going to be on welfare forever. I'm going to do something—I'm going to be a nurse—do something.

SARA (*to Peggy*): That's what I would like to be—a nurse—

PEGGY: I'm going to be something—I'm not going to be a welfare recipient forever—

HELEN (*To group*): I'd like to be a nurse—

PEGGY (*To self*): —and I'm going to do it.

HELEN (*To group*): A regular RN, too—not an LPN, but an RN.

PEGGY (*To group*): I don't care what I am— a bedpan flunky or something—I'm going to do something.

MOLLY (*To group*): They could stick me out in the laundry—I wouldn't care.

HELEN (*To group*); No, really, I'd like—I'd like to go into the hospital and go right into the kitchen and cook—become a dietitian cook. Because I enjoy cooking.

MOLLY (*To group*): I want to go to work in a library—that's what I want to do.

PEGGY (*To group*): Because I'm not going to get married—I can see that nobody's going to support me. (*Group laughter.*)

WORKER: I wish we had the time this morning to talk more about these things you'd like to do—but, of course, each one of your social workers will help you with plans for training and jobs. (*Pause.*) I do want to say that I've enjoyed working with you as a group during these twelve weeks. We're not really saying good-bye, because I'll probably see most of you many times again—and I'll hear about you from your social workers. (*Pause*) Because of our meetings, they know a lot more about the ways they can help you—and I have the feeling all of you know better how to ask for help—and you can go on helping each other.

Group members seem to be saying, "I want to be productive," whether it is being a nurse or working in the laundry. They have higher aspirations for their futures. The group worker, in a broad invitation to pull together what has happened in the last twelve weeks, puts the responsibility on the group members to evaluate their progress. They talk about how their behavior has changed and how they anticipate acting in the future. The group worker discusses how they might use their assigned agency social worker in further planning for training and jobs. The group has served the purpose of increasing their receptivity to regular agency services—one of its original goals. There are increased feelings of self-esteem and a more positive attitude as the clients leave the group.

27. Refer Group Members to Other Services.

WORKER ACTIVITY: *When it seems desirable and needed, suggest that group members initiate contact with other professionals for specific services. Contact the service provider beforehand to explain that the client will be calling (if appropriate). Accompanying the client to another agency in order to facilitate the referral may also be appropriate. For the most part, the client will be expected to assume responsibility for making the arrangement.*

Not all group members will need and want additional services once the group has ended. But this possibility should be considered for some, and the worker will want to become familiar with community resources that might be useful to those in the group. In some cases, contacts with referral sources might be made before the ending of the group. In this way the group member will have support for taking the initiative in exploring new goals.

Today the trend is toward short-term groups, and if this continues, intragroup goals for clients are necessarily limited. This makes other services even more useful. It is up to the client whether to pursue a referral, but the group worker can help him or her explore whether such a commitment is desirable. This might be done in the group, as part of the planning phase of termination, or in an individual conference to discuss just this issue. The group worker may or may not want to accompany the member to another agency. If at all possible, the member should take on as much responsibility as possible to initiate and follow through on such contacts.

When another agency person has become involved in a referral, this person and the group worker become a working team on behalf of the client. The worker will continue to maintain contact with the agency source until the referral has become a reality. Depending on the needs of the client and his or her wishes, there may or may not be continued communication with this other agency—it depends on whether it will serve the interests of the client. Once other agencies are involved, there is also a question of confidentiality: Will the client be willing to release information that is the basis for communication in the continuing team effort? If the client understands the purpose of sharing the information, it is more likely that he or she will agree to its use.

☐ *Example of the Task.* In the analysis of the Group in Transition presented in Chapter 6, the group of mentally retarded young men had weekly meetings at a YMCA while they were still living at a residential school. Since a primary purpose of the group was to help the group members become more able to live independently, the meeting at the Y and involvement in community activities were steps toward the transition to more autonomy. While the group was meeting at the agency, there were built-in opportunities for the young men to have experiences with the regular membership at the Y, such as contacts during swimming, Ping-Pong, eating in the cafeteria, and playing pool. Because of some of their interests, such as swimming, the group worker met with the Y staff about whether it would be feasible for some of the young men to participate in a swimming class. With approval from the Y, the group worker asked the group members if they would like to participate in the swimming program on their own. Some of them agreed. When the group ended, there was a natural continuation of their social experiences at the community agency. The swimming class served several goals. It helped them learn swimming skills, which would add to their feelings of competence, provide social contacts within a class structure so that expectations were very clear, and learn about other activities at the Y, so that there could be additional opportunities when they were ready for continued independent functioning.

The referral was made to help the young men continue the gains they'd made in the group and expand their social experiences toward increased independence and community awareness. The types of group activity available at the Y were carefully considered. Swimming was ideal. It allowed for individualized learning, and yet it was part of a group activity. There was a minimum expectation for social competence. And yet, since swimming lessons were based on an interest the boys already had, the lesson could be a source of motivation for risking social experiences outside the structure of the young men's group. Moreover, they had a beginning relationship with staff at the Y, and this facilitated the referral.

Hepworth and Larsen (1986, 593) present guidelines to assist the practitioner in making referrals. They mention (1) determining client's readiness for a referral by exploring thoughts and feelings about such an action, (2) matching the best resources to meet the client's particular needs, (3) offer your recommendation but respect the client's right of self-determination, (4) offer optimism but not false or unrealistic promises, and (5) avoid telling the next practitioner what to do. However, it would be professionally responsible to confer with staff at the agency where the client was being referred, so that there could be joint thinking about a working plan.

UNPLANNED ENDINGS

All that has been said so far presupposes that the group worker and group are aware of when the group will terminate. However, there are instances when group members leave the group suddenly or the group worker may not be able to continue.

Dropouts

Bostwick (1987) examined studies on dropouts from group treatment. About one-third of the participants in the studies cited left the group prematurely (range of 15 percent to 70 percent). There were few definitive findings about the reasons for dropouts. Client psychological characteristics seem to be the dominant factor in discontinuance, such as difficulty with self-disclosure or being angry. An important consideration for continuance was whether the worker liked the client. Pregroup preparation seemed to help clients get started in treatment, and it is suggested the clients continue to get help in learning how to be a group member once treatment begins.

When there is some notice that a person will be separating from the group, even if it is just during a current session, the person and group should be encouraged to discuss it. If the person has been disruptive and had a negative impact, the notice about leaving may be welcomed by the others. The more usual reaction is that group members will be angry, disappointed, and perhaps guilty that they have contributed to the departure. Group members and the group worker should avoid putting the prospective dropout on the defensive with probing or attacking questions. This person may have good reasons for wanting to leave, and his or her self-determination should be respected. However, it could be helpful to invite the discontinuing member to share any thoughts and feelings about wanting to leave, and for the rest of the group to discuss their reactions. The discussion should take a positive direction in focusing on future plans the discontinuing group member has or on helping him or her consider appropriate alternatives. If the ending is handled positively, it is more likely that this person will be receptive to joining another group.

When persons simply do not show up in the group anymore, the group worker should attempt to obtain individual interviews with the absent members, to discuss their leaving or, if this is not possible, at least to make telephone contact to find out their reasons for dropping out and offer help in exploring future plans. If it is acceptable to the departing client, his or her reasons for leaving the group should be discussed with group members at the next meeting. Even if the reasons for the member's departure must be kept confidential, it is advisable for the group to discuss the group's feelings about the person's absence.

Group Worker Departure

When the group worker leaves the group, it can be a source of great anxiety for the members, especially if members have strong feelings of attachment to the worker. Such a departure could open old wounds among some members, stir up feelings of loss or abandonment that were part of their life experiences. If the worker has some advance opportunity to discuss the departure, it should be brought up for discussion. The group members need to share their thoughts and feelings, both positive and negative. It would be desirable to express affection, if it is sincerely felt, as well as expressions of loss. When the worker accepts these feelings without hostility or defensiveness, it demonstrates to the group members that it is safe to bring out their feelings. The worker could be modeling how to accept feedback. Obviously, the worker will also have feelings about leaving the group, and these should be brought out as well.

If the worker is replaced by a new staff person, it would be beneficial for the next worker to allow some time for leftover feelings about the departure. Unless this is done, the new worker may find group members showing signs of anger, resentment, or resistance to group involvement. If the worker leaves so suddenly that there is no opportunity to discuss the departure, it is especially important for the next worker to discuss the meaning of the loss.

TRANSFORMATION

There are times when groups that are preparing for termination will shift their focus and want to recontract for another purpose. Some practitioners may consider this development as resistance to separation and sidestep any discussion of the group or certain members continuing. However, it may be desirable for group members to use the gains they have made in the group and their cohesiveness to set new sights. Greenfield and Rothman (1987) discuss this changing direction as transformation, an extension of the stage of group development beyond termination. If group members, for instance, started in a treatment group and, after satisfying such a personal agenda, wanted to become a group with a social-action emphasis, they would transform themselves into this community-minded group. They would then develop a working agreement that aimed at this new goal. If it is a feasible arrangement for the same worker to continue with the group, this might be done or a new staff person might become the group worker. If the agency cannot accommodate this new kind of group, it may be possible to refer them to another agency more suitable to these changed interests. Still another possibility is for the group to meet as a self-help group with their own indigenous leadership to guide them.

Some group members may continue to see one another informally as a means of expanding their helping network. They know that, when it becomes necessary, there is someone to depend upon—someone to talk to about a problem. Some of their continued contacts may just be for social relationships. Whether or not group members continue to see one another after the group ends, the group experience has presumably increased their feelings of self-worth so that is becomes easier to reach out to others without as much fear of rejection.

SUMMARY

For each phase of group development, there is emotional involvement in relationships and success or failure in solving problems or completing tasks. The ending has special meaning, because it is associated with the feelings of loss and accomplishment, often experienced as ambivalence. The group worker is aware that as each group session ends there needs to be some form of closure— a recognition of the time being over, a review of what has happened, a preview of what comes next, and perhaps some expression by group members and the worker about the meaning of the group experience. The reasons for closure are to prepare people for the physical and emotional withdrawal of an event in their lives. Life is composed of new and changing experiences. The structure of beginning and ending enables the person to invest and divest energy from an incident in order to prepare himself or herself for the next episode.

Usually endings are planned, and sufficient time is allowed to prepare for termination. With enough time, group members are able to bring out feelings and ideas that will make it more possible to integrate their group experiences with other life events. New values from the group become incorporated into their belief system, adding an increased dimension to their self-concept. During an ending period, there is a shift to the individual, as in the beginning. It is part of helping the person to make the separation from group to individual once again. However, all three areas—the person, group, and environment—are still within the framework of practice.

There are also unplanned endings, which need to be considered and handled with care. An unplanned separation can be particularly traumatic, whether the loss is for a group member or the worker. The agency should recognize its impact and have staff available to discuss it with the group. Transformation is another way that the group can change its focus during an ending phase, to develop another purpose for continuing.

REFERENCES

Blatner, H. A. (1973). *Acting-in: Practical applications of psychodramatic methods.* New York: Springer.

Bostwick, G. J. (1987). "Where's Mary?" A review of the group treatment dropout literature. *Social Work with Groups, 10*(3), 117–132.

Corey, G., Corey, M. S., Callanan, P. J., & Russell, J. M. (1988). *Group techniques* (rev. ed.). Pacific Grove, CA: Brooks/Cole.

Corey, M. S., & Corey, G. (1987). *Groups: Process and practice* (3rd ed.). Monterey, CA: Brooks/Cole.

Fox, E. F., Nelson, M. A., & Bolman, W. M. (1969). The termination process: A neglected dimension in social work. *Social Work, 14*(4), 53–63.

Fried, E. (1970). Individuation through group psychotherapy. *International Journal of Group Psychotherapy, 20*(4).

Garland, J. A., Jones, H. E., and Kolodny, R. L. (1973). A model for stages of development in social work groups. In S. Bernstein (Ed.). *Explorations in group work: Essays in theory and practice* (pp. 17–71). Boston: Milford House.

Garvin, C. D. (1987). *Contemporary group work* (2nd ed.). Englewood Cliffs, NJ: Prentice-Hall.

Greenfield, W. L., & Rothman, B. (1987). Termination or transformation? Evolving beyond termination in groups. In J. Lassner, K. Powell, & E. Finnegan (Eds.), *Social group work: Competence and values in practice.* New York: Haworth Press.

Henry, S. (1981). *Group skills in social work.* Itasca, IL: F. E. Peacock.

Hepworth, D. H., & Larsen, J. (1986). *Direct social work practice: Theory and skills* (2nd ed.). Chicago: Dorsey Press.

Kolb, D. A., & Fry, R. (1975). Towards an applied theory of experiential learning. In C. L. Cooper (Ed.), *Theories of group process.* New York: John Wiley.

Mayadas, N., & Glasser, P. (1985). Termination: A neglected aspect of social group work. In M. Sundel, P. Glasser, R. Sarri, & R. Vinter (Eds.), *Individual change through small groups* (2nd ed.). New York: Free Press.

Toseland, R. W., & Rivas, R. F. (1984). *An introduction to group work practice.* New York: Macmillan.

Trainee's handbook: A case history of a public assistance client group (1968). Manhattan Beach, CA: Mehring productions and the California State Department of Social Welfare.

Wayne, J., & Avery, N. (1979). Activities for group termination. *Social Work, 24*(1), 58–62.

TEACHING AND LEARNING IDEAS

1. Participate in a role play of a group that is preparing for separation. What are the tasks that are performed by the worker during this ending period? After the role play, discuss what happened and offer feedback to the worker about tasks and techniques that were most helpful.

2. Interview persons who have been in social work type groups. Ask them about their experiences in the group during a separation phase. What was most helpful to them at that time?

3. Think about your own endings with relationships. Try to get in touch with what it was like for you. How can you make use of these personal experiences and empathize with group members who are separating from the group?

4. Meet in small groups within the class and discuss how you want to prepare for endings with groups. How would you handle sudden endings when members leave the group while the group is ongoing?

CHAPTER 11

Social Action and System Development

During the early and formative years of group work, there was a strong commitment to social action and community change (see Chapter 2). Personal growth, group development, and social action were envisioned as complementary. Through projects to improve neighborhood conditions, group members became strengthened and groups more cohesive. Papell and Rothman (1966) identified this form of group work as the social goals model, emphasizing democratic participation, citizen responsibility, and socially approved values. Coyle's writings (1947, 140), in particular, highlighted the role of the group worker as social statesman and educator of social values. Social action was a responsibility of the agency, the profession, and the small group. Its purpose was to develop needed resources and prevent "social disabilities" (p. 140). Barker (1988, 151) defines social action as

> A coordinated effort to achieve institutional change in order to meet a need, solve a social problem, correct an injustice, or enhance the quality of human life. This effort may occur at the initiative and direction of professionals in social welfare, economics, politics, religion, or the military, or it may occur through the efforts of the people who are directly affected by the problem or change.

A related activity is system development, whereby the social worker "helps to create organizations and resources to meet the psychosocial needs of consumers" (Lister, 1987, 384). Social action and system development, especially in working with persons experiencing poverty, are not as prevalent in social work now as in previous decades (Reeser and Epstein, 1987). However, these methods of community and organizational change are recognized as important functions for the direct practitioner. Lister (1987) found that the advocate, broker, enabler, mediator, negotiator, and research roles were often taught in direct practice—all professional responsibilities that could be associated with the person/group/environment transaction. These roles are typically used in community organization, a form of social work that uses task groups to achieve community change. When direct practitioners use social action or system development, it blurs the distinction between micro and macro social work.

The difference is that in group work the social action activity of the group may develop as a means of challenging the barriers to group members' personal growth. It may also take place as a way of reaching people who might not respond to a declared therapeutic orientation. For instance, Paster (1986) uses a social action model for minority populations and those experiencing poverty who ordinarily do not make use of established social agencies. In the SAM (social action model) approach, persons are invited to participate in a socially relevant project that has value to themselves and the community. The process of accomplishing the task leads to increased personal competence, group bonding, recognition from others, and social networking in their association with community persons. Community organization starts with a social need or problem and forms the task group with that purpose in mind. The community organizer needs to make use of knowledge and skills with small groups in order to maintain an effective group (Bakalinsky, 1984). Even with the apparent differences in direct practice and community organization, work with groups for social change projects or to develop community resources is becoming more common for all social workers. It may be indicative of a continuing trend toward the integrative practice of a generalist social worker.

System development to create a more therapeutic environment to support growth and change has had a long tradition in social work (Maier, 1965), and the more recent work with social networks (Maguire, 1983; Moore, 1978) continues attention to the environment as a vital connection with the helping process. A review of literature in group work (Zimpfer, 1984) identifies some recent writings on the use of networks with groups and a continuation of the long-standing tradition of using milieu therapy, or the concept of the therapeutic community within institutional settings, as a major form of patient or resident care.

Social action and system development is being described in this chapter as encompassing the different forms of organizational or community engagement. Some writers, such as Garvin, Glasser, Carter, English, and Wolfson (1985), Frankel and Sundel (1978), Cnaan and Adar (1987), and Schwartz (1976) describe a methodology for environmental change. The extragroup means of influence, proposed by Vinter and Galinsky (1985), is a framework for conceptualizing group work and the environment. It includes understanding social roles of members prior to being in the group, the significant persons in their lives, the social systems to which they belong, and the social environment of the group. For agencies that recognize social problems and wish to initiate community action to resolve these problems, Frankel and Sundel (1978) propose a systemic methodology for the practitioner. The various steps start with assessment of community needs, determining why the problem may exist, who is affected, and existing sources of support and services. This is followed by the development of program goals (in measurable terms), using knowledge and appropriate leadership skills to effect service delivery, evaluation, and how to maintain the services.

A SOCIAL ACTION AND SYSTEMS DEVELOPMENT MODEL

The rationale for the phases of this model makes use of systems concepts, small group theory, and learning theories that were described earlier (see Chapter 4). It offers the practitioner involved in environmental work a systematic means of using social action to achieve system development and change.

Identification of Need or Problem. This is usually considered the presenting problem, where a person or group identify a need or problem and seek help from an agency. It may also be a social problem within the community that is cause for concern, such as widespread use of drugs, lack of affordable housing, or racial tension. For organizations, it may be an administrative issue that needs attention, like increasing burnout of staff.

Even though a group meets for personal change or educational or socialization reasons, there may come a time when problems in the community or organization have an equally high priority. In this case, the group may redefine its purposes to include social action and system development. For instance, a socioeducation group of adolescents were meeting because of problems adjusting to the high school. Some were on probation, and others were having academic problems or feeling socially isolated. In the course of meeting together, they complained about the lack of community recreational facilities for youth. The group worker helped them to find out more about the problem by talking to other teens and knowledgeable adults in the community, so they could decide whether to make a proposal for action to remedy the situation. If and when this happens, the group's purpose includes community action as well as personal growth.

The initial identification of a need or problem is the beginning definition of its boundary. The perception of this boundary will create a further assessment. However, the way people conceptualize this need or problem will shape the future directions for thinking and action. This is why further assessment of a beginning request for help is so important.

Assessment and Planning. Once the need or problem has been recognized as requiring attention, further exploration must be carried out about its meaning and who is part of the problem. This could be a time for mapping personal networks, as suggested by Maguire (1980), in order to identify potential sources of support. At this time persons are identified who may be in a position to influence the environment in a positive direction.

The intake interview might be used to focus on the presenting problem and examine the fuller implications for the person and those in the immediate surroundings. Some agencies will use a needs assessment, whereby persons are asked about their interests in and preferences for certain groups, or to rank community problems in order of importance, to decide on the use of limited resources. The assessment includes a planning dimension, if possible in collaboration with the person or group that has brought the need or problem to the attention of the agency. Garvin (1987, 56–57) describes a Group Needs Assessment Questionnaire, which surveys potential group member interests, areas for possible discussion, and personal characteristics, which are checked off to indicate a behavioral profile.

As more information becomes known and feelings are expressed, the original conception of the need or problem may be altered or reframed to look differently. The boundary could be modified to include a different arrangement of people and a changed focus in dealing with the problem. For instance, a child's disruptive behavior in the classroom may take on new meaning as information is gathered. It now appears that the parents, teacher, and playground supervisor have conflicting expectations of the child, and any plan for intervention should include the collaboration of these three, so that there are consistent expectations and similar goals to help the child. Boundary clarification could also include partializing and setting priorities for one small area of the environment as an initial form of intervention.

Selection of Planning and Action Group. When the environmental issue has been brought up in an existing group, the planning and action takes place within the group itself. It uses a problem-solving approach to consider the next steps: either changing group-member behavior to interact with the environment in a more effective way, or to modify that part of the environment that seems to be contributing to the problem.

When the identification of the environmental problem is emanating from one individual, perhaps as a presenting problem at an agency, a group could be formed with others who share an interest or concern about the same kind of problem. One of the purposes of their group would be to resolve the particular issue that brought them together. For instance, homeless persons from a shelter meet together to consider how they will find housing arrangements or jobs that will enable them to pay rent for a place to live. Hardy-Fanta (1986) discusses the importance for Hispanics to become involved in groups that are related to their immediate interests and concerns. These might be issues of migrant workers, illegal immigrants, bilingual education, health services, staffing of agencies to include more Hispanics, and ways to increase political power (p. 120).

The need to deal with community concerns may come from agency staff, interested citizens, or government or business organizations. A planning and action group is usually formed to clarify the meaning of the problem and work toward change. Persons to be selected for this group should have a strong interest in the problem, represent some diversity in their views, be able to reach others and accessible in terms of time and commitment. This should be a small, working group that meets for purposes of social action or system development. The planning and action group should have the necessary organization and energy to mobilize further efforts to accomplish its purposes. Because of the particular strength of its composition, this group should be able to involve others in the process of change. Cnaan and Adar (1987) identify several stages of development in forming and working with a group for community change purposes. Within each stage, the worker is guided by *values*, such as the importance of involving persons who are experiencing the problem, *organizational factors*, including the establishment of procedures for meeting and carrying out responsibilities, *the operational dimension*, which involves planning strategy and implementation, and the *interpersonal area* that is attentive to group dynamics and cooperative relationships. These factors are all necessary to consider in working with a planning and action group.

Further Involvement. One of the responsibilities of the planning and action group is to interest those who may be in a position to influence change and induce them to participate. These are the persons who may be less accessible at first or even demonstrated resistance when they were first approached. But if their help is important to the implementation of a plan, it could be worthwhile to include them. For instance, in response to problems of burnout of nurses in a hospital, the administration supported the formation of stress-management groups. Besides helping nurses with personal techniques to lessen stress, the groups recognized that the work environment needed to be modified. The planning and action group, composed of key administrators, recommended the implementation of the program, but the head nurses on the floors, who were informed of the intentions but not directly involved in the planning, claimed the modification interfered with ward routine. These middle-management nurses were crucial to the successful operation of the change, so their cooperation had to be gained. This is an example of the need to involve this next layer of influential people.

Forming coalitions, whereby groups who have a common interest join together, is another way of increasing involvement and using additional resources. Gentry (1987, 49) highlights the need for collaboration, horizontal power distribution, and effective communication as essential elements of stable coalition relationships. In some cases publicity in the media can stimulate interest and favorable attitudes toward the issue under consideration. This is also the phase when potential recipients of a service would be involved in further planning. For instance, when planning for a teenage recreation program in response to adolescent delinquency or underachievement, representatives of the intended teenage population should participate, so that they can contribute their thinking and action to the project.

There is continued and expanded energy as more persons commit themselves and take responsibility for implementation of proposals for action. When there is this exchange of energy, a process of linkage takes place. Linkage, as described in Chapter 4, means connections among people in common pursuit of a solution to needs or problems. There is strength and power in this collective activity, especially when these forces for change are moving in the same direction. Linking is what Maguire (1980) describes as making contacts with persons from a client's personal network in order to expand the client's helping system.

Change and Stabilization. Support for change comes from active participation of persons who are affected by the problem. With increased communication, clarification about common goals, and strategies for implementation, support for change is likely to build up. Change may occur on at least three levels: personal attitudes and skills learning to react to the environment in a more effective way; group developing empowerment and capacities for problem solving; and environment being restructured to accommodate the needs of group members or those most affected by the social problem. In this process, the patterns of communication and arrangements of relationships in the person/group/environment constellation will be modified. It is a developmental process, starting with identification of the need or problem, moving to assessment and then incremental steps of involvement by persons in a position to find solutions.

Linkage with key persons should activate forces for change. The particular combination of influential persons will provide additional weighting, or leverage, toward meeting needs or solving problems. When change occurs, it will mean a new balance of relationships, perhaps in how roles are perceived and performed. This "state of balance or adjustment, typically achieved through opposing actions" is called equilibrium (Chess and Norlin, 1988, 126). When the equilibrium is established in a new position, instead of being returned to a former level, it is called dynamic equilibrium (Chin, 1961, 205). If support and reinforcement of these new relationships and structures are continued, the new equilibrium has a better chance of being maintained. A sufficient number of persons, especially those who have the power to influence decision making, need to be involved in the change process in order for it to succeed.

TECHNIQUES OF INTERVENTION

To use the model outlined above, the worker needs a specific set of techniques. Two phases of the model will be highlighted—work with the planning and action group, and further involvement of persons related to the issue or problem. Although the focus will be on what the group worker does, it is also important to realize that group members are also using these techniques to initiate and sustain improvements in their environment. Social action and system development involve power and control shared between the worker and group members. A goal of the worker is to help group members use problem-solving techniques.

Actions of the Worker and Group Members

When a group prepares to effect change in the environment, it is taking on a planning and action function. This may happen when a treatment or socioeducation group recognizes obstacles in the environment that they would like to overcome, or when a group is specially formed to deal with an organizational or community issue. The planning and action group needs to be focused on its task. Techniques of planning, already mentioned in the beginning and middle phases (Chapters 8 and 9), will be elaborated upon.

1. *Sharing of perceptions, values, feelings and ideas about the issue, needs or problem.* The worker is open to hearing about environmental concerns and validates them. Participation and elaboration are encouraged. Diverse thinking is welcomed to bring out various sides of an issue.

2. *Identifying common themes and defining the issue, need or problem from the collective thinking of the group.* On the basis of a mutual exchange of views and a fuller explanation of problems, the group engages in clarifying the meaning and implications of their areas of concern.

3. *Seeking further information to clarify the nature of the problem.* Additional information is sought for further clarification, if necessary. The group worker and/or group members take responsibility for collection of evidence outside the group to substantiate the defined problem.

4. *Reaching agreement on what the group will work on together.* With the preliminary fact gathering about the definition and meaning of the problem, the worker seeks to reach agreement with the group about its agenda—a phase of contracting.

5. *Partializing issue or problem for accessible and manageable tasks.* The strategy that is developed by the worker and group includes an exploration of component parts of the problem and locating areas that seem more attainable, at least at first.

6. *Considering alternatives for action and problem solving.* The group reflects on different approaches to implement a plan. Members are helped to

weigh the consequences of alternative ways of thinking or acting. Priorities are considered and available resources for different courses of action are identified.

7. *Making decisions and determining responsibility for action.* The worker elicits varying shades of opinion and any reservations or questions about the plan before a decision is reached. Once a decision is made, however, the group is encouraged to take responsibility for implementing it. If members have many personal deficits and can assume only limited responsibility, the worker will take a more active and responsible role in providing leadership.

These techniques are identified with task accomplishment (see Chapter 6). However, it is also necessary to use support and involvement techniques to help the group in its development. Conflict may occur as the group struggles to negotiate its differences and find solutions to the social action agenda. In these cases, the worker will use an array of techniques that includes awareness of individual and group behavior. These techniques are used to help group members deal more effectively with the developmental growing pains of group life, as well as problems with people who may present barriers to problem solving. In discussing working groups, Ephross and Vassil (1988, 143–163) also discuss a full range of what they call technologies, covering the socioemotional and task dimensions of the group. In many cases, these are similar to the techniques discussed in Chapter 6, but they also include useful approaches such as role playing, dividing into subgroups, using supposals ("what ifs"), working in the member's idiom (within their cultural context), grading activities from the simple to more complex, pacing or timing the amount of anxiety to allow in the group in helping them accomplish their task, and synthesizing to locate common themes among diverse strands of thought.

GROUP AS PART OF THE ENVIRONMENT

Groups that are part of a living or work situation (families, hospitals, institutions, housing units, camps, workplace, etc.) are influenced by the openness or restrictions on growth in the larger system. Being able to negotiate with persons who represent the wider environment can be an opportunity for resolving issues of authority, power, and control. What may seem like someone's personal problem could actually be a response to social disorganization within a system (a dysfunctional family, an oppressive organization, or conflicting cultural expectations, etc.). In a study by Sarri and Vinter (1985), it was found that problems exhibited by students in secondary schools were often the result of conflictive interactions between the student and the school. When students were identified as malperformers, some schools offered help, others restrictions. The definition and treatment of deviance will depend on how the behavior is perceived in the social environment or by the agency practitioner. Even the collecting and ordering of data during an assessment period will depend upon what is perceived as useful. Auerswald (1984) differentiates between what a "system" practitioner will be looking for (adaptation, transactions, social context of problem) and the "interdisciplinary" team, which is intent on finding information from various disciplines to label an illness. The social worker needs to consider deviance within the context of the social situation. It is necessary to modify the environment as well as personal awareness and self-fulfillment, in order for change to occur.

Groups that are part of the environment may be natural groups, which are associations of people who select one another, perhaps because of interest, similar characteristics, or physical proximity. In any living, work, or educational environment, where persons need to interact because of the physical and social occasion, a natural selection takes place. These groups are sometimes called informal groups. Within them there are indigenous leaders who have more influence than others in the group. When an agency attempts to do social action or make organizational change, these indigenous leaders can be helpful in mobilizing others for planning and implementation of proposals.

The informal or natural group may be the best way of reaching Hispanics (Hardy-Fanta, 1986, 119) and other minority populations who may be fearful of the formal structure of an agency. It is sometimes necessary to locate these groups in their neighborhoods, schools, local recreation areas, or houses of worship. Meeting with them on an outreach basis lessens resistance to social work intervention. A group formed in the neighborhood may feel more safety and less cultural conflict than does the formed agency group.

The various steps in this model will now be illustrated in dealing with the living situation of elderly adults from an urban area.

Identification of Problem
Loneliness, fear, dependence

Assessment and Planning
Need for involvement, mutual aid; locate indigenous leadership

Planning and Action Group
Group worker and selected floor captains (indigenous leaders)

Example: In an eleven-story senior citizens apartment building, located in a large urban community, many of the residents were lonely and fearful. Federally funded for those in the lower income, it was racially and ethnically mixed. The group worker assigned to the building was on the staff of an adjacent neighborhood center. She initially selected two floor captains for each eleven-unit floor. Initially, the floor captains would distribute flyers about events in the building and community, take complaints from the residents to the staff, and discuss problems in the building. As the floor captains became more comfortable in their role, they organized the Helping Hand

Further Involvement
Formation of other
groups to meet
specific needs;
expanding leadership
potential

Friends, a group that would water plants, do shopping, or collect mail for those who were away or unable to perform these activities.

The Tenant's Association was organized as more of the residents were willing to assume responsibility for governance. This group was also formed initially by the group worker. It was composed of cochairpersons, other officers, and a chairperson of the floor captains. After a year and a half the residents held their own elections. Groups started to form, such as a three-session group to deal with death and dying, a women's group called Life Experiences, and eventually a regular weekly Rap Group, which was open to all the residents. Young children from a local school started to visit each week to help with a gardening project.

Change and Stabilization
Mutual aid,
involvement, more
accessible
communication from
residents to staff,
assertiveness by
residents

When one of the well-liked building managers was asked to leave because of mismanagement, the residents expressed anger and disappointment. The Tenant's Association discussed the problem, and they called a meeting for residents to discuss the situation more fully. The group worker helped them bring out their thoughts and feelings and explained the reasons why the employee was asked to leave.

The initial boundary of the problem was the individual loneliness and fear of being able to manage in a new location. Through further assessment and planning, the boundary was expanded to include the need to feel included, form relationships, and have some control of their environment. The worker recognized that there was leadership potential among the residents and the capacity for them to help each other. From her observations of the informal network of relationships and communication patterns, she selected floor captains who would be acceptable as communicators and be able to demonstrate the necessary warmth and support of others. This choice was based on the worker's assessment of the social organization in the building. These indigenous leaders, who had great influence with the residents and were in close proximity to them, were able to generate enough energy to mobilize a helping network. They helped increase involvement and expanded linkage possibilities among the residents and with the housing staff. Change occurred in the restructuring of how groups were formed to include more active participation of the residents in formal and informal groups and an accessible system of communication from apartment occupants to management. The mutual-aid possibilities increased. Traditional barriers that sometimes exist because of racial or ethnic differences were less important, since the tenants were helping one another in regard to common issues and problems. During all this time the roles of the group worker included mediator, advocate, administrator (interpret agency policies), counselor, and broker.

GROUPS ORGANIZED IN RELATION TO ENVIRONMENTAL NEED OR PROBLEM

This type of group has social action or system change as its main function, although the process of reaching that goal can also have empowering effects on the group members and the group as a whole. The focus for change could be the amelioration or prevention of a social problem, the provision of a new service, or the restructuring of an organization. The problem may be identified by persons, by groups, or by organizations within the community.

The setting for this illustration is a high school where there is the development of new resources to meet the presenting needs and problems of some of the students.

Identification of Problem
Poor school
  performance and
  behavior problems

Assessment and Planning
Unclear expectations,
  low self-esteem,
  little support within
  school for incoming
  students

Example: Guidance counselors at a high school became increasingly aware of the difficult adjustment incoming freshmen were having. Many of them had academic problems, felt intimidated by the older students, and demonstrated negative behavior in classes. The high-school social worker talked to the guidance counselors at the high school and middle school to find out more about the problems. He also spoke to some of the freshmen to hear what they had to say. The social worker learned that, although there was a large meeting at the middle school to inform the students about the high school, the ninth graders still had little idea about what was expected of them. They were intimidated by the older students. In many cases, they felt too young and awkward to participate in extracurricular activities. For some, both parents were working, and they were by themselves or with friends for several hours until their parents returned.

Planning and Action Group
Key persons from middle school and high school; considering systemic as well as student aspects of problem

The social worker met with representatives (principals and guidance counselors) from the middle and high schools to discuss the problem and seek solutions. These persons were in a position to make administrative decisions or at least to initiate change by involving others at both schools. The idea of a peer leadership program was introduced as one means of dealing with the problem. This would involve junior and senior students as support persons to the freshmen. It was envisioned as something like a big brother and big sister program.

Further Involvement
Wider array of participants, more diversity in group composition

To become more fully engaged in planning and implementation, this initial administrative group brought together other persons to sound them out on the proposed plan. This larger group included students from the high and middle schools, other guidance counselors, and some teachers who were particularly interested in the concept of peer support.

Interested sophomore and junior students were recruited as a peer leadership group and participated in a series of training sessions, including a weekend away from school at a camp. Each peer leader was assigned to a small group of freshmen. The role of the peer leader was defined as providing a helping relationship with ninth-grade students in the areas of academic enrichment, recreation, and socialization, and referral to school or community activities. Training sessions continued to help peer leaders deal with issues and problems in their relationships with the younger students.

Change and Stabilization
Enhanced self-image, more active in school activities, improved academic work

In an evaluation of the program using a standardized instrument (Jesness Behavior Checklist), there were positive findings in all the measurable characteristics of behavior compared to a control group. There were also

parent groups, family treatment, and a
professionally led counseling group for some
of the freshmen. It was found that the peer
leaders also benefited greatly from the overall
experience.

In this example, the social worker starts with the broader social and
behavioral problem—poor school performance and behavior problems by ninth
grade students. Although it is certainly necessary to individualize the needs of
each of these pupils, the environments of the middle and high schools are
considered the largest part of the problem. But the schools also have the potential
to be part of the solution. In this way the boundary of the problem is
reconceptualized to include the school environment. Once the planning and
action group meets, they clarify the problem according to the broader context—
student/environment interplay. Within this framework, an array of solutions is
sought. Persons who have the capacity to influence policy decisions or provide a
more direct source of support are involved as part of a helping network. The idea
of a peer leadership program is a natural consequence of this kind of thinking.
Other possibilities include preparation of parents to offer specific kinds of
supportive help, in-service training of ninth-grade teachers, after-school academic enrichment classes, or a series of meetings while the pupils are still in the
eighth grade, regarding expectations for the high school. There might also be
support/socialization groups led by guidance counselors. Combinations of the
above possibilities would be useful. In all these approaches, the child is not
singled out as the problem. When the pupil is not burdened with a deviant label,
the environment will contribute to a healthier self-image and enable the child to
join in efforts to improve school conditions as a collaborator rather than a victim.
    It was mentioned in the illustration that the peer leaders (junior and seniors)
benefited greatly from this experience. It enabled them to take on the role of
helper and was a step in their transition to adulthood. They learned beneficial
problem-solving skills for use in their everyday life. The advantage for the peer
leaders as helping persons is also true for others who are mobilized to provide
support, energy, and resources to those in need. The fact that the helpers are
helped tends to be overlooked. The purpose of their involvement is not to enrich
them personally, but this often happens as a side effect. They become more
socially conscious citizens and resourceful helpers for others.
    The group worker takes on more of the coordinator role, emphasizing
adequate communication and facilitating linkages. The worker recognizes the
importance of organization—the system term for clarity of purposes, roles, and
the accompanying structure—and energy to generate interest and ideas. The
concept of linkage, perhaps using coalitions or helping people to join together, is
basic to resolving social problems in the environment. The persons in the
planning and action group are influential enough to exercise leverage in the

linking process. An important reason to involve key administrative or community persons, who are part of the target for change, is that their power will assure more stability of change, since they have been involved in decision making about solutions.

SUMMARY

Social action and system development are professional functions for all social workers. When group members are involved in community-change projects, it enables them to take more control of their environment and develop greater self-esteem in accomplishing desirable social goals. They also learn problem-solving skills that can be applied to other aspects of their lives. It has been found that persons normally resistant to therapeutic intervention within the formal structure of a social agency are receptive to community service and action projects that are relevant to their interests and needs. This is especially true for ethnic minorities with social and cultural differences that may not be fully understood by agency staff.

The practice model for social action and system development contains elements of a problem-solving method, which starts with the need for clarity about the nature of the issue or problem, follows with assessment for increased understanding of the meaning of the problem, and goes on to locate persons in the environment who can influence a change process. The planning and action group, composed of the worker and some of these key individuals, develops a strategy for involving the next layer of persons who can implement a plan of action or set up barriers to it. Indigenous leadership of formal and informal groups are sought out for their guidance, support, and decision-making abilities.

The roles of the social worker who is engaged in environmental change are more varied than in any other type of practice. He or she might be mediator, educator, advocate, broker, counselor, consultant, or coordinator. Environmental change requires a good knowledge of resources that are related to the need or problem and of when to use them. The worker might use the power, control, and authority of his or her position but must be prepared to share it with the broadening base of persons who are willing to take responsibility for planning and implementing action proposals. It is only as others can exercise influence that change will occur.

REFERENCES

Auerswald, E. H. (1984). Interdisciplinary versus ecological approach. In B. R. Compton & B. Galaway (Eds.), *Social work processes* (3rd ed.). Homewood, IL: Dorsey Press.
Bakalinsky, R. (1984) The small group in community organization practice. *Social Work with Groups, 7* (2), 87–96.

Barker, R. L. (1988). *The social work dictionary*. Silver Spring, MD: National Association of Social Workers.

Chess, W. A., & Norlin, J. M. (1988). *Human behavior and the social environment: A social system model*. Boston: Allyn & Bacon.

Chin, R. (1961). The utility of system models and developmental models for practitioners. In W. G. Bennis, K. D. Benne, & R. Chin (Eds.), *The planning of change* (pp. 201–214). New York: Holt, Rinehart & Winston.

Cnaan, R. A., & Adar, H. (1987). An integrative model for group work in community organization practice. *Social Work with Groups, 10*(3), 5–24.

Coyle, G. L. (1947). *Group experience and democratic values*. New York: Woman's Press.

Ephross, P. H., & Vassil, T. V. (1988). *Groups that work*. New York: Columbia University Press.

Frankel, A. J., & Sundel, M. (1978). The grope for group: Initiating individual and community change. *Social Work with Groups, 1*(4), 399–405.

Garvin, C. D. (1987). *Contemporary group work* (2nd ed.). Englewood Cliffs, NJ: Prentice-Hall.

Garvin, C. D., Glasser, P. H., Carter, B., English, R., & Wolfson, C. (1985). Group work intervention in the social environment. In M. Sundel, P. Glasser, R. Sarri, & R. Vinter (Eds.), *Individual change through small groups* (pp. 277–293). New York: Free Press.

Gentry, M. E. (1987). Coalition formation and process. *Social Work with Groups, 10*(3), 39–54.

Hardy-Fanta, C. (1986). Social action in hispanic groups. *Social Work, 31* (2), 119–123.

Lister, L. (1987). Contemporary direct practice roles. *Social Work, 32* (5), 384–391.

Maguire, L. (1980). The interface of social workers with personal networks. *Social Work with Groups, 3*(3), 39–49.

———. (1983). *Understanding social networks*. Beverly Hills, CA: Sage.

Maier, H. W. (ed.). (1965). *Group work as part of residential treatment*. New York: National Association of Social Workers.

Moore (1983). The group-in-situation as the unit of attention in social work with groups. *Social Work with Groups, 6*(2), 19–31.

Papell, C. P., & Rothman, B. (1966). Social group work models: Possession and heritage. *Journal of Education for Social Work, 2*(2), 66–77.

Paster, V. S. (1986). A social action model for difficult to reach populations. *American Journal of Orthopsychiatry, 56* (4), 625–629.

Reeser, L. C., & Epstein, I. (1987). Social workers' attitudes toward poverty and social action: 1968–1984. *Social Service Review, 61* (4), 610–622.

Sarri, R., & Vinter, R. (1985). Beyond group work: Organizational determinants of malperformance in secondary schools. In M. Sundel, P. Glasser, R. Sarri, & R. Vinter (Eds.), *Individual change through small groups* (pp. 408–434). New York: Free Press.

Schwartz, W. (1976). Between client and system: The mediating function. In R. W. Roberts & H. Northen (Eds.), *Theories of social work with groups* (pp. 171–197). New York: Columbia University Press.

Vinter, R. D., & Galinsky, M. H. (1985). Extragroup relations and approaches. In M. Sundel, P. Glasser, R. Sarri, & R. Vinter (Eds.), *Individual change through small groups* (pp. 266–276). New York: Free Press.

Zimpfer, D. G. (1984). *Group work in the helping professions* (2nd ed.). Muncie, IN: Accelerated Development.

TEACHING AND LEARNING IDEAS

1. Locate a social-action group that is meeting in your community. Interview a group member and the group worker of this group. Compare their expectations for the group. How will a similarity or dissimilarity of their expectations affect the possible outcome of their efforts?

2. Think of the class as an organization. Assign roles that are appropriate for its structure (administrator, supervisor, direct service worker, etc.). Decide on a problem in the organization, such as staff burnout. Who should be on the planning and action group? Conduct a meeting of such a group and determine the next steps.

3. Visit an agency, such as a settlement house or place that may be engaged in social action. Meet with the staff person who had the responsibility for a social-action type group and determine to what extent the model discussed in the chapter is similar to what is being done in the agency.

4. Meet with an administrator of an agency and discuss how decisions about organizational change are carried out in the agency. How are staff groups used in this decision-making process?

Index

Abrams, V., 144
Abramson, M., 85. *See also* Self-determination
Acosta, F., 107
Action, 94, 240, 241. *See also* Intervention, techniques; Continuum of behavior
Action, taking. *See* Taking action for change
Action-oriented groups. *See* Social action, groups
Active intervention, 103–105. *See also* Intragroup process
Activeness of worker, 15, 23, 24
Activity, 98, 99. *See also* Planning
groups, 146
group therapy, 34
use of, 41, 98, 99
Adar, H., 235
Addams, J., 30. *See also* Hull House
Administrative groups, 3, 55–57
Adult education, 31
Advocacy. *See* Change, advocacy for
Alissi, A., 35, 36, 150, 161. *See also* Group, therapy
American Association of Group Workers, 33, 34
Anderson, J., 37
Anderson, R., 50, 66, 67. *See also* Boundaries; Energy
Andragogy, 77, 78

Arrangement of room, 150, 151
Assessment 7, 8, 170, 171, 237. *See also* Social action; Understanding presenting needs or problems
Association for the Advancement of Social Work with Groups, 40
Attitudes, positive. *See* Positive attitudes
Auerswald, E., 242
Avery, N., 221

Bakalinsky, R., 235
Balgopal, P., 112, 146, 185
Barker, R., 47, 67, 84, 234. *See also* Code of ethics; Linkages
Beginning. *See* Stages of groups, beginning
Behavior, meaning of, 60. *See also* Leadership, differences
Behavior modification, 39. *See also* Models of practice
Behroozi, C., 175
Benne, K., 36. *See also* T Group
Berman-Rossi, T., 105
Bernstein, S., 85, 86, 200. *See also* Self-determination
Bertcher, H., 112, 147
Biddle, B., 74
Birnbaum, M., 144
Black empowerment, 103

Blanchard, K., 60. *See also* Situational leadership
Blatner, H., 219
Bolman, W., 219
Bostwick, G., 230
Boundaries, 66. *See also* Social systems
Boyd, N., 31, 34, 35. *See also* Therapeutic group work
Bradford, L., 36. *See also* T Group
Brainstorming, 55
Bremner, R., 29
Breton, M., 99, 152. *See also* Outreach
Brown, L., 42, 97, 108, 161
Building relationships, 59, 166, 204, 205. *See also* Social group workers, Roles
Burn-out, 42. *See also* Social supports and health

Callanan, P., 219, 220
Cantor, L., 177
Caplinger, T., 147
Carter, B., 235
Carter, I., 50, 66, 67. *See also* Boundaries; Energy
Casey, R., 177
Casper, M., 150, 161
Catalina, J., 144
Caudill, W., 75
Change, advocacy for, 107, 212–214, 239. *See also* Environmental support; Social action
Chess, W., 239
Chin, R., 68, 163, 239. *See also* Conflict; Intersystem model
Chu, J., 94, 104
Clarity of purpose, 18, 19, 172
Clausen, J., 8. *See also* Development, influences on
Clear guidelines, 99
Closed groups, 150
Closure of group session, 219, 220. *See also* Stages of groups, ending
Club work, 31
Cnaan, R., 235, 238
Co-worker relationships, 155
Co-worker teams, 56. *See also* Administrative groups
Code of Ethics, 84, 85
Cohen, M., 105
Cohesion, group. *See* Group, cohesion
Coit, S., 29

Collaboration with staff and other professionals, 137, 138, 214–216
Collaborative process, 85. *See also* Values
Collins, A., 9. *See also* Networks, helping
Commonality of purpose, 163
Community organization, 38, 235
Composition, 11, 143, 147, 148. *See also* Planning, process model
Compton, B., 83
Concrete needs, 105, 106. *See also* Intragroup process
Conditions
for group meetings, 150–152
for growth, 19
Confidentiality, 86. *See also* Values
Conflict, 68, 162, 163, 199–202. *See also* Tension
resolution of, 71, 199–202
Conrad, A., 84
Constructive difference, 86. *See also* Values
Consultation and prevention, 7
Contact with persons in environment, 60, 61. *See also* Leadership, differences
Continuum of behavior, 92–94
Contract, independent. *See* Independent contract
Contracting with involuntary group members, 175, 176
Contracts, 12, 203
Control, 71
Controversy, 200. *See also* Conflict
Cooley, C., 30. *See also* Primary group
Corazzini, J., 154. *See also* Pregroup training
Corey, G., 177, 219, 220
Corey, M., 177, 219, 220
Coven, C., 148
Coyle, G., 30, 33, 34, 234

Decision making, 103, 198. *See also* Intragroup process
information. *See* Information for decision making
skills. *See* Skills
Defense, 83. *See also* Ego psychology
Delgado, M., 99
Departure of group worker, 230, 231
Development
influences on, 8, 9
of environment, 59. *See also* Social group workers, roles
Devine, E., 29
Devore, W., 95

Dewey, J., 20, 30, 31
Differences,
   discussion of, 101, 102. *See also* Intragroup
     process
   group. *See* Group, differences
   mediation of. *See* Mediation of differences
Differentiation, 73. *See also* Maturation
Disadvantaged groups. *See* Oppressed groups
Distress, 68. *See also* Stress
Doty, M., 108
Drop-outs, 230
Dynamic equilibrium, 239

Education groups, 50. *See also* Socioeducation
   groups
Edwards, E., 98, 102
Edwards, M., 98, 102
Ego psychology, 80–83
Employee involvement, 55
Empowerment, 191. *See also* Enhancing
   self-esteem
Empowerment, black. *See* Black empowerment
Encounter group, 36. *See also* Group, relations
Ending. *See* Stages of groups, ending
Energy, 67. *See also* Social systems
English, R. 235
Enhancing self-esteem, 190, 191
Environment, groups in the. *See* Natural
   groups
Environmental needs, 244–247
Environmental support, 106–108. *See also*
   Practice principles
Ephross, P., 241
Epstein, I., 235
Equilibrium, 72, 239. *See also* Dynamic
   equilibrium; intimacy
Erhard, W., 36. *See also* Est group
Erikson, E., 77, 82, 191
Est group, 36. *See also* Group, relations
Ethics, 84. *See also* Values
Eustress, 68. *See also* Stress
Evaluation, 21, 224, 225
Evaluation, reflective. *See* Reflective
   evaluation
Expectations 168, 169, 172
   realistic. *See* Realistic expectations
   shared. *See* Shared expectations

Feelings, 93, 94. *See also* Continuum of
   behavior
   expressions of. *See* Expressions of feelings
Feldman, R., 37, 147

Field theory, 37. *See also* Lewin, K.
Fischer, J., 204, 205
Flexible stance, 60. *See also* Social group
   workers, roles
Follet, M. 30, 210
Formative stage, 70. *See also* Group,
   formation
Fox, E., 219
Frankel, A., 235
Freeman, E., 100
Freud, A., 83
Fried, E., 221
Fry, R., 223
Functions, balance of, 58, 59. *See also* Social
   group workers, roles
Further involvement, 238, 239. *See also*
   Social action
Future. *See* Planning

Galaway, B., 83
Galinsky, M., 56, 69, 70, 72, 73, 235
Garbarino, J., 185
Garland, J., 69, 72, 73, 162, 220
Garvin, C., 37, 51, 112, 220, 235, 237. *See
   also* Group work research
Gazda, G., 145
Gentry, M., 238, 239
Gershenfeld, M., 145
Gestalt therapy, 36. *See also* Group, relations
Getzel, G., 96, 143. *See also* Planning,
   process model
Gibb, J., 36. *See also* T Group
Gitterman, A., 41, 145, 154, 190
Glasser, P., 218, 235
Glassman, V., 112
Goldberg, G., 4, 112. *See also* Social group
   work, versus social work with groups
Goldberg, T., 40
Gottlieb, B., 41. *See also* Social supports
   and health
Greenfield, W., 231
Group
   arrangements. *See* Technical aspects
   cohesion, 204, 205
   commonalities, 11
   counseling, 35. *See also* Group, therapy
   development, 17, 136, 137
   differences, 11
   facilitator, 4
   formation, 70
   functioning, 72. *See also* Intimacy
   guidance, 35. *See also* Group, therapy

interaction, reflection. *See* Reflection on
group interaction
leader, 4
members
involuntary. *See* Contracting with
involuntary group members
planning. *See* Planning, with group
members
preparation of. *See* Preparation, for the
group
planning. *See* Planning, with group
members
process, 17, 18, 24, 69–74
psychotherapy, 35. *See also* Group, therapy
purposes, 58, 171, 172. *See also* Social
group workers, roles
relations, 35, 37
Relations Conference, 36
resistance. *See* Resistance
resources. *See* Resources for the group
service agencies, 29
services. *See* Services for the group
size, 151
structure, 161–163
tasks. *See* Tasks, group
therapy, 34, 35
work, 4
work in social work. *See* Social group work
work research, 37
worker tasks. *See* Tasks, group
Groups, 3
activity. *See* Activity, groups
educational. *See* Education groups
in direct practice, 40, 41
reasons to form, 144, 145
social action. *See* Social action, groups
socialization. *See* Socialization groups
socioeducation. *See* Socioeducation groups
support. *See* Support groups
task. *See* Task groups
treatment. *See* Treatment groups
Groupthink, 17, 165
Guidelines, clear. *See* Clear guidelines
Gunther, B., 36. *See also* Sensory awareness
group

Hanson, P., 77, 78. *See also* Resistance
Hardy-Fanta, C., 237, 238, 242
Hare, A., 151
Harris, G., 175
Hartford, M., 28, 38, 60, 69, 70, 72, 151.
See also Flexible stance; Social
group work, purposes

Hartmann, H., 81
Head Start, 186
Health
psychological. *See* Psychological health
social. *See* Social health; Social supports
and health
Hearn, G., 40
Henry, S., 112, 221
Hepworth, D., 229
Hersey, P., 60. *See also* Situational leadership
Heterogeneity, group, 147. *See also* Group,
differences
Hidalgo, H., 96
Hirayama, H., 191
Hirayama, K., 191
Ho, M., 107
Holism, 185
Holistic social work, 25
Hom, A., 95
Homogeneity, group, 147
Hull House, 30
Humm-Delgado, D., 99
Hunter, J., 101
Hurley, D., 177

Identity, 82, 83. *See also* Ego psychology
In-group feelings, 72. *See also* Intimacy
Inclusion, 70
Independent contract, 221
Indigenous leaders, 67, 107, 108, 162. *See
also* Environmental support
Individual issues, 195–197
Individualizing, 59, 60. *See also* Social group
workers, roles
Informal groups. *See* Natural groups
Informal leaders. *See* Indigenous leaders
Information for decision making, 19, 20
Information sharing, 114. *See also* Techniques
Integration, 71. *See also* Superordinate goals
Integrative practice, 4, 5, 21, 22, 39. *See also*
Models of practice
Intermediate phase, 71
Interrelationships, 163, 164
Intersystem model, 163
Intervention, 65
active. *See* Active intervention
techniques, 240, 241
Interviews, pregroup. *See* Premeeting
interview
Intimacy, 71, 72. *See also* Stages of groups,
middle
Intragroup process, 71, 99–106. *See also*

Intermediate phase; Practice principles
Involuntary group members, 153. *See also* Contracting with involuntary group members
Involvement, 78, 114, 115. *See also* Learning theories; Techniques

Janis, I., 17, 165. *See also* Groupthink
Jones, H., 69, 70, 72, 73, 162, 220
Juan, G., 95
Justice, B., 20, 41. *See also* Social supports and health
Kahn, R., 55
Kaiser, C., 30
Kates, L., 112
Katz, D., 55
King, M., 108
Kisthardt, W., 100
Kivlighan, D., 154. *See also* Pregroup training
Knowledge, 65, 66
Knowles, M, 77, 78. *See also* Relevance
Kohn, A., 85
Kolb, D., 223
Kolodny, R., 69, 70, 72, 73, 162, 220
Konopka, G., 38
Kurland, R., 143. *See also* Planning, process model

Lamont, A., 40
Lang, N., 40
Larsen, J., 229
Lawler III, E., 42. *See also* Quality Circle
Leaders, indigenous. *See* Indigenous leaders
Leadership, 37
  differences, 60, 61
  preparation, 154
Learning theories, 76–80
Lee, P., 95
Length of meetings, 150
Leverage, 67. *See also* Social systems
Lewin, K., 37
Lieberman, J., 33
Lindeman, E., 31. *See also* Adult education
Linkage, 67, 239. *See also* Social systems
Lippitt, R., 37, 67. *See also* Leadership; Leverage
Lister, L., 234, 235
Long-term groups, 150
Lopez, D., 96
Lynn, M., 105

McGovern, T., 154. *See also* Pregroup training

McRoy, R., 100
Maeroff, G., 186
Maguire, L., 9, 235, 237, 239. *See also* Networks, helping
Maier, H. , 235
Maintenance phase, 72. *See also* Intimacy
Maluccio, A., 12, 172. *See also* Contracts
Manor, O., 152
Maple, F., 147
Marathon group, 36. *See also* Group, relations
Mares, W., 55
Marlow, W., 12, 172. *See also* Contracts
Martin, M., 105
Maslow, A., 77, 153. *See also* Motivation
Maturation, 72, 73. *See also* Stages of groups, middle
Mayadas, N., 218
Mayer, H., 76. *See also* Role, behavior
Meadow, D., 152
Mediation of differences, 209–212
Meetings
  conditions for. *See* Conditions, for group meetings
  length. *See* Length of meetings
  number. *See* Number of meetings
  place. *See* Place of meeting
  time. *See* Time of meeting
Meyer, C., 41. *See also* Social supports and health
Middle. *See* Stages of groups, middle
Middleman, R., 4, 41, 112. *See also* Social group work, versus social work with groups
Minahan, A., 40
Modeling, 79. *See also* Learning theories
Models of practice, 39, 40
Mohrman, S., 42. *See also* Quality Circle
Moore, E., 235
Moreno, J., 35. *see also* Group therapy
Motivation, 77, 81, 82. *See also* Ego psychology; Learning theories
Mutual aid, 86, 190. *See also* Values

Napier, R., 145
National Association for the Study of Group Work. *See* American Association of Group Workers
National Association of Social Workers, 34, 84, 85
  group work section, 38
National Conference of Social Work, 33

Natural groups, 241–244
Natural leaders. *See* Indigenous leaders
Nayowitz, S., 105
Need, 143, 220. *See also* Planning, process model
Needs assessment, 237
Needs, concrete. *See* Concrete needs identification of, 236. *See also* Social action
Negotiation of differences, 163
Nelson M., 219
Networks, helping, 9, 10
New York Charity Organization Society, 29
Newstetter, W., 30, 33
Nisinzweig, S., 144
Norlin, J, 239
Norming, 72. *See also* Intimacy
Norms, 85. *See also* Values clarification of, 206, 207
Northen, H., 39, 68, 112. *See also* Conflict; Models of practice
Number of meetings, 150

Olsen, M., 66. *See also* Social systems
Open groups, 219, 220
Open systems, 66. *See also* Social systems
Open-ended groups, 150
Oppressed groups, 91–110
Organization. *See* Structure
Origin stage, 70
Others, significant. *See* Significant others
Outreach, 6, 7, 108, 152, 153. *See also* Environmental support

Papell, C., 39, 40, 234. *See also* Models of practice
Parsons, T., 75
Participation, 78, 145–147. *See also* Learning theories
Participatory management, 55
Paster, V., 235
Paterson, T., 96
Performing, 73. *See also* Maturation
Perls, F., 36. *See also* Gestalt therapy
Pernell, R., 191
Perrault, E., 153
Physical structure, arrangement of, 183, 184
Pincus, A., 40
Piper, W., 153. *See also* Pregroup training
Place of meeting, 150, 151, 184
Planned endings, 220, 221. *See also* Stages of groups, ending
Planning, 97–99, 181–183, 226–228, 237,

238, 240, 241. *See also* Practice principles; Social action and action groups, 237, 238. *See also* Social action
pregroup. *See* Pregroup planning process model, 143, 144
with group members, 12, 13, 23
clear guidelines, 99
contracting with involuntary group members, 175, 176
contracts, 12, 203
independent contract, 221
Polsky, H., 66. *See also* Boundaries
Positive attitudes, 20
Power, 71
Practice developments. *See* Models of practice
Practice principles, 94–106
Pre-affiliation, 70. *See also* Group, formation
Pregroup contact, 144. *See also* Planning, process model
Pregroup interview. *See* Premeeting interview
Pregroup phase, 70. *See also* Origin stage
Pregroup planning, 143–158
Pregroup training, 153, 154
Premeeting interview, 11, 152
Preplanning, 61. *See also* Leadership, differences
Preliminary interview. *See* Premeeting interview
Preparation for leadership. *See* Leadership, preparation
Preparation for the group, 5–7, 10–12, 22, 23, 152–154
arrangement of the room, 150, 151
composition, 11, 143, 147, 148
conditions for group meetings, 150–152
contact, 5–7, 22, 60, 61, 144, 157, 158
premeeting interviews, 11, 152
purpose, 10, 11, 143, 146, 202–204
recruitment, 149, 150
staff receptivity, 11, 12
technical aspects, 12
Presenting needs. *See* Understanding presenting needs or problems
Primary group, 30
Problems, identification of. *See* Need
Problem solving, 17, 18, 24, 59, 207–209. *See also* Social group workers, roles
Procedures, 112. *See also* Techniques
Professional self-awareness, 13, 14, 23, 163, 164
Progression, 80. *See also* Learning theories

Psychoanalytic theory, 80
Psychodrama, 35
Psychological health, 18–21, 24
Psychology, ego. *See* Ego psychology
Publicity for group, 150
Purpose, 10, 11, 143, 146, 202–204. *See also* Planning, process model

Quaim, J., 29
Quality Circle, 36, 41, 42. *See also* Group, relations

Radin, N., 51
Ramsey, G., 76
Rapp, C., 100
Ratner, J., 30
Readiness, 81. *See also* Ego psychology
Realistic expectations, 97. *See also* Self-preparation
Recapitulation, 74. *See also* Separation
Receptivity, staff. *See* Staff receptivity
Reciprocal model, 39. *See also* Models of practice
Recontracting, 231
Recreational group therapy, 35
Recruitment, 149, 150
Reeser, L., 235
Referrals, 149, 150, 228, 229
Reflection on group interaction, 21
Reflective evaluation, 79. *See also* Learning theories
Refreshments, 184
Regression, 74. *See also* Separation
Reid, K., 29, 33
Relationships, building. *See* Building relationships
Relevance, 77. *See also* Learning theories
Remedial model, 39. *See also* Models of practice
Research Center for Group Dynamics, 36
Resistance, 77, 78, 83, 102, 103, 148, 149, 176–179. *See also* Intragroup process; Learning theories
Resources for the group, 9, 10, 23, 184, 185
Respect for human dignity, 85. *See also* Values
Responsibility, taking, 60, 197–199. *See also* Leadership differences
Review of progress, 222, 223
Revision phase, 71. *See also* Intermediate phase
Rhodes, R., 103

Rice, A., 36. *See also* S Group
Richmond, M., 31
Rivas, R., 55, 112, 220, 221. *See also* Brainstorming
Roberts, R., 39. *See also* Models of practice
Rogers, J., 77, 78
Role
  behavior, 75, 76
  conflict, 75
  play, 20, 21, 180
  set, 75
  theory, 74–76
Roles, 171, 172. *See also* Social worker roles
  clarification of, 206, 207
  definition of, 50, 74. *See also* Social group workers, roles
Romero, S., 97
Rose, S., 39. *See also* Models of practice
Rothman, B., 39, 40, 231, 234. *See also* Models of practice
Rules for the group, 151
Russell, J., 219, 220
Ryland, G., 34

S Group, 36. *See also* Group, relations
Salmon, R., 143. *See also* Planning, process model
Sammons, M., 102
Sarri, R., 69, 70, 72, 73, 241
Schaecher, R., 102
Schlesinger, E., 95
Schopler, J., 56
Schutz, W., 70
Schwartz, W., 37, 39, 145, 152, 190, 210, 235. *See also* Models of practice
Screening of applicants for groups, 146. *See also* Assessment
Sculpting, 224
Seabury, B., 176
Self-awareness, 96, 97, 116, 117. *See also* Self-preparation; Techniques
  professional. See Professional self-awareness
Self-determination, 85, 86. *Also see* Values
Self-esteem, 82, 83. *See also* ego psychology
  enhancing. *See* Enhancing self-esteem
Self-examination, 21
Self-help group, 36, 41. *See also* Group, relations; Support groups
Self-preparation, 96, 97. *See also* Practice principles
Self-understanding, 192–195

Sensory awareness group, 36. *See also* Group, relations
Separation, 73, 74, 221, 223–226
Sequencing, 80. *See also* Learning theories
Services
  for the group, 184, 185
  mandates to seek, 6
  on-site, 7
  voluntarily seeking, 6
Shared expectations, 12, 13
Shiffman, B., 38. *See also* Social group work, definition
Short-term groups, 150
Shulman, L., 41, 112, 145, 148, 152, 154, 175, 190
Shutz, W., 161
Significant others, 8, 9, 106, 107. *See also* Environmental support
Silverman, M., 37
Simmons, J., 55
Siporin, M., 146, 164
Situational leadership, 60. *See also* Social group workers, roles
Size of group. *See* Group, size
Skills, 112. *See also* Techniques
Slavson, S., 33, 34. *See also* Group, therapy
Slocum, Y., 152
Small group theory, 69–74
Smith, B., 76
Social action, 98, 99, 234–247. *See also* Planning; system development
  groups, 3, 52–55, 149
  model, 235
Social goals model, 39, 234. *See also* Models of practice
Social group work, 31–34
  branches, 31–38
  definition, 4, 38
  history, 28–43
  models, 37
  purposes, 28
  roots, 28–31
  versus social work with groups, 4
Social group workers
  roles, 58–61
Social health, 18–21, 24
Social networks, 235
Social supports and health, 41
Social systems, 66—69
Social work with groups, 3, 4
  essential elements, 5–21
  goals, 25

Social worker roles, 16, 17, 24. *See also* Roles
Socialization groups, 50, 150
Socioeducation groups, 3, 50–52, 146, 151
Sociogram, 35
Solomon, B., 103. *See also* Black empowerment
Somers, M., 77, 79, 182. *See also* Motivation; Reflective evaluation
Stabilization, 239. *See also* Social action
Staff receptivity, 11, 12
Stages of groups
  beginning, 161–186
  middle, 189–216
  ending, 218–232
Standards for the Classification of Social Work Practice, 84, 85
Storming, 71. *See also* Intermediate phase
Strengths, use of, 99–101. *See also* Intragroup process
Stress, 68. *See also* Tension
  management groups, 42.. *See also* Social supports and health
Structure, 105, 106, 143, 179–181. *See also* Intragroup process
Studt, E., 164
Study Group. *See* S Group
Sub-groups, 162
Sub-systems. *See* Social systems
Sue, S., 94, 104
Sullivan, W., 100
Summary of progress, 222, 223
Sundel, M., 235
Superordinate goals, 71
Support, 114, 115. *See also* Techniques
  environmental. *See* Environmental support
Support groups, 36, 50, 150. *See also* Group, relations; Self-help group
Supportive persons, involvement of, 185, 186
Symposium for Empirical Group Work, 37
System development, 234–247. *See also* Social action
Systemic linkage, 66. *See also* Boundaries; Social systems

T Group, 35, 36. *See also* Group, relations
Taking action for change, 20, 21
Task accomplishment, 116, 117. *See also* Techniques
Task groups, 150
Tasks, 112. *See also* techniques
  person, 165–171, 190–199, 222, 223

group, 171–175, 199–209, 223–226
environment, 183–186, 209–216, 226–229
Tavistock Institute, 36. *See also* Rice, A.
Team building, 56
Teams, 56. *See also* Administrative groups
Technical aspects, 12
Techniques, 112–138
  information sharing, 114
  involvement, 78, 114, 115
  self-awareness, 96, 97, 116, 117
  support, 114, 115
  task accomplishment, 116, 117
Tension, 67–69
Tension release, 200
Termination, 74. *See also* Separation
Testing activity, 70
Therapeutic group work, 38, 48. *See also*
      Treatment groups
Therapy, definition of, 47
Thinking, 93. *See also* Continuum of behavior
Thomas, E., 74
Time of meeting, 150
Time-limited groups. *See* Short-term groups
Toseland, R., 55, 112, 146, 220, 221. *See
      also* Brainstorming
Toynbee Hall, 29
Training group. *See* T Group
Training, pregroup. *See* Pregroup training
Transference, 200
Transformation, 231
Treatment groups, 3, 47–50, 146, 150
Tropp, E., 41, 145
Trosvold, D., 55
Trust, 82. *See also* Ego psychology
Tsui, A., 102
Tuckman, B., 69, 70, 72, 73

Types of groups, 47–61
  administrative groups, 3, 55–57
  social action groups, 3, 52–55, 149
  socioeducation groups, 3, 50–52, 146, 151
  treatment groups, 3, 47–50, 146, 150

Understanding presenting needs or problems,
      7–9, 22. *See also* Assessment
University Settlement, 29, 30
Unplanned endings, 229–231

Values, 65, 83–86
Vassil, T., 112, 146, 185, 241
Vinter, R., 37, 39, 235, 241. *See also* Models
      of practice
Vulnerable groups, 91–110

Wanamaker, C., 33
Ward, N., 107
Watkins, D., 175
Watson, J., 67, 221. *See also* Leverage
Weick, A., 100
Western Reserve University, 33
Westley, B., 67. *See also* Leverage
White, R., 81. *See also* Motivation
Williamson, M., 30
Wilson, G., 30, 34
Wolfson, C., 235
Woodman, N., 96

Yalom, I., 35, 145, 146, 151, 200
Yamamoto, I., 107

Zelman, A., 103
Zerin, E., 68
Zerin, M., 68
Zimpfer, D., 28, 40, 235